Wensdy Whitehead's
Origami Portfolio

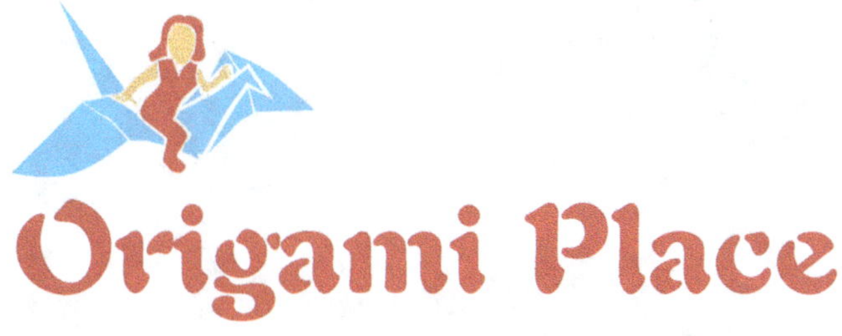

Origami Place

Wensdy Whitehead (1971-2023) created this portfolio of her work.
Her wish was that her origami be folded and shared. If you would
like to fold and recreate her work, many diagrams can be found here:

https://origamimuseum.org/wensdy-whitehead/

It is the publisher's wish that this collection inspires you to try your
hand with these great works. Enjoy!

Table of Contents

No Cuts!

No Glue!

Origami Flora and Fauna

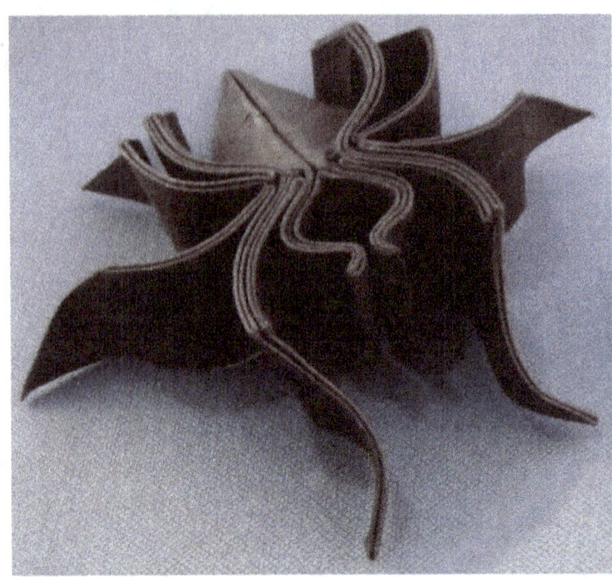

Spider
One uncut 1:4 rectangle
Published in <u>Creased</u> issue 5

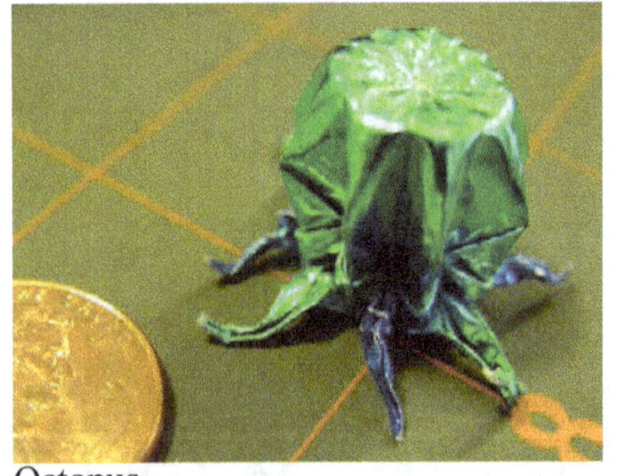

Octopus
Two uncut squares of foil-backed paper
Unpublished as of 19 September 2017

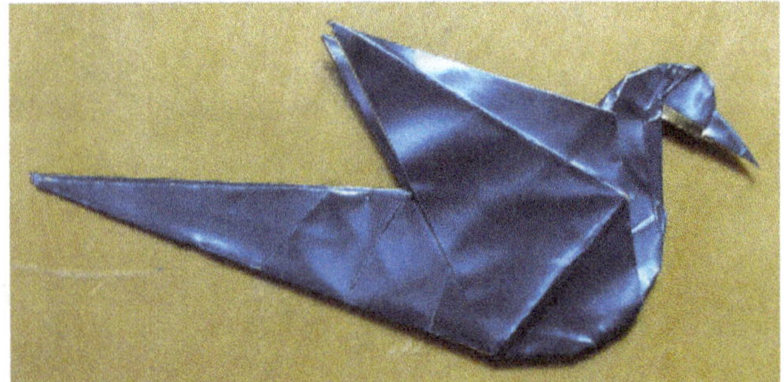

Barn Swallow
One uncut square
Unpublished as of 19 September 2017

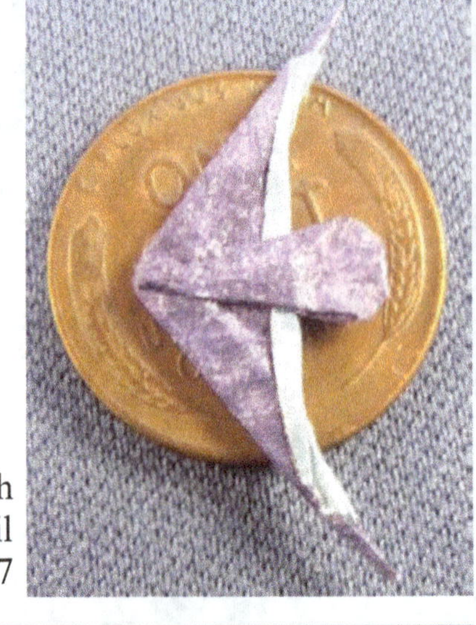

Angelfish
One uncut square of tissue foil
Unpublished as of 19 Sept. 2017

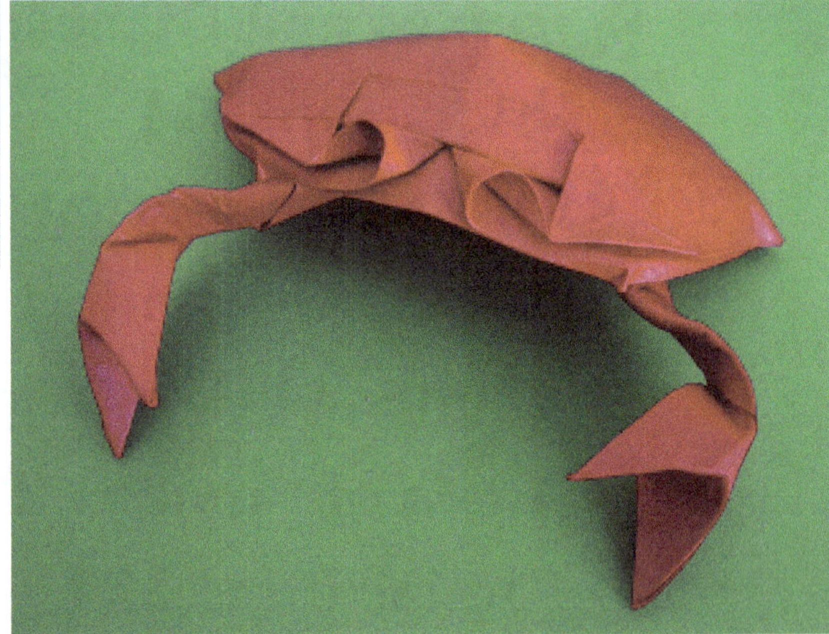

Kani – the Happy Crab
One uncut U.S. letter (or approximately 3:4) rectangle
Unpublished as of 19 September 2017

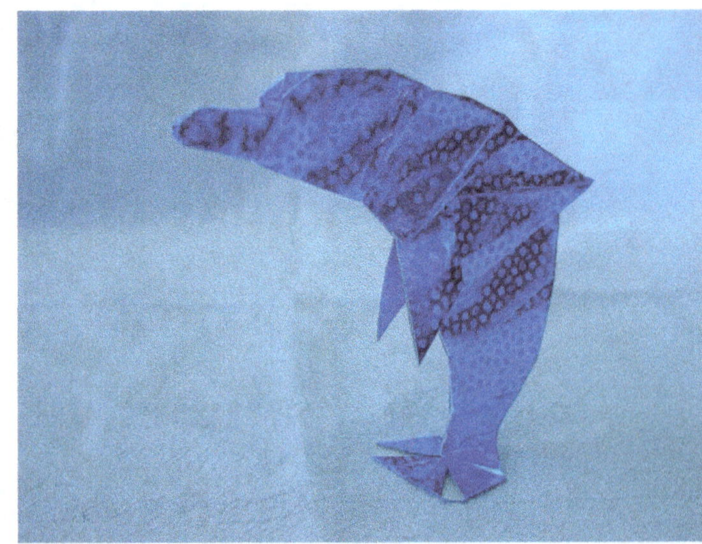

Dolphin
One uncut square foil-backed paper
Unpublished as of 19 Sept. 2017

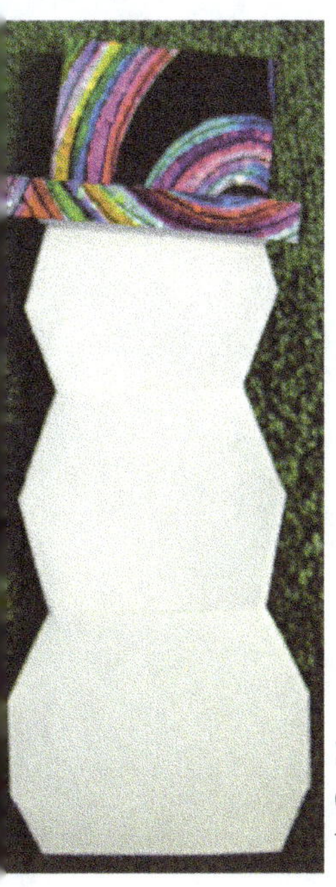

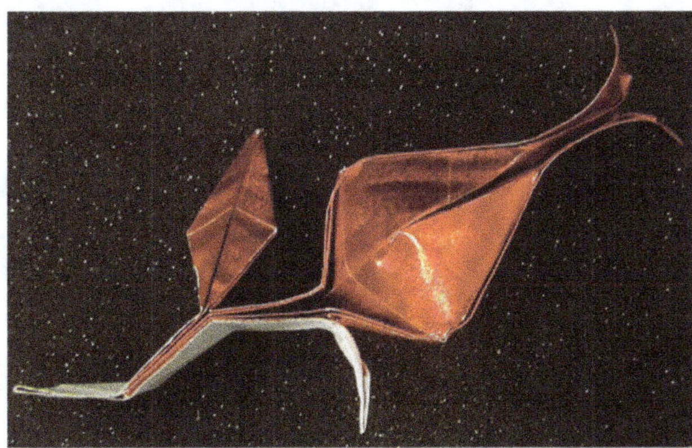

Long-Stemmed Rose with Thorn
One uncut square of foil-backed paper
Unpublished as of 19 September 2017

Snowman
One uncut rectangle
Unpublished as of 19 Sept. 2017

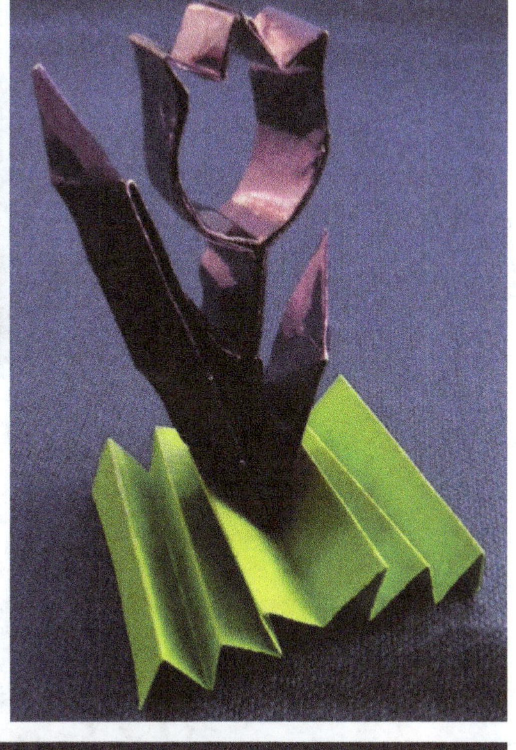

Tulip
One uncut square for the tulip and an uncut rectangle for the flowerbed
Published in the 2010 Mennorode convention book

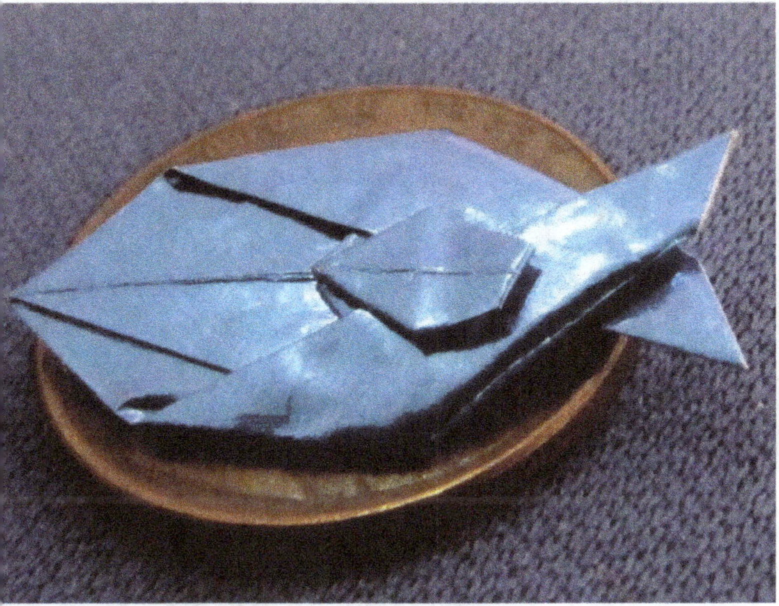

(Annual Meeting) Fish
One uncut square of foil-backed paper
Unpublished as of 19 September 2017

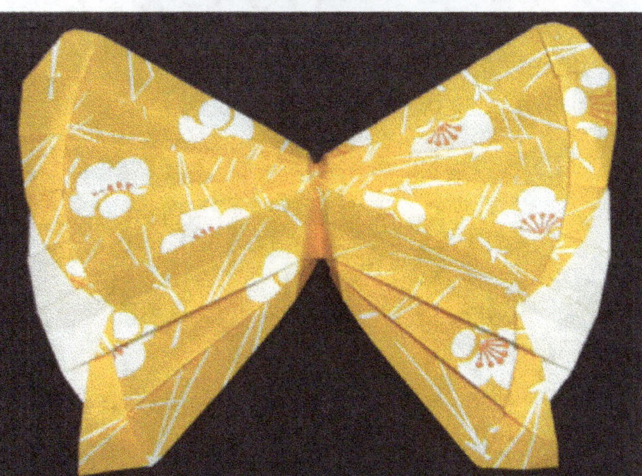

Spiral Butterfly
One uncut rectangle
Unpublished as of 19 Sept. 2017

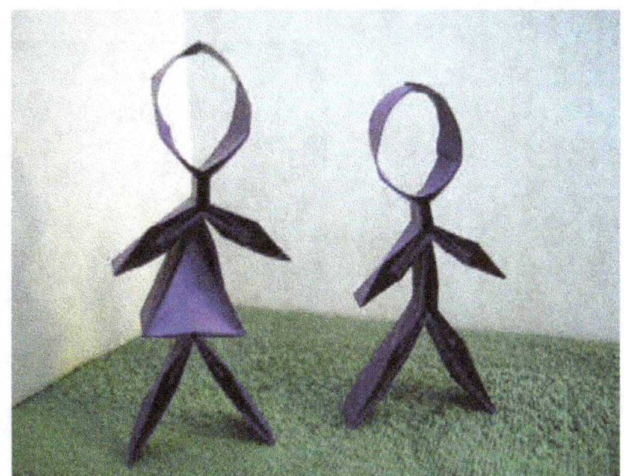

Stick Figures
One uncut 1:2 rectangle each
Published in the 2009 Mennerode convention book

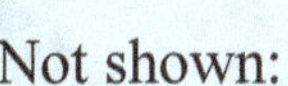

Not shown:

Acorn (see example
diagrams)
Flutterby
Cactus Pencil Topper

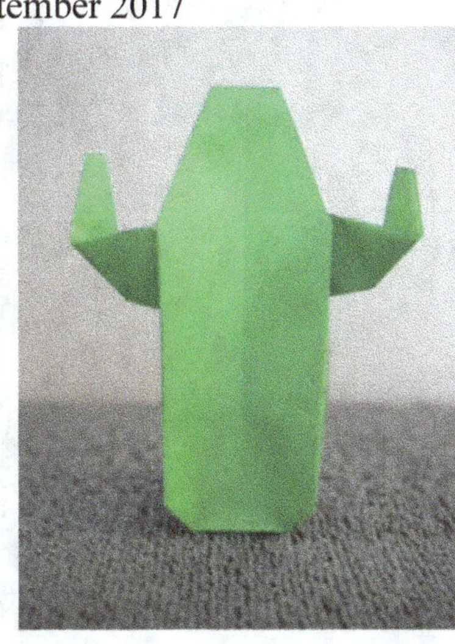

Cactus
One uncut square of kami (origami paper)
Unpublished as of 19 September 2017

Love & Peace

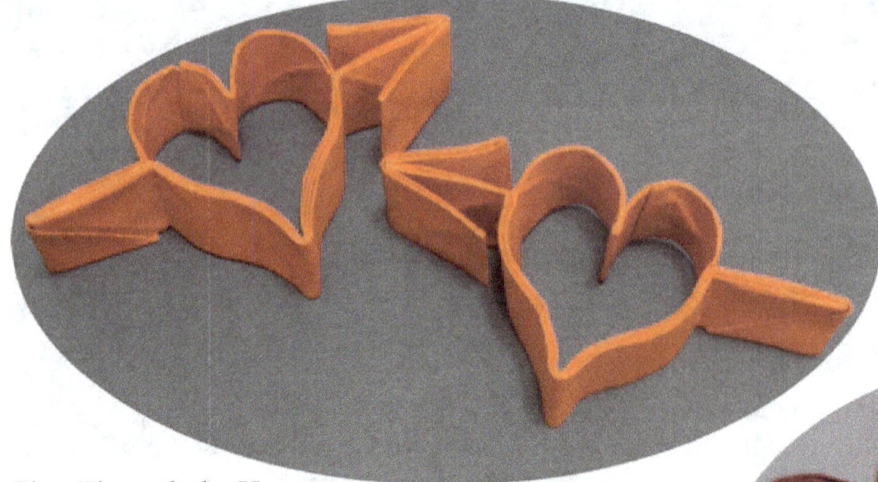

Shot Through the Heart
One uncut square
Unpublished as of 19 September 2017

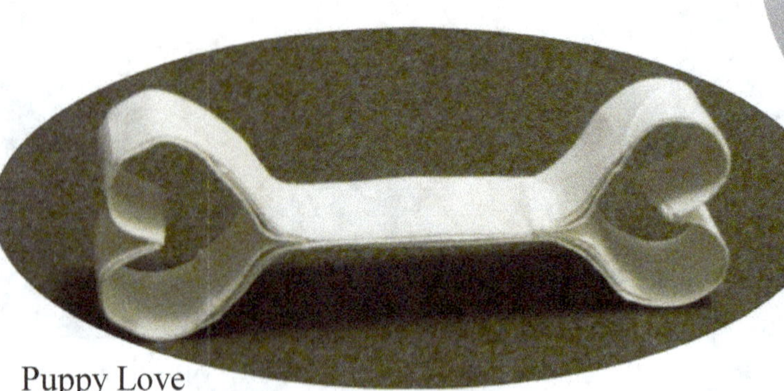

Puppy Love
One uncut rectangle
Unpublished as of 19 September 2017

Heart to Heart
One uncut square
Unpublished as of 19 September 2017

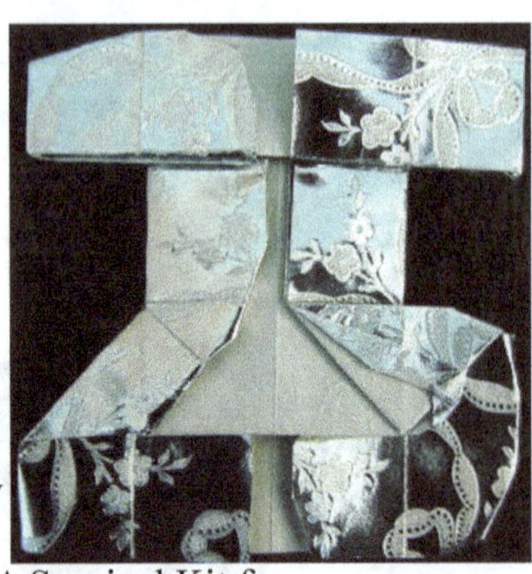

Silver Anniversary
One uncut square
Published in OUSA Survival Kit for
their 25th anniversary convention
and The Paper issue 91

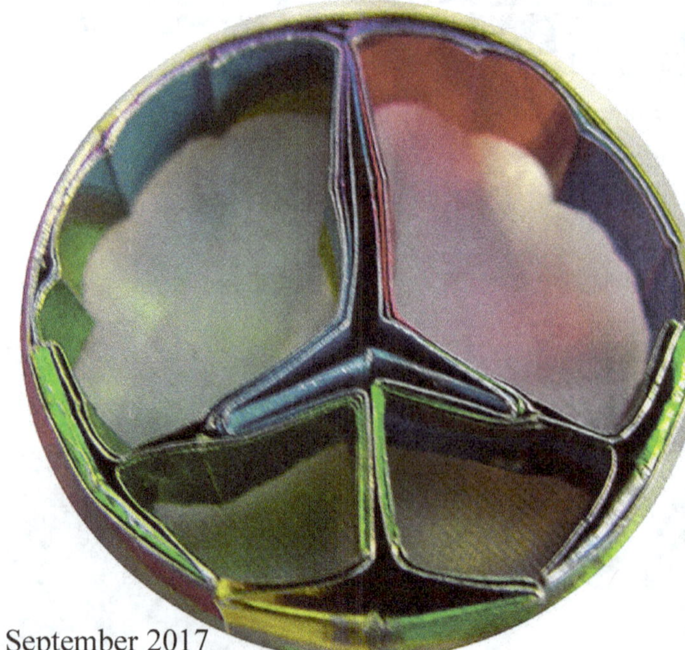

Peace of Paper
One uncut square
Unpublished as of 19 September 2017

Heart Transplant Origami

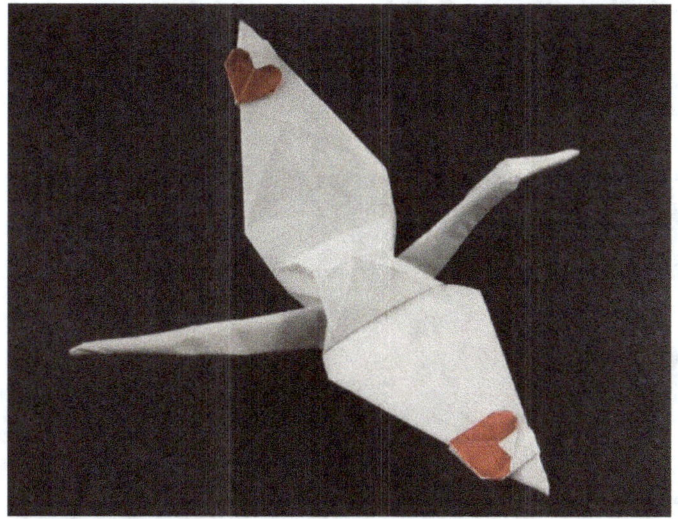

My Heart Soars
One uncut square of foil-backed paper
Variation on the traditional Crane
Unpublished as of 19 September 2017

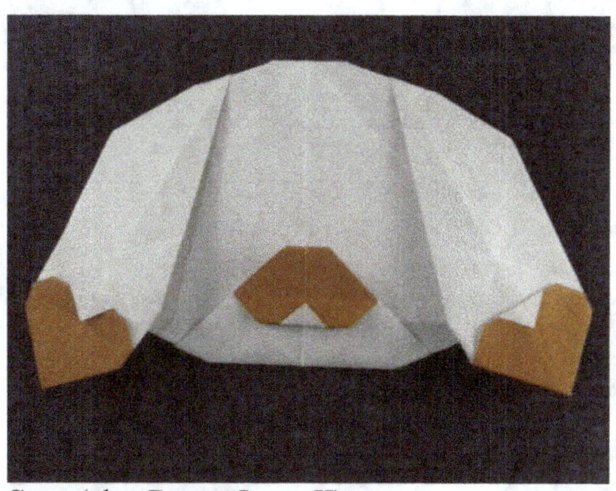

Spot (also Puppy Love II)
One uncut square of kami (origami paper)
Variation on the traditional Dog
Unpublished as of 19 September 2017

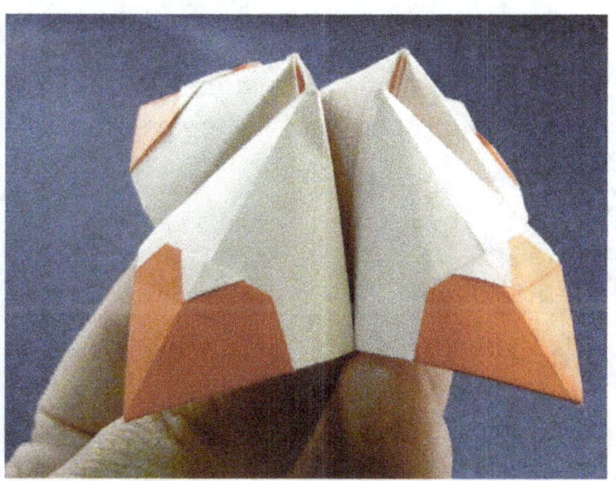

Fortune's Fancy
One uncut square of kami (origami paper)
Variation on the traditional Fortune Teller
Unpublished as of 19 September 2017

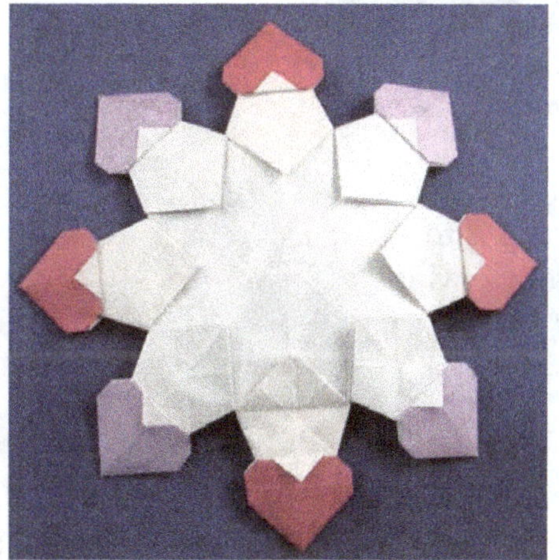

Heart Shuriken
Two uncut squares of kami
Unpublished as of 19 Sept. 2017

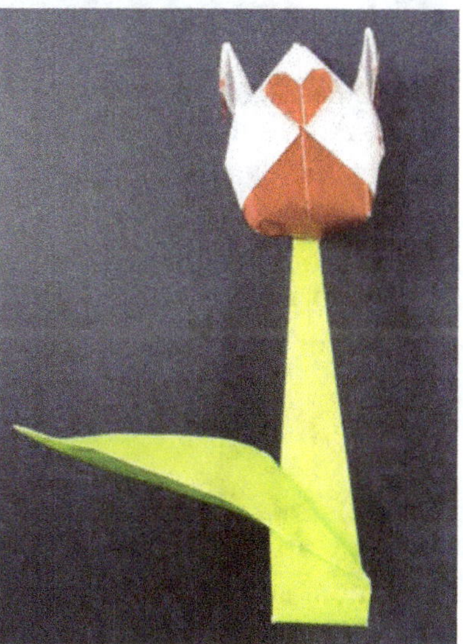

Lovely Tulip
One uncut square of foil-backed paper
and one uncut square of kami
Variation on the traditional Tulip
Unpublished as of 19 September 2017

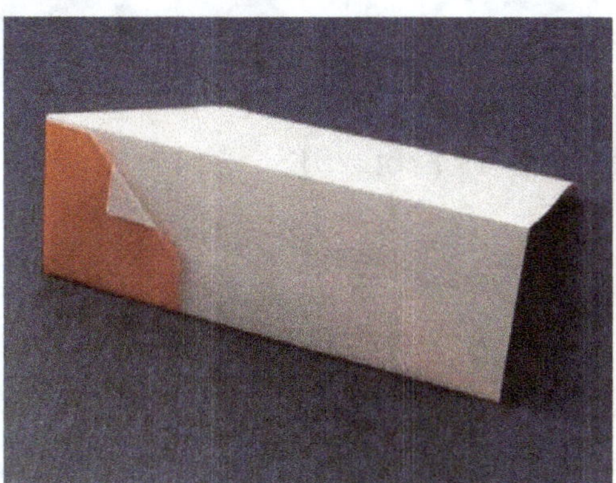

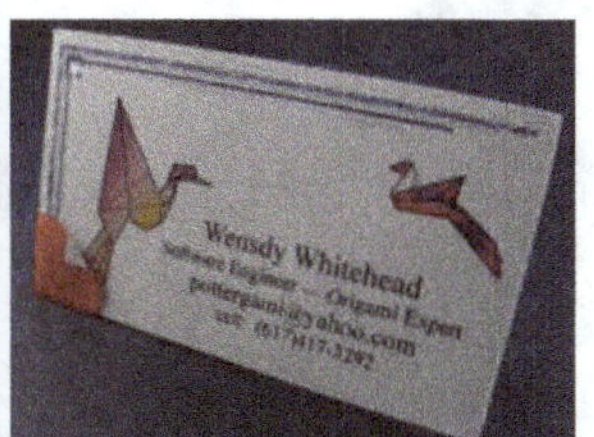

Heart Place Card Holder
One uncut square of kami (origami paper)
Unpublished as of 19 September 2017

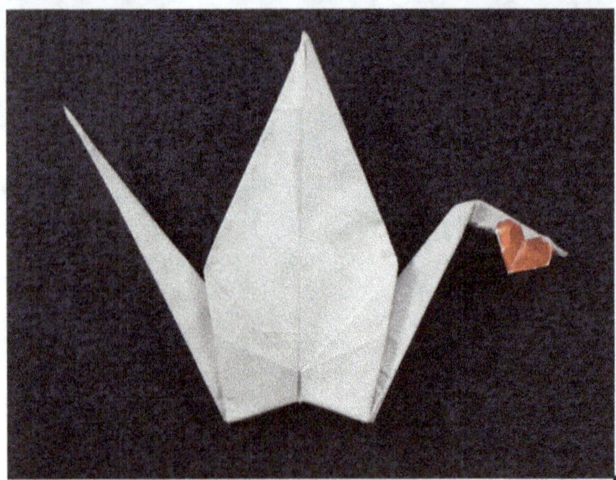

Crane Carrying Valentine
One uncut square of foil-backed paper
Variation on the traditional Crane
Unpublished as of 19 September 2017

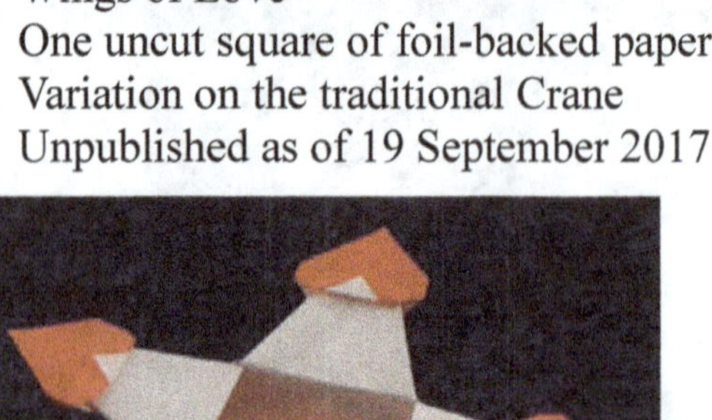

Wings of Love
One uncut square of foil-backed paper
Variation on the traditional Crane
Unpublished as of 19 September 2017

Heart Star Dish
One uncut square of kami
Variation on the traditional Star Dish
Unpublished as of 19 Sept. 2017

Heart Star Dish II
One uncut square of foil-backed paper
Variation on the traditional Star Dish
Unpublished as of 19 September 2017

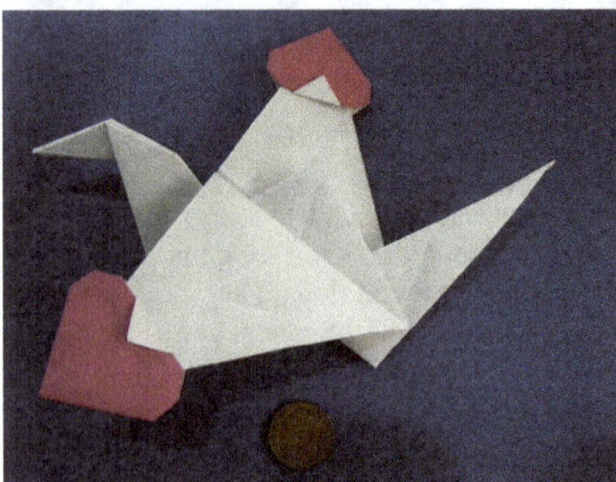

Hearts All A-Flutter
One uncut square of kami (origami paper)
Variation on the traditional Flapping Bird
Action model! Pull the tail to flap the wings
Unpublished as of 19 September 2017

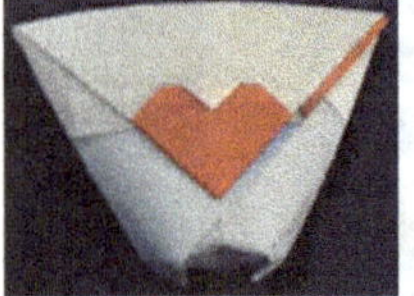

Loving Cup
One uncut square of harmony paper
Variation on a traditional cup
Unpublished as of 19 Sept. 2017

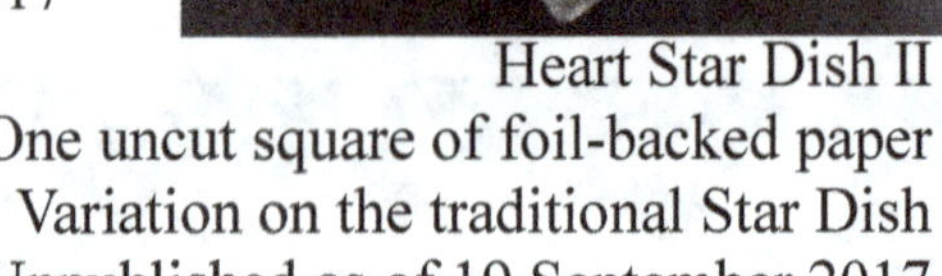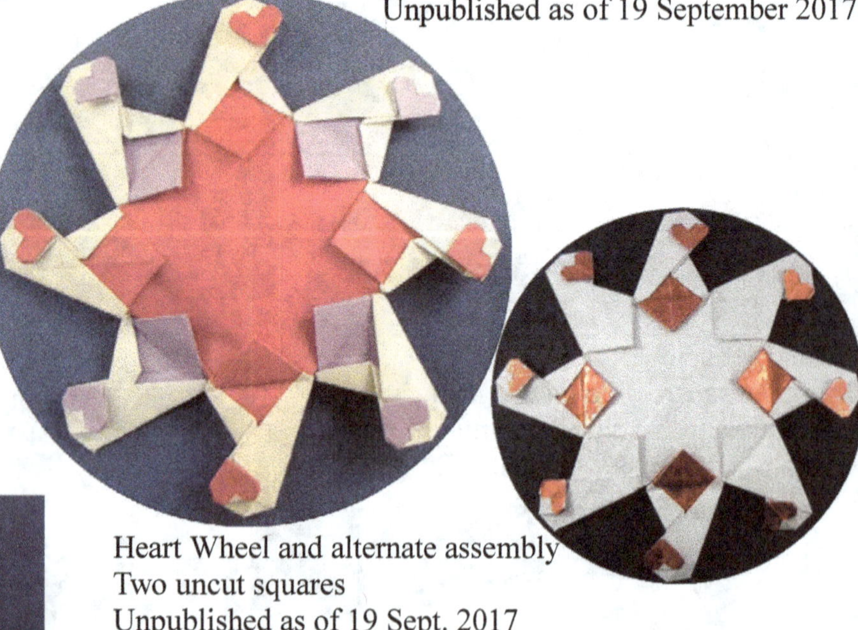

Heart Wheel and alternate assembly
Two uncut squares
Unpublished as of 19 Sept. 2017

...and that Shamrock
w/o its Star Dish

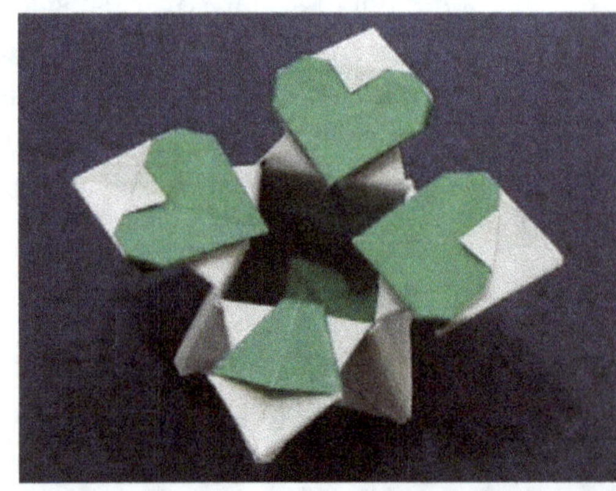

Shamrock Star Dish
One uncut square of kami
Variation on the traditional Star Dish
Unpublished as of 19 Sept. 2017

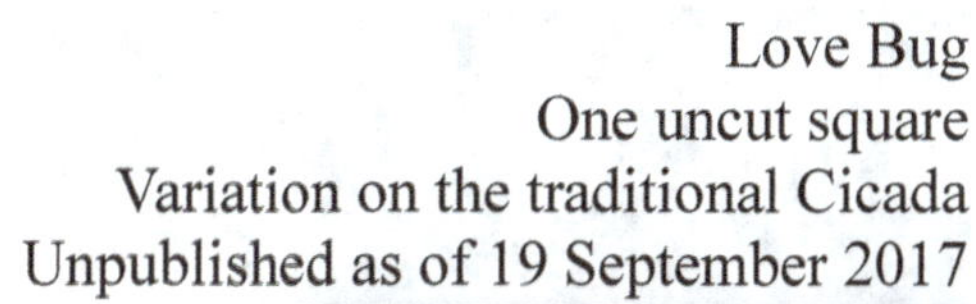

Love Bug
One uncut square
Variation on the traditional Cicada
Unpublished as of 19 September 2017

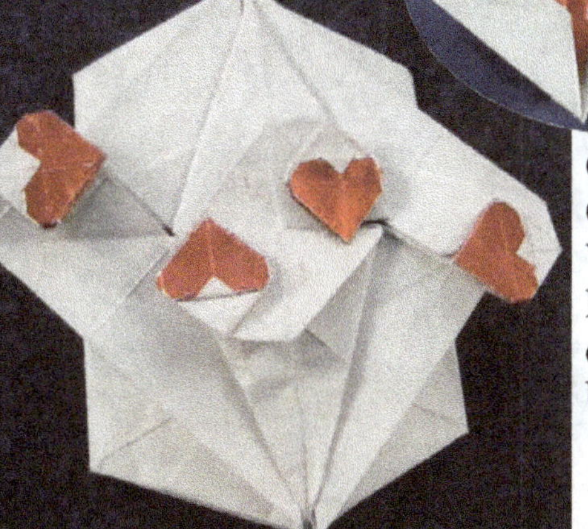

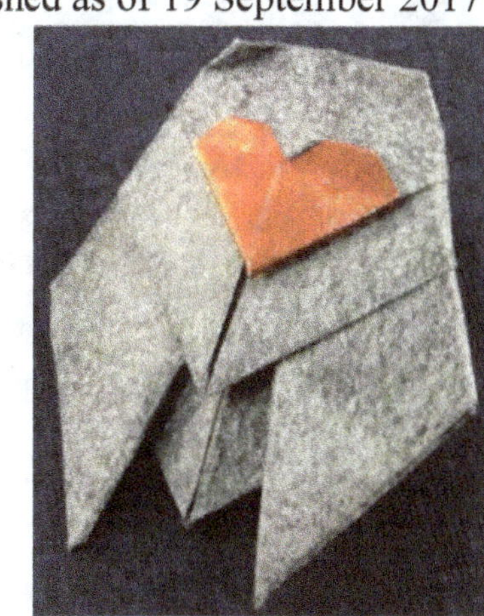

Crazy Tato
One uncut square of foil-backed paper
Variation on the traditional Tato
Model opens, closes and holds small
objects such as pins or stamps
Unpublished as of 19 Sept. 2017

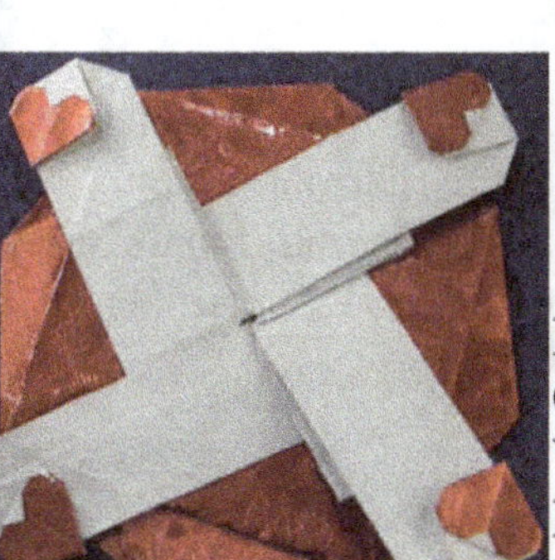

More Heart Transplant Tatos
One uncut square each
Variation on various Tatos
Models open, close and hold small objects like pins or stamps.
Unpublished as of 19 Sept. 2017

Red Hot Crane
One uncut square
Variation on the traditional Crane
Unpublished as of 19 Sept. 2017

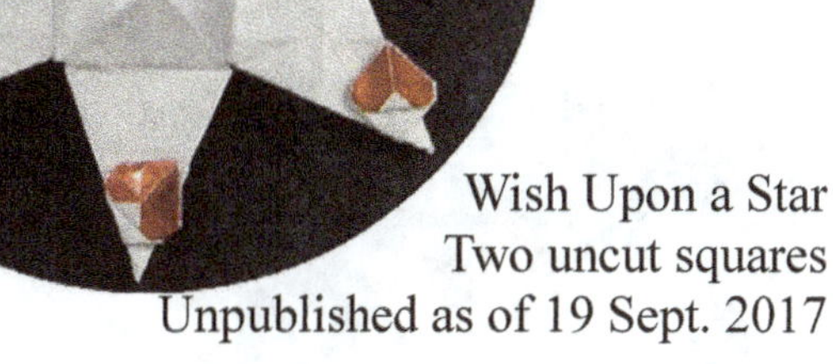

Heart Transplant Masu
One uncut square each
Variation on the traditional Masu box
Unpublished as of 19 Sept. 2017

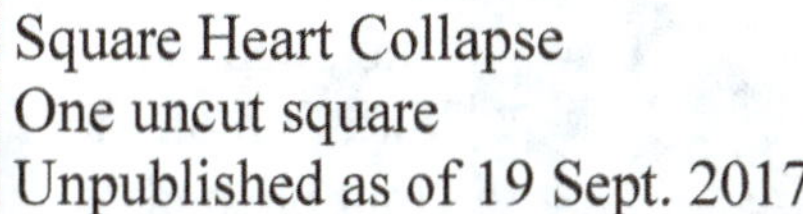

Wish Upon a Star
Two uncut squares
Unpublished as of 19 Sept. 2017

Square Heart Collapse
One uncut square
Unpublished as of 19 Sept. 2017

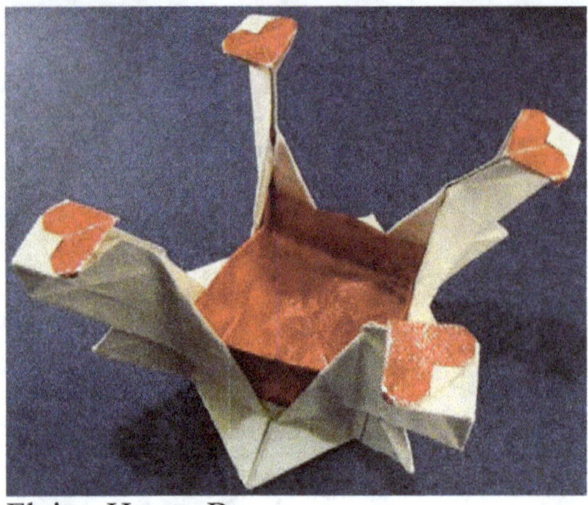

Flying Hearts Box
One uncut square
Variation on the traditional Spanish Box
Unpublished as of 19 September 2017

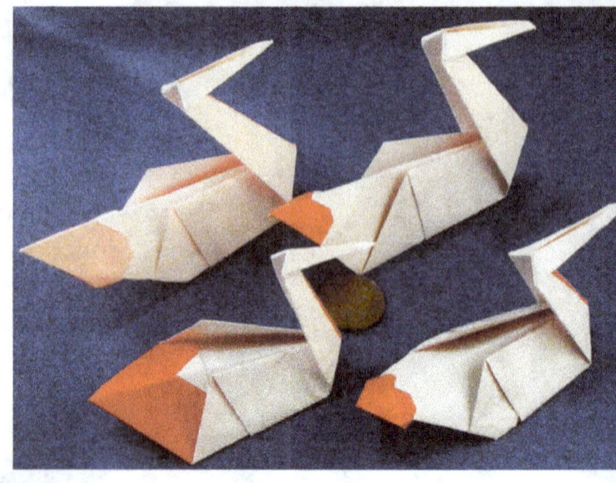

Heart Transplant Swans
One uncut square each
Variations on the traditional Swan
Unpublished as of 19 September 2017

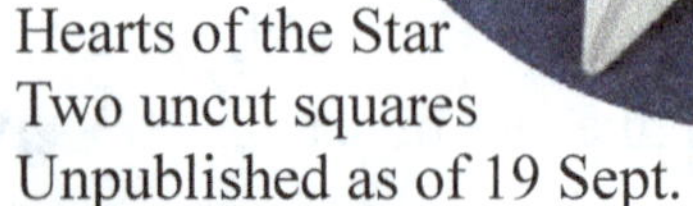

Hearts of the Star
Two uncut squares
Unpublished as of 19 Sept. 2017

Heart Transplant Kabutos (Samurai Helmets)
One uncut square (harmony, kami) each
Variations on the traditional Kabuto
Unpublished as of 19 September 2017

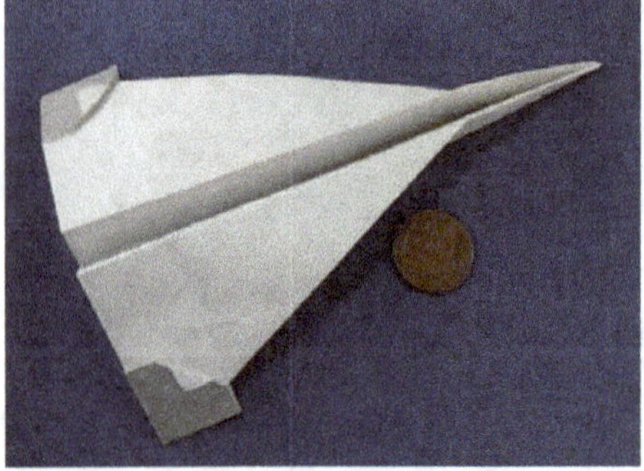

Airplane with Hearts
One uncut square
Variation on a traditional Airplane
Unpublished as of 19 Sept. 2017

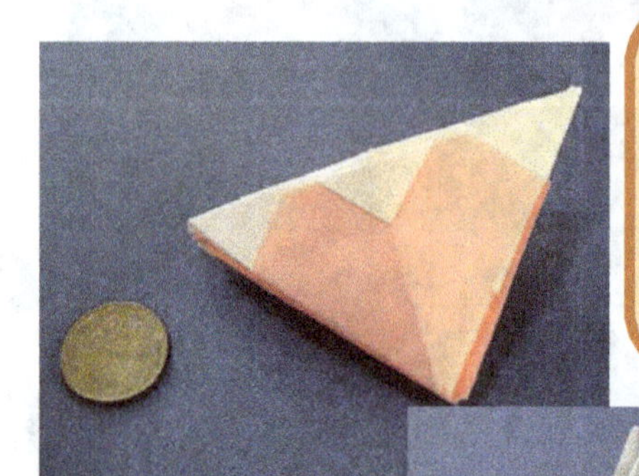

Harmony paper provides an extra color change by fading from one color to another on the front side of the paper.

Heart Transplant Pointy Hat/Cup
One uncut square each
Variation on a traditional Hat or Cup
Unpublished as of 19 September 2017

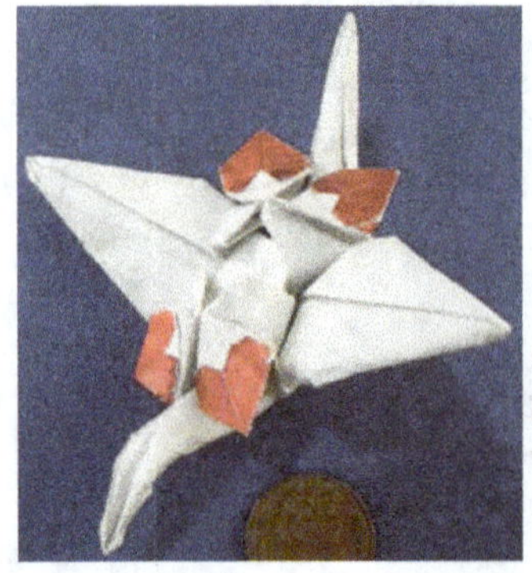

Crane in a Cloud of Hearts
One uncut square
Variation on the traditional Crane
Unpublished as of 19 Sept. 2017

Boxes and Dishes

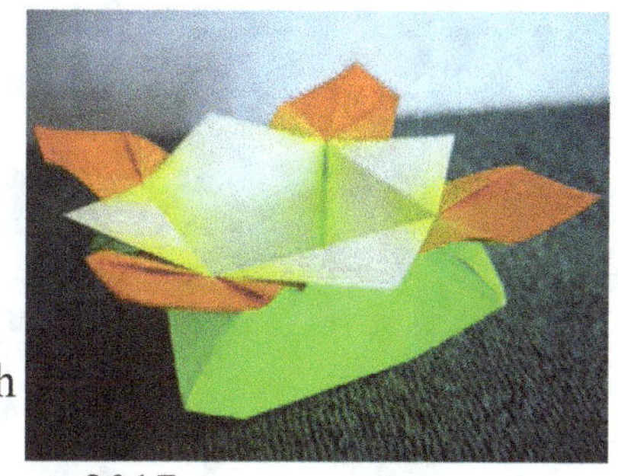
Yet Another Fancy Dish
One uncut square
Unpublished as of 19 Sept. 2017

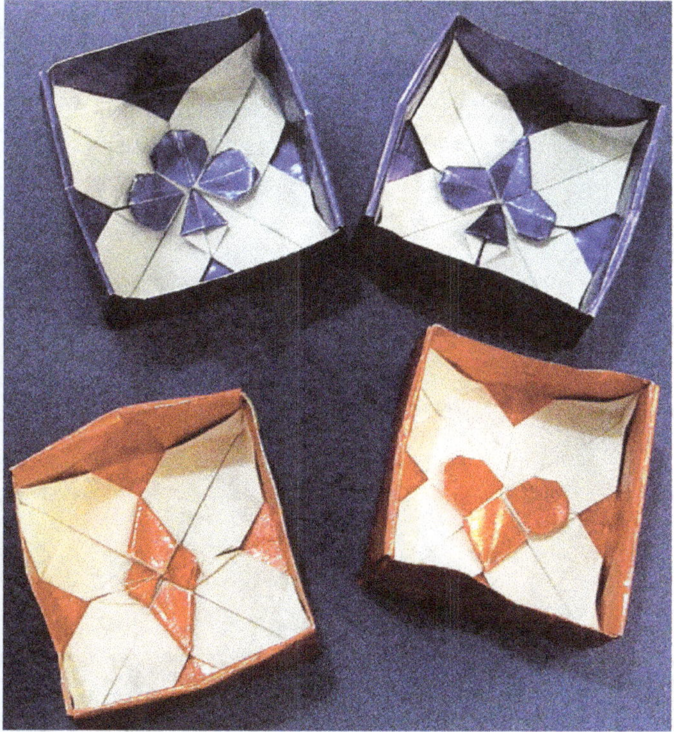

Card Suit Masu
One uncut square each
Variations on the traditional Masu box
Unpublished as of 19 Sept. 2017

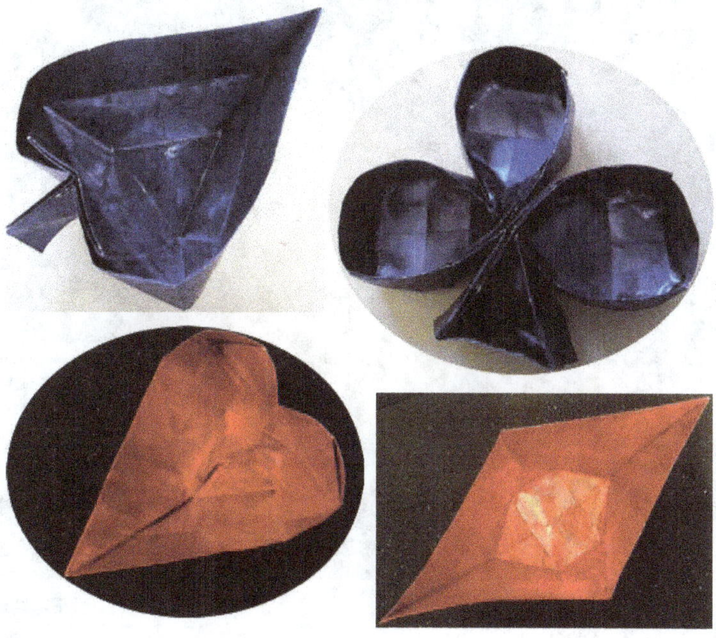

Card Suit Dishes
One uncut square each
Unpublished as of 19 Sept. 2017

Swan Dish
One uncut square
Variations on a traditional Swan
Unpublished as of 19 Sept. 2017

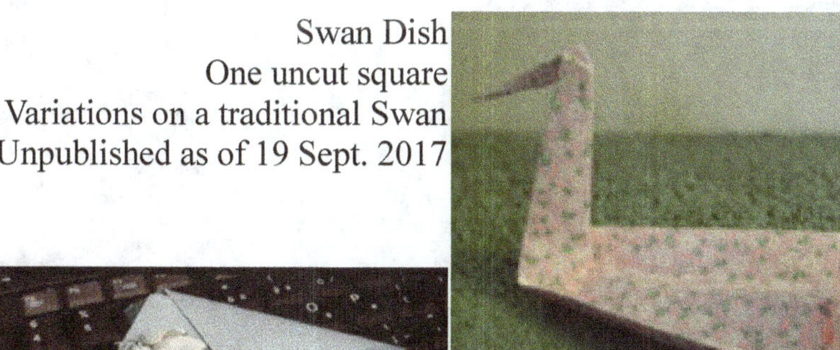

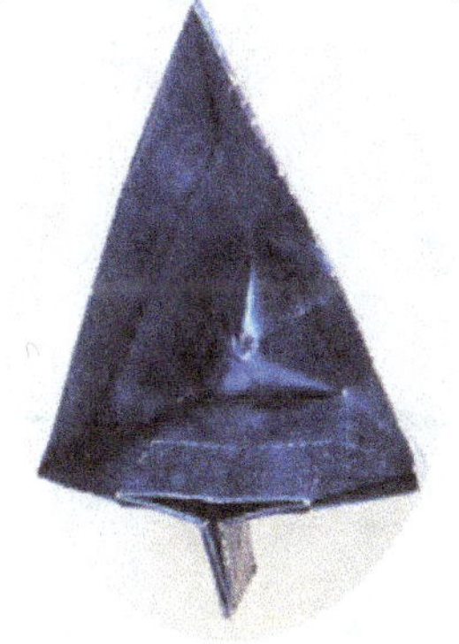

Tree and Leaf Dishes
One uncut square each
These are variations on the Spade Dish
Unpublished as of 19 Sept. 2017

Locking Tato Box
One uncut square
Unpublished as of 19 Sept. 2017

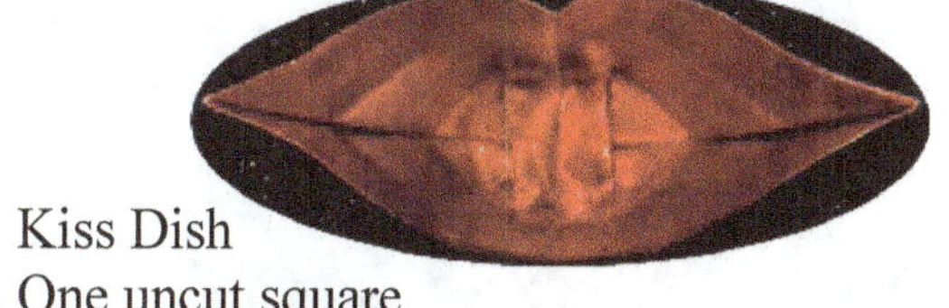

Kiss Dish
One uncut square
This is a slight variation on the Diamond Dish
Unpublished as of 19 Sept. 2017

Storigami

Storigami is storytelling with origami. Each fold moves a bit of the story forward. Some such stories are used to make a folding sequence memorable for beginning folders. Other stories are meant to entertain. Often the model is an action model, whose action becomes the last segment of the story. My stories for these two original action models and three traditional models are meant to entertain.

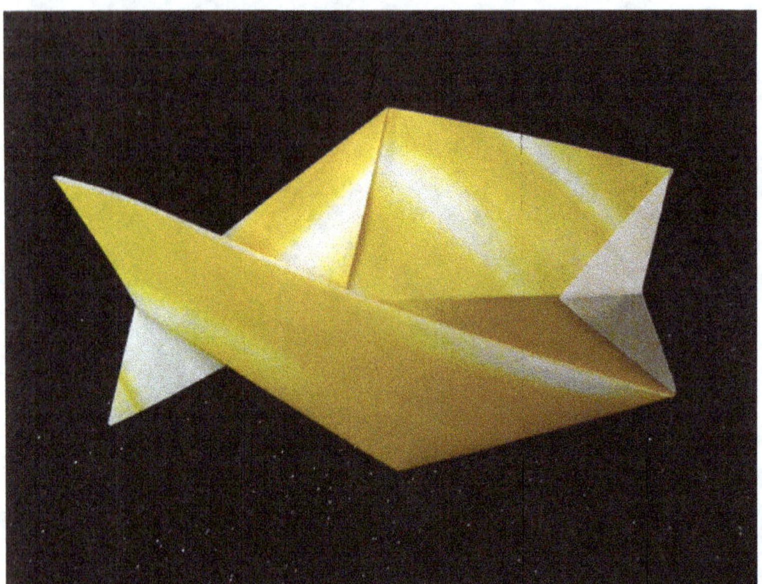

Gabby Guppy
One uncut square
Action model: The mouth opens and closes.
Unpublished as of 19 September 2017

Also have stories for the traditional models:

Pajarita
American Jumping Frog
Waterbomb

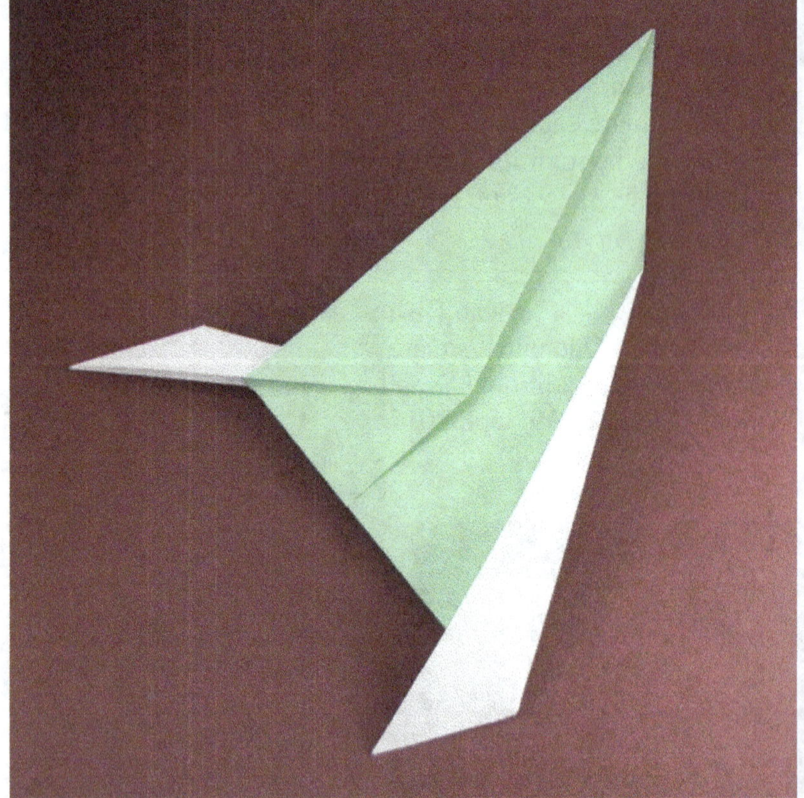

Flapping Hummingbird
One uncut square
Action model: The wings flap.
Unpublished as of 19 September 2017

Say It With Origami

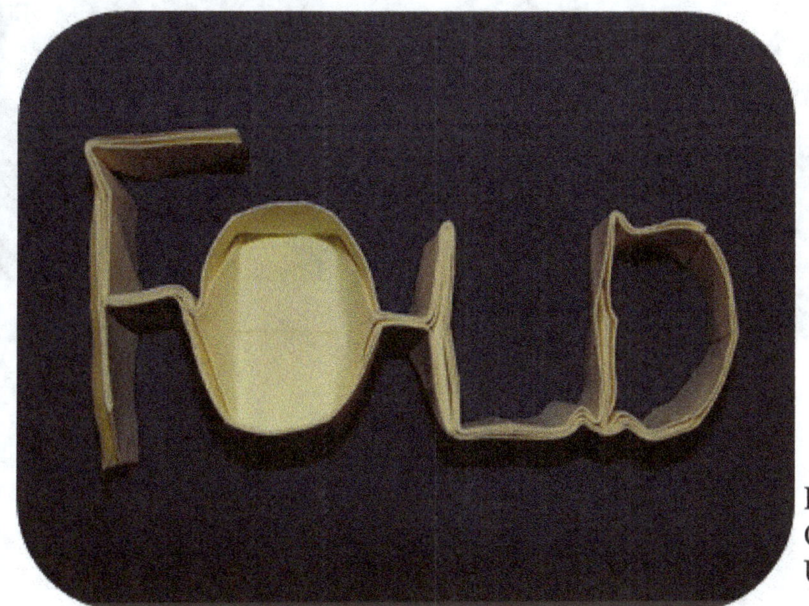

Supercalifragilisticexpialidocious
One uncut 2:45 rectangle (using an 8x180 grid)
Unpublished as of 19 September 2017

Fold
One uncut 1:2 rectangle
Unpublished as of 19 September 2017

This original blend of origami and calligraphy is systematic. Using it, I can design and fold practically any word using the English alphabet, including extraordinarily long words like "Supercalifragilisticexpialisdocious" and personalized names. The Dollar Puns section provides many more examples. The subroutines that form the various letters are based on my shovel-folding approach to box-pleating suited to models of line drawings such as my stick figures.

Boo!
One uncut 1:2 rectangle of foil-backed paper
Published in the <u>OrigaMIT 2013 Convention Book</u>

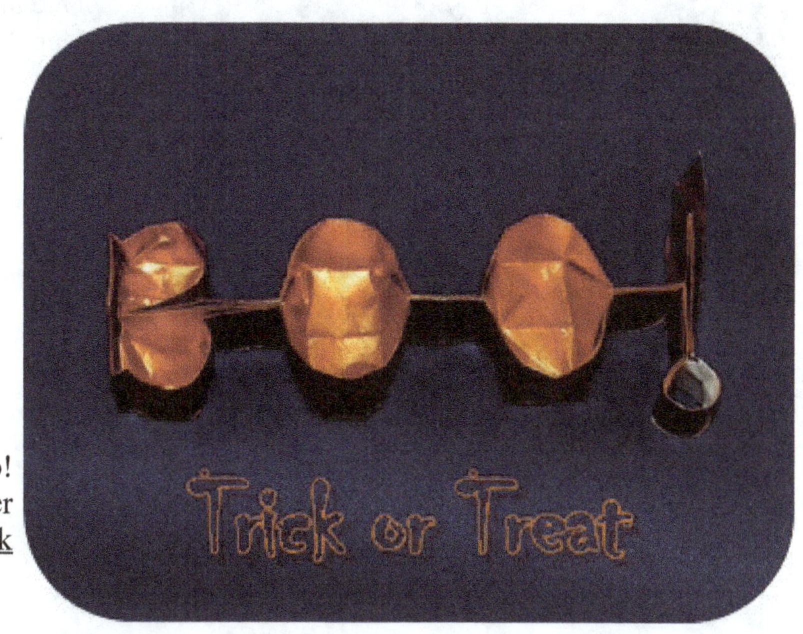

Dollar Origami
(Orikane)

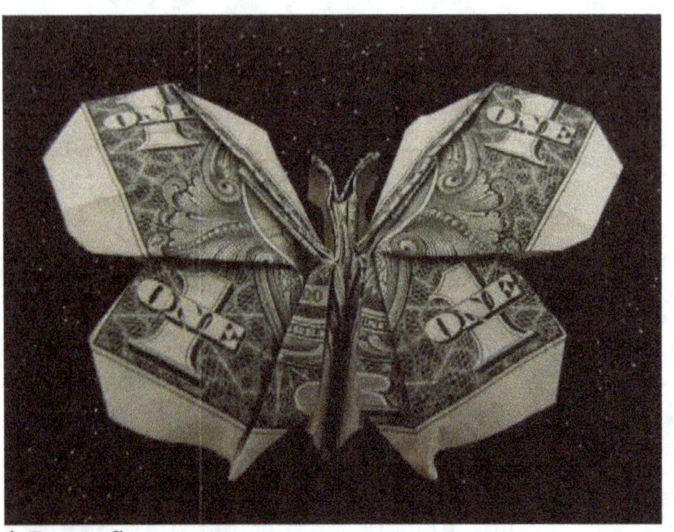

$ Butterfly
One uncut U. S. dollar bill
Unpublished as of 19 September 2017

Honest Abe
One uncut U. S. dollar bill
Unpublished as of 19 September 2017

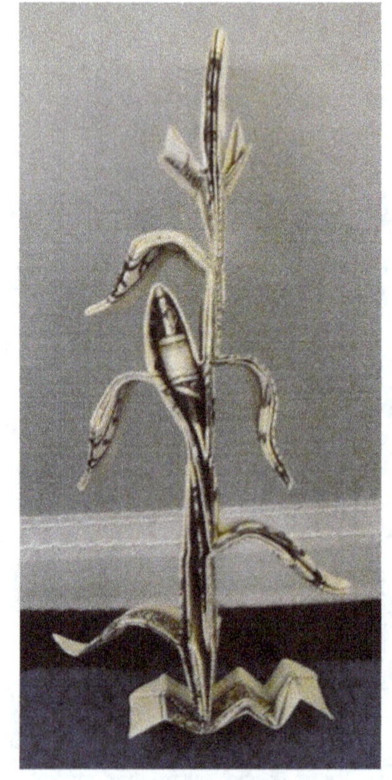

Corn Ready To Harvest
One uncut play U. S. dollar bill
Unpublished as of 19 September 2017

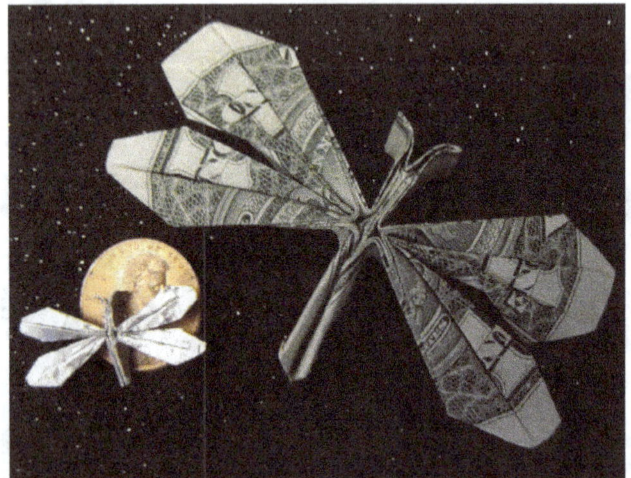

$ Dragonfly w/ Variation for 1:2 rectangle
One uncut U. S. dollar bill (Right)
1:2 paper-backed foil rectangle (Left)
Unpublished as of 19 September 2017

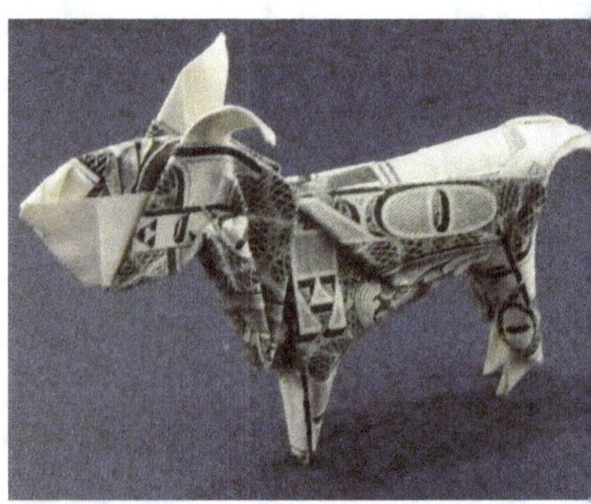

Donkey
One uncut U. S. dollar bill
Unpublished as of 19 September 2017

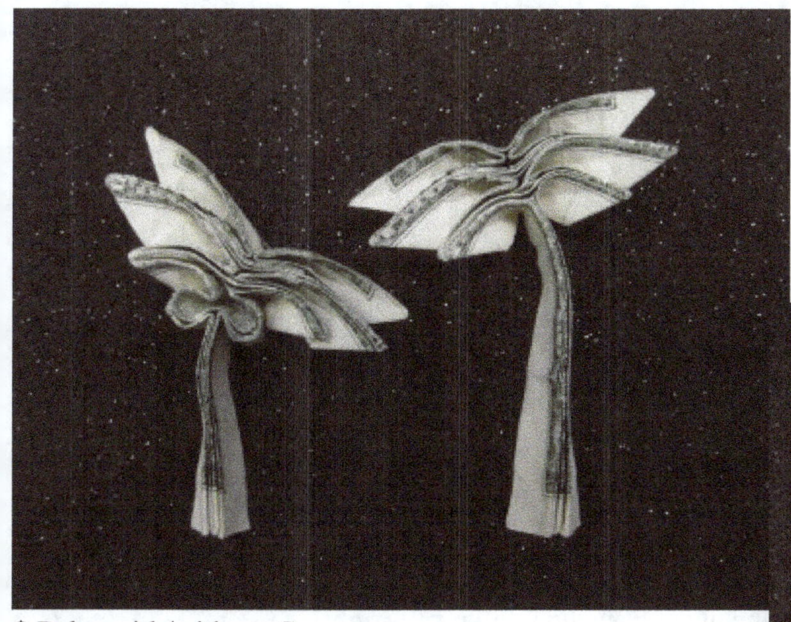

$ Palm with/without Coconuts
One uncut U. S. dollar bill (per tree)
Unpublished as of 19 September 2017

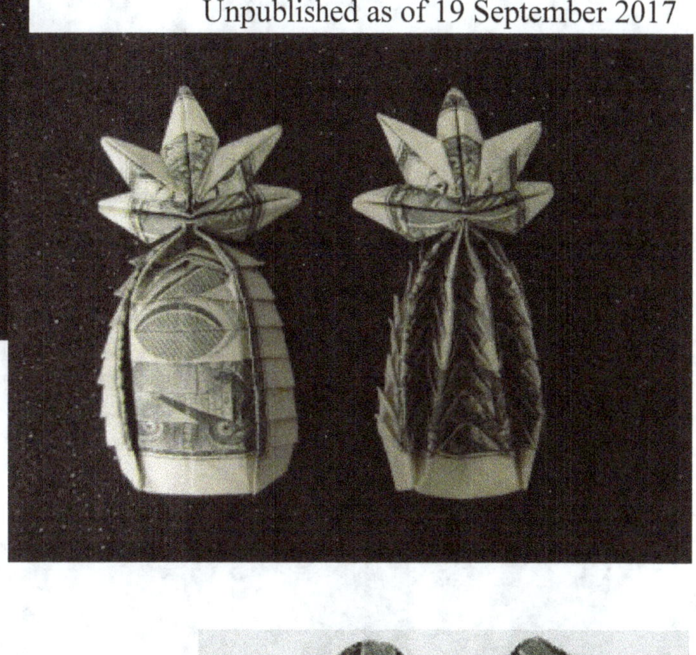

$ Pineapples
One uncut U. S. dollar bill (per pineapple)
Unpublished as of 19 September 2017

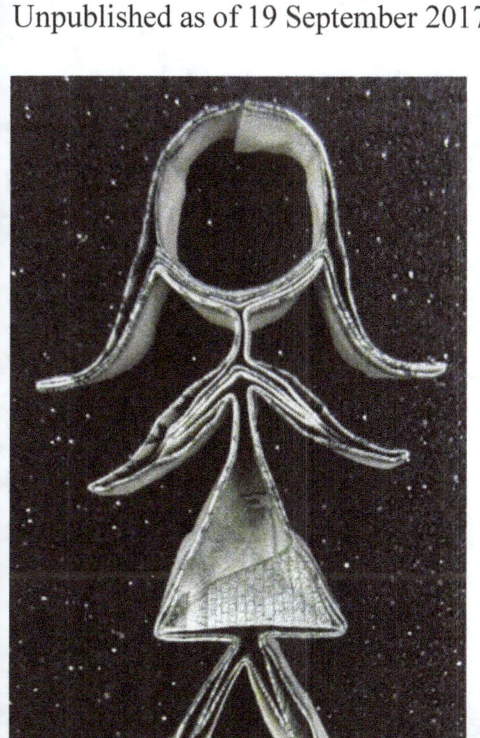

$tick Figure Girl
One uncut U. S. dollar bill
Unpublished as of 19 September 2017

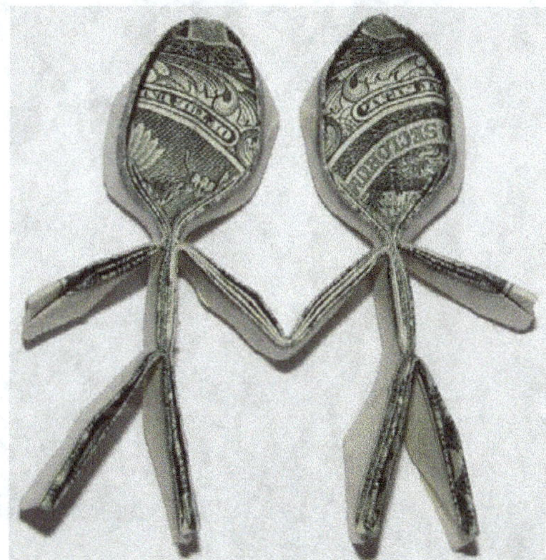

Friends Forever
One uncut U. S. dollar bill
Unpublished as of 19 September 2017

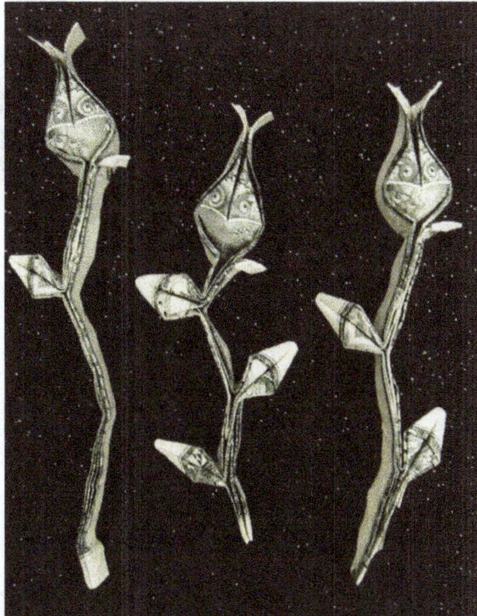

$ Long-Stemmed Roses with Thorns
One uncut U. S. dollar bill (per rose)
Unpublished as of 19 Sept.2017

14.

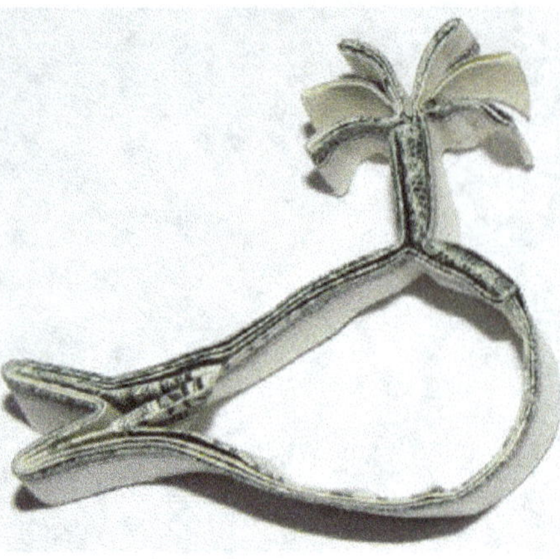

$pouting Whale
One uncut U. S. dollar bill (left)
Unpublished as of 19 September 2017

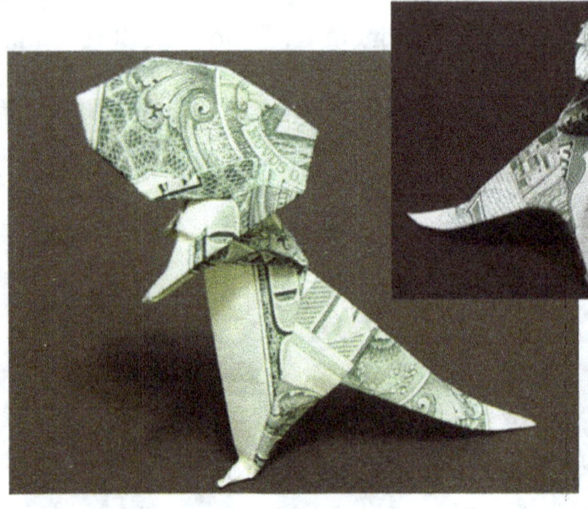

$ Tyrannosaur
One uncut U. S. dollar bill (left)
One uncut Canadian dollar bill (right)
Unpublished as of 19 September 2017

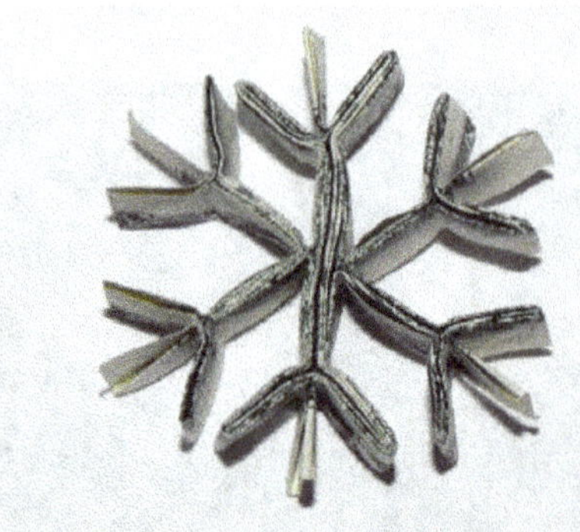

$nowflake
One uncut U. S. dollar bill
Unpublished as of 19 Sept. 2017

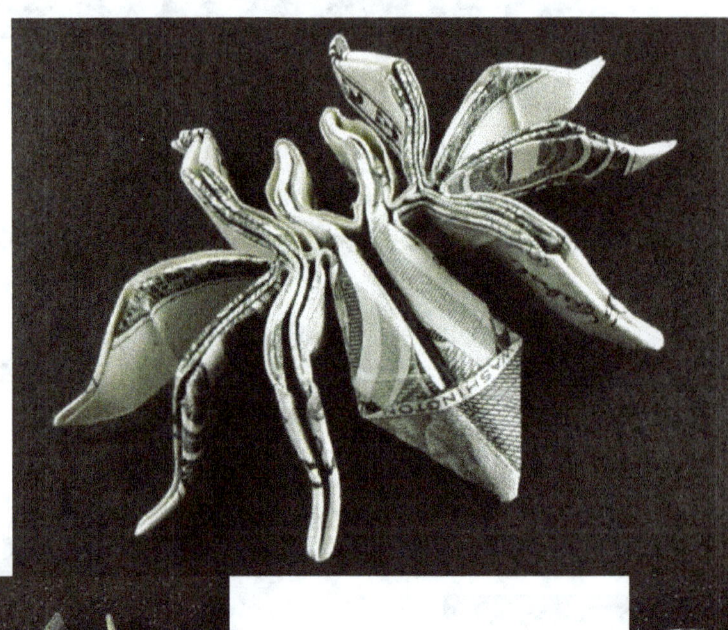

$pider
One uncut U. S. dollar bill
1:4 variant published in Creased issue 5

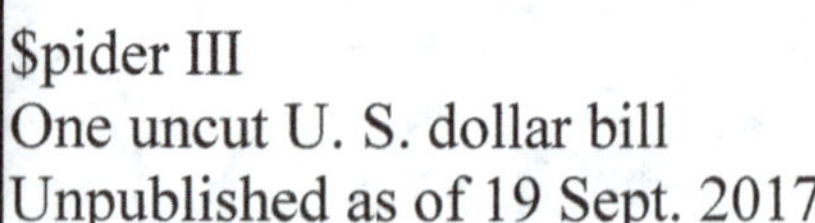

$pider II
One uncut U. S. dollar bill
Unpublished as of 19 Sept. 2017

$pider III
One uncut U. S. dollar bill
Unpublished as of 19 Sept. 2017

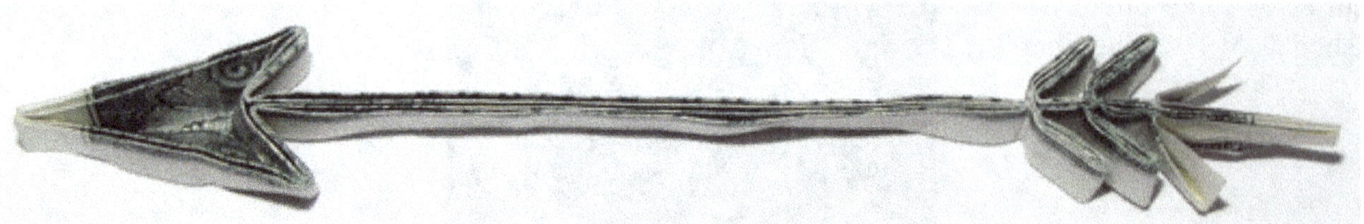

Arrow
One uncut U. S. dollar bill
Unpublished as of 19 Sept. 2017

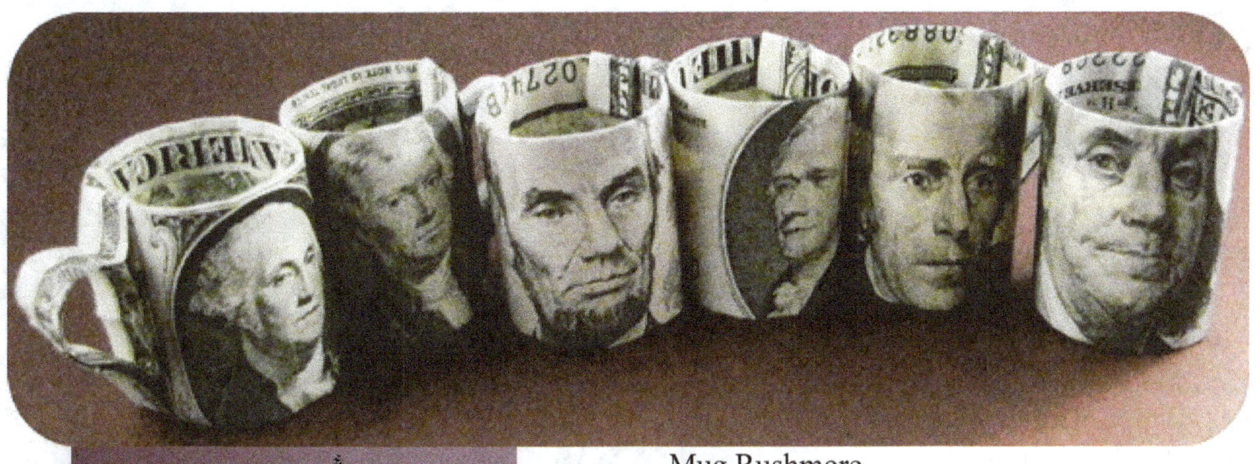

Mug Rushmore

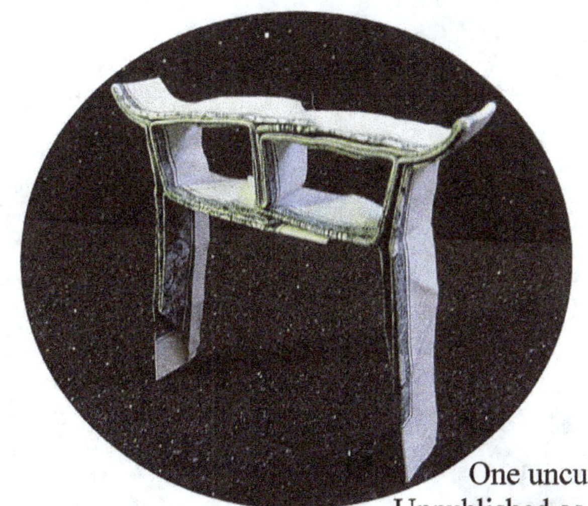

Bottomless Cup of Coffee
One uncut U. S. dollar bill
This model can also use somewhat longer or shorter rectangles.
Unpublished as of 19 September 2017

Torii Gate
One uncut U. S. dollar bill
Unpublished as of 19 Sept. 2017

Pagoda
One uncut U. S. dollar bill
Unpublished as of 19 Sept. 2017

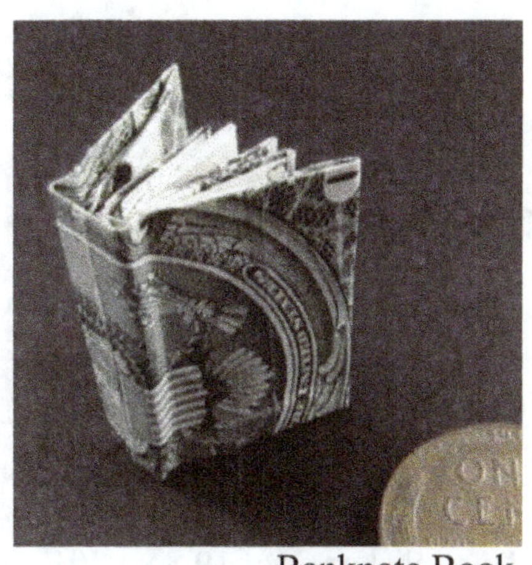

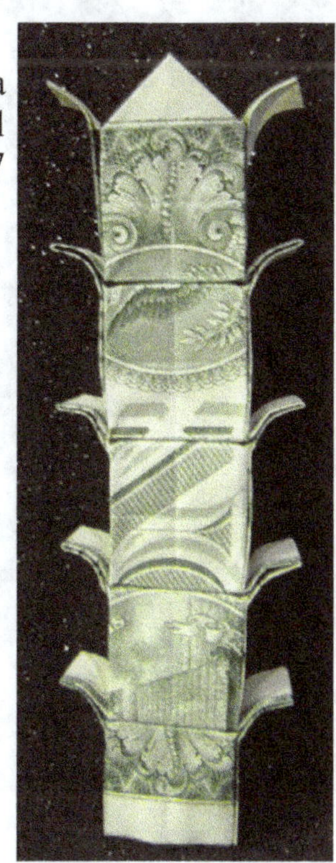

Tepee
One uncut U. S. dollar bill (left)
Unpublished as of 19 September 2017

Banknote Book
One uncut U. S. dollar bill
Unpublished as of 19 Sept. 2017

16

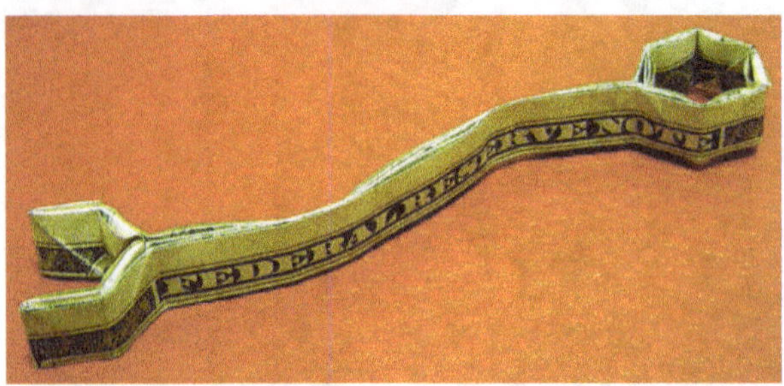

Combination Wrench
One uncut U. S. dollar bill
This model can use any banknotes or other
long rectangles. Ends can be either open or
closed ends for various wrenches.
Unpublished as of 19 September 2017

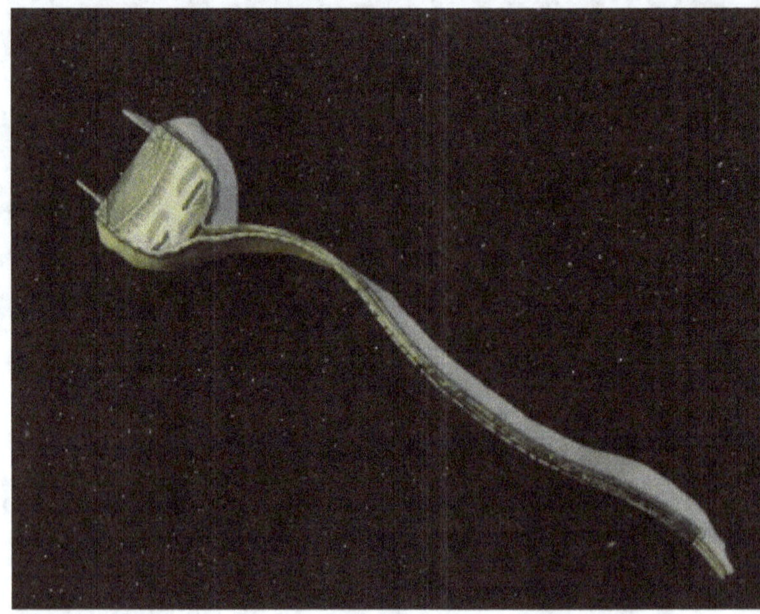

Electric Bill
One uncut U. S. dollar bill
This model can use any banknotes or other long rectangles.
Unpublished as of 19 September 2017

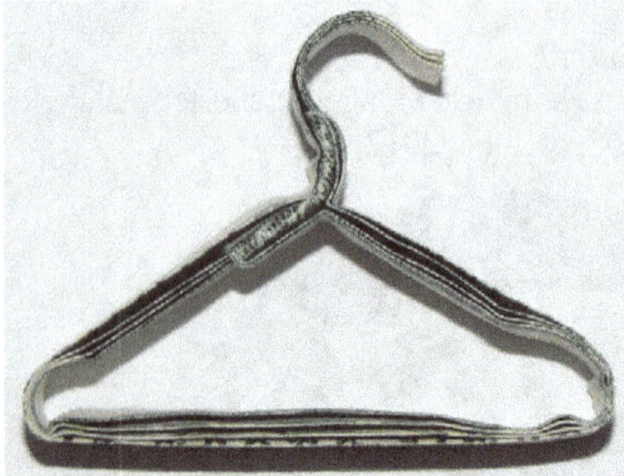

Coat Hanger
One uncut U. S. dollar bill
This model can use other long rectangles.
Unpublished as of 19 September 2017

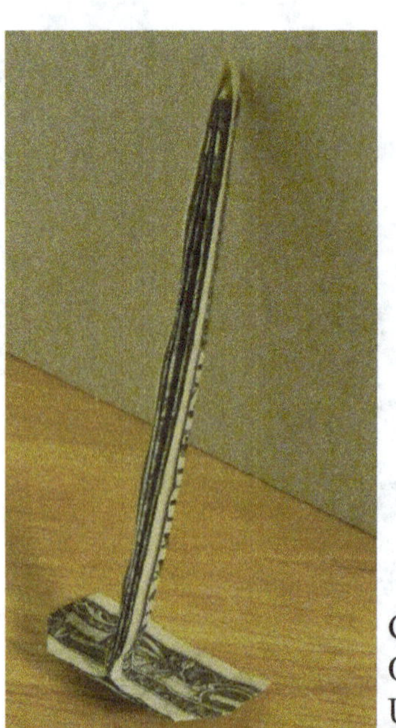

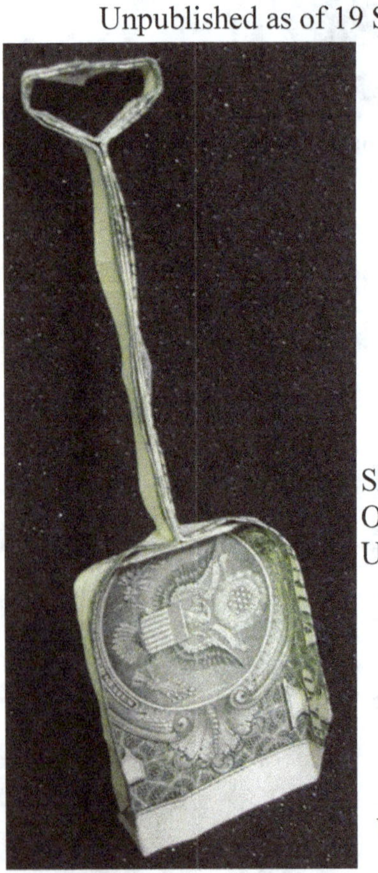

Shovel
One uncut U. S. dollar bill
Unpublished as of 19 Sept.2017

Garden Hoe
One uncut U. S. dollar bill
Unpublished as of 19 Sept.2017

End Wrench
One uncut U. S. dollar bill
Unpublished as of 19 Sept.2017

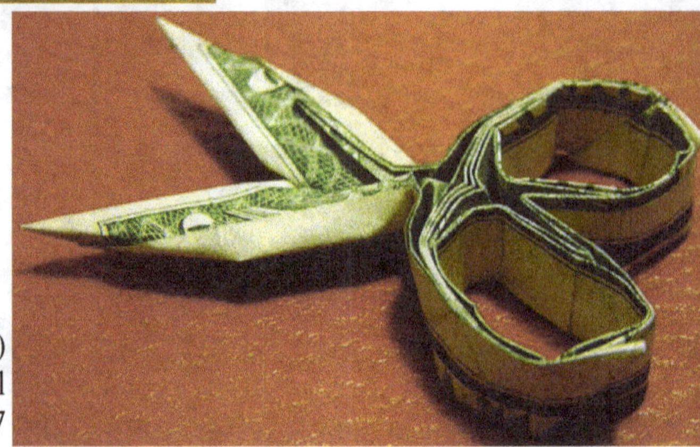

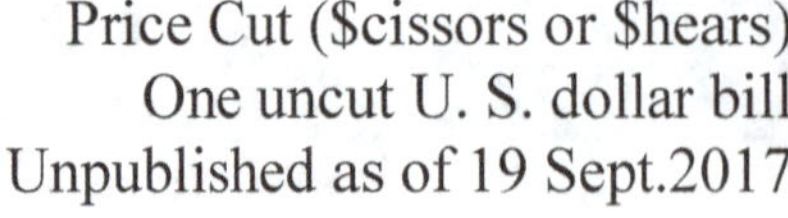

Price Cut ($cissors or $hears)
One uncut U. S. dollar bill
Unpublished as of 19 Sept.2017

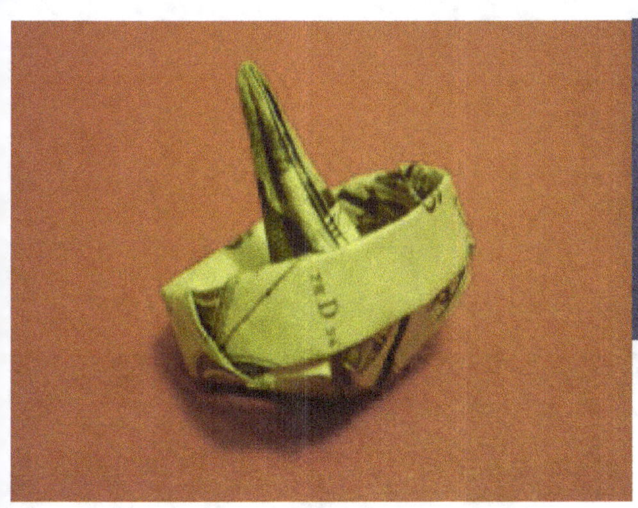

[$pinning] Tip Top
Action model: it spins
One uncut U. S. dollar bill
Unpublished as of 19 Sept. 2017

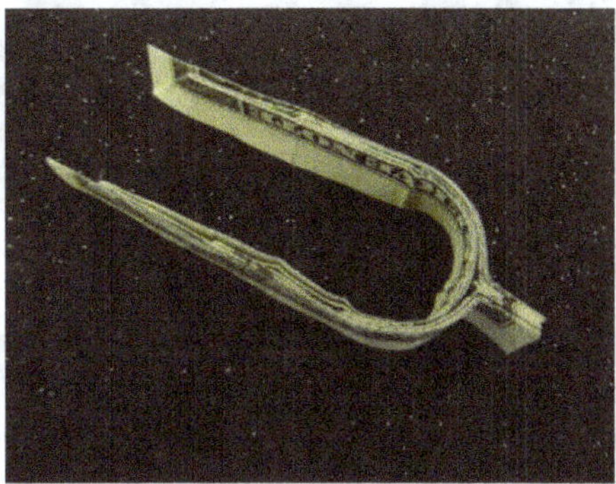

Tuning Fork
Action model: vibrates
One uncut U. S. dollar bill
Unpublished as of 19 Sept. 2017

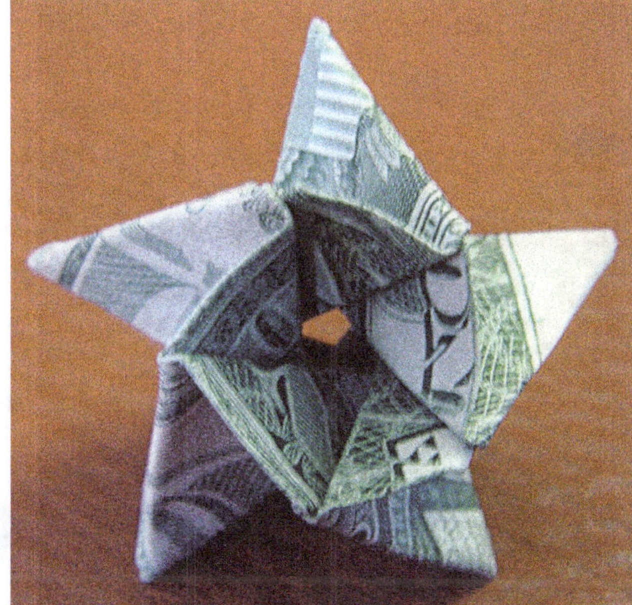

$pinning $tar
Action model: it spins on a toothpick
One uncut U. S. dollar bill
Unpublished as of 19 Sept. 2017

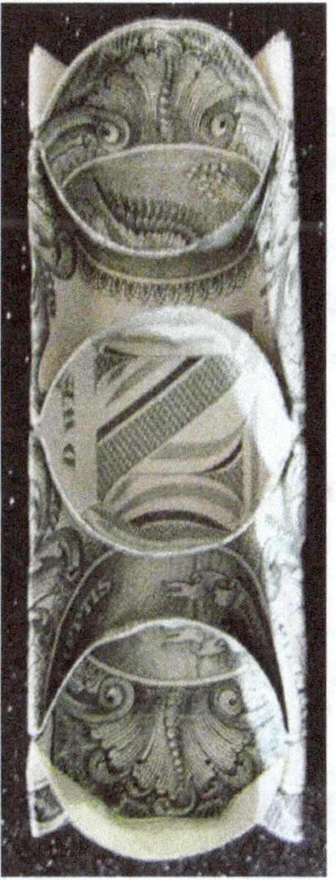

Traffic $ignal
One uncut U. S. dollar bill
Unpublished as of 19 Sept. 2017

Not shown:

Wand
Shallow Box
Wild Boar
Dangling Spider

Mom & Pop Origami (Orikane)

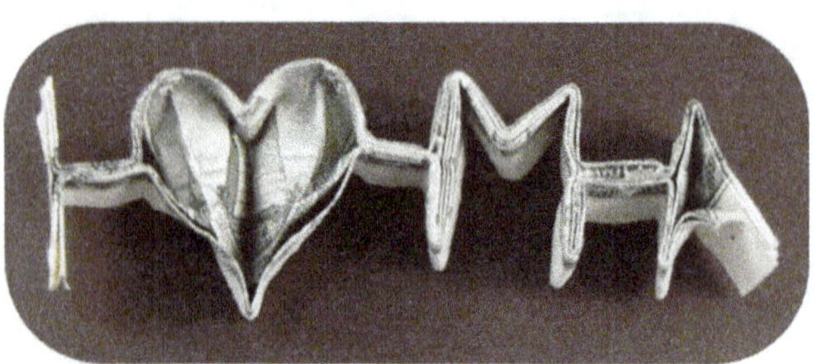

I-♥-Ma (or I-♥-MA for Massachusetts)
One uncut U. S. dollar bill
Unpublished as of 19 September 2017

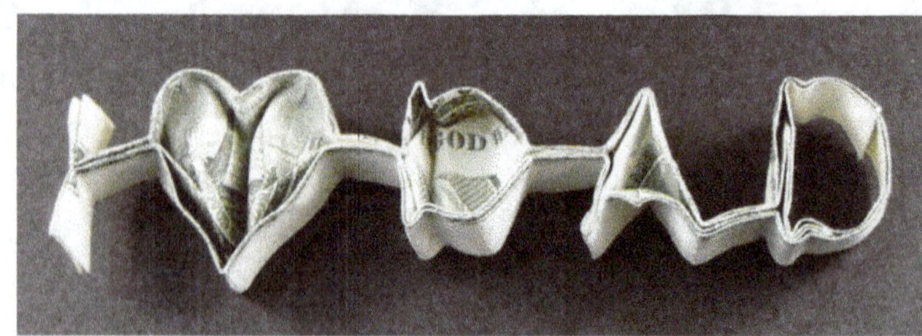

I-♥-Dad
One uncut U. S. dollar bill
Unpublished as of 19 September 2017

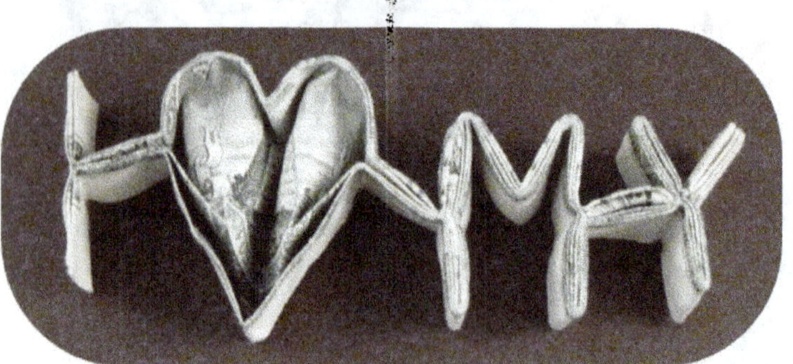

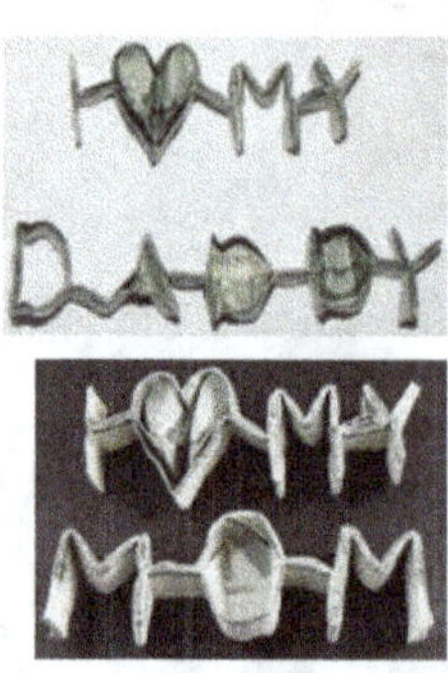

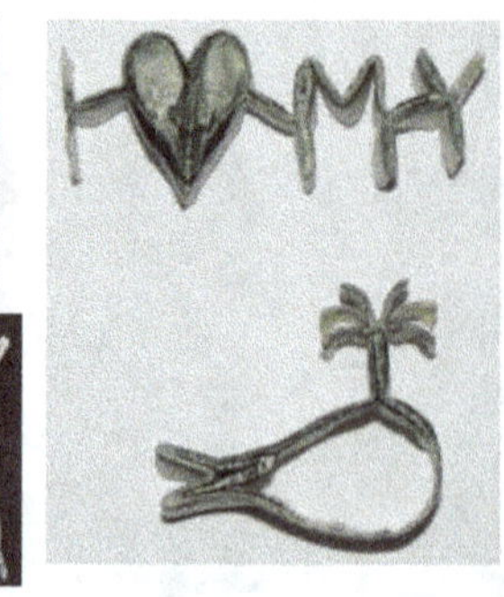

I-♥-My ___________ (pair with another model)
One uncut U. S. dollar bill
Unpublished as of 19 September 2017

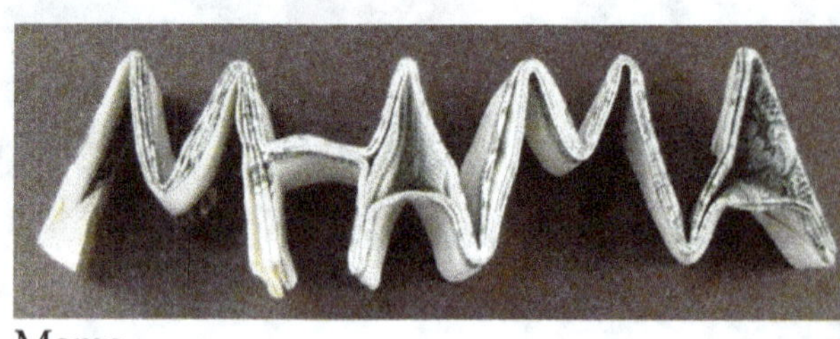

Daddy
One uncut U. S. dollar bill
Unpublished as of 19 September 2017

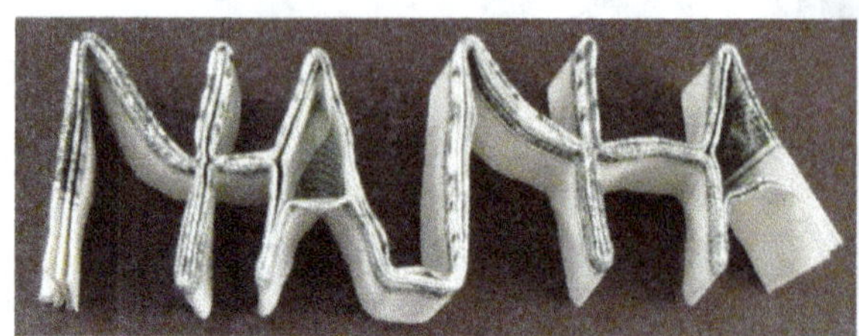

Mama
One uncut U. S. dollar bill
Unpublished as of 19 September 2017

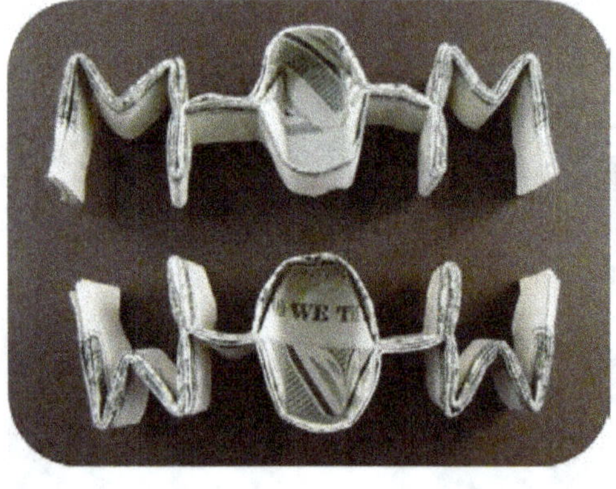

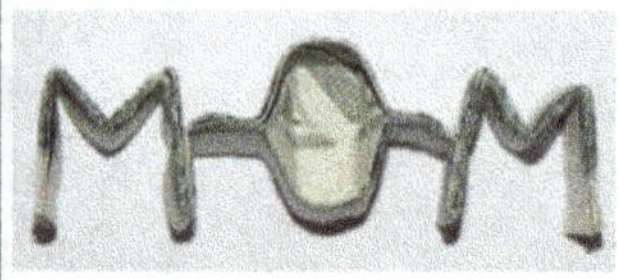

Mom=Wow
One uncut U. S. dollar bill
Unpublished as of 19 September 2017

Nana
One uncut U. S. dollar bill
Unpublished as of 19 September 2017

Love of Money (Orikane)

These models are designed for U. S. currency, but fake banknotes other 8:19 rectangles also work. The models do not depend on the printed design of the bills.

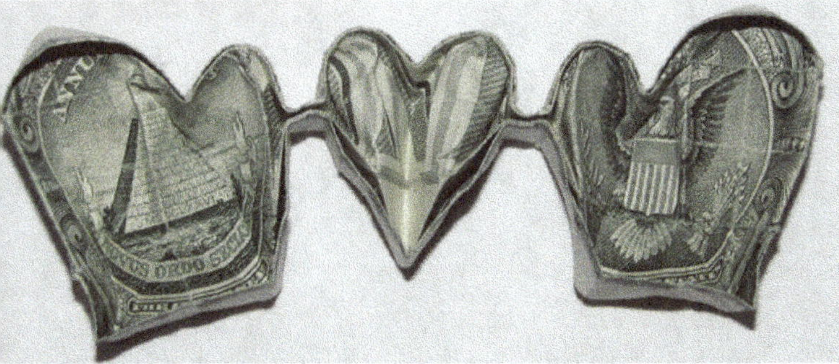

I-♥-U
One uncut U. S. dollar bill; it also looks good in red
Unpublished as of 19 Sept. 2017

Cold Hands, Warm Heart
One uncut U. S. dollar bill
Unpublished as of 19 September 2017

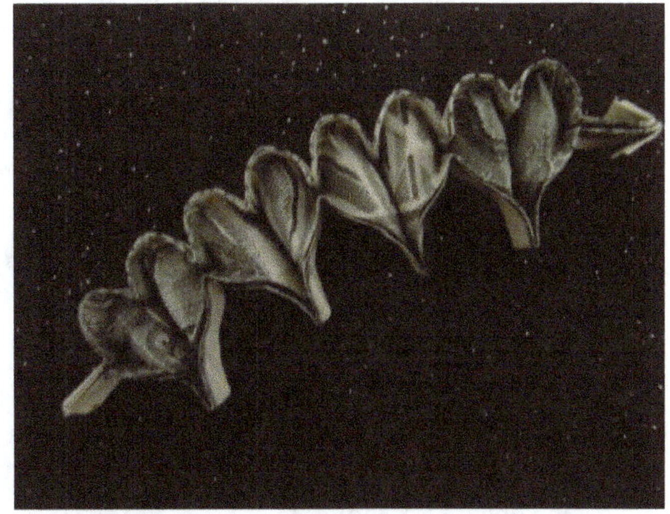

Heart Ka-Throb
One uncut U. S. dollar bill
Unpublished as of 19 September 2017

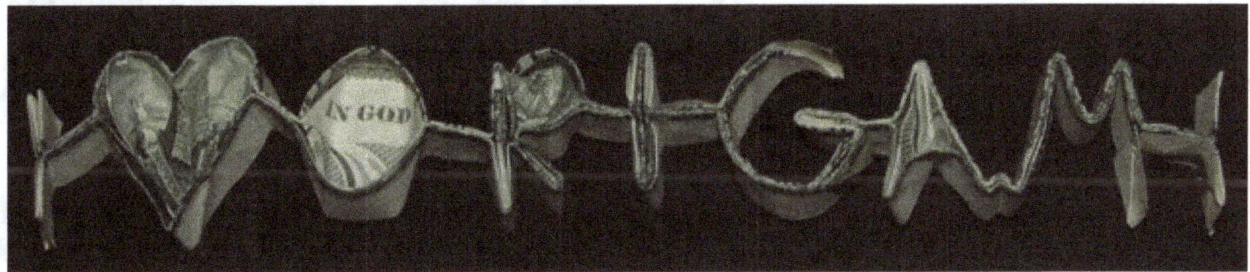

I-♥-Origami
Two uncut U. S. banknotes, joined fairly solidly by folding (no glue)
Unpublished as of 19 September 2017

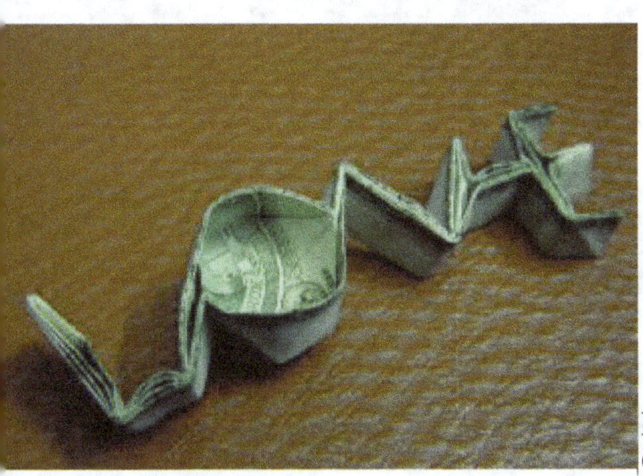

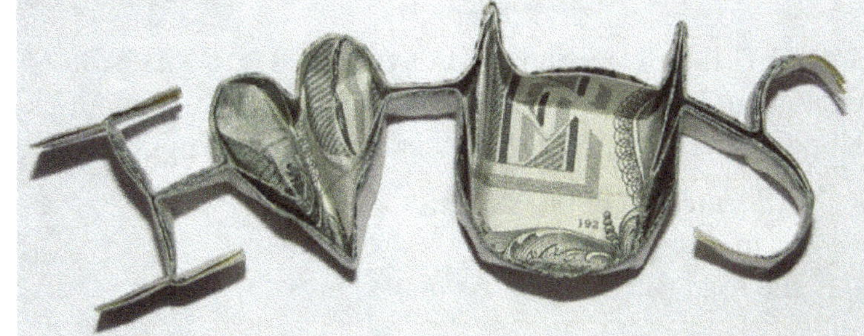

I-♥-Cats
Onr uncut U. S. dollar bill
Unpublished as of 19 September 2017

Love of Money
One uncut U. S. dollar bill
Unpublished as of 19 September 2017

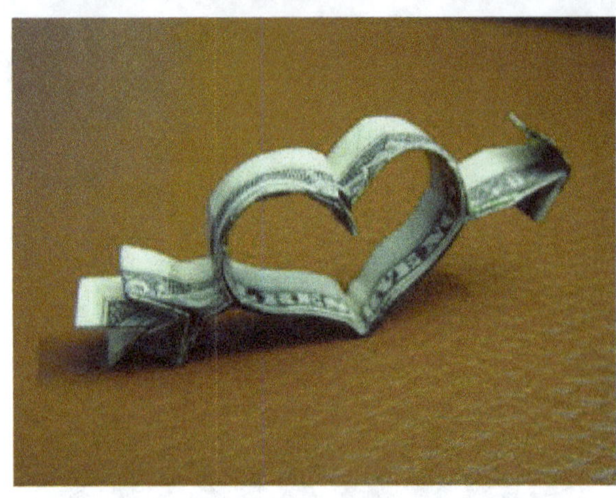

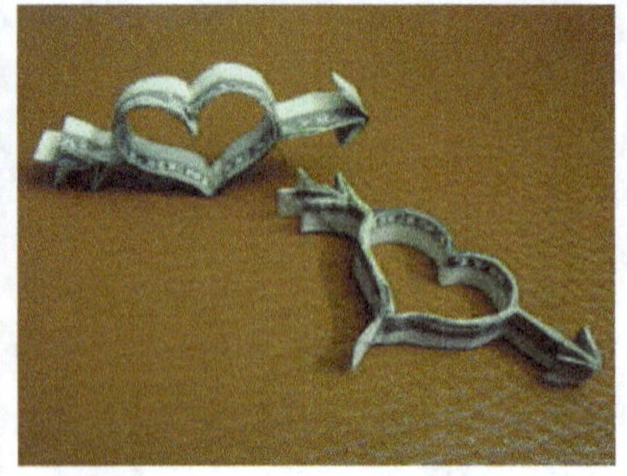

Love You Can Bank On
One uncut U. S. dollar bill
Published in <u>Love Origami Convention 2008</u>

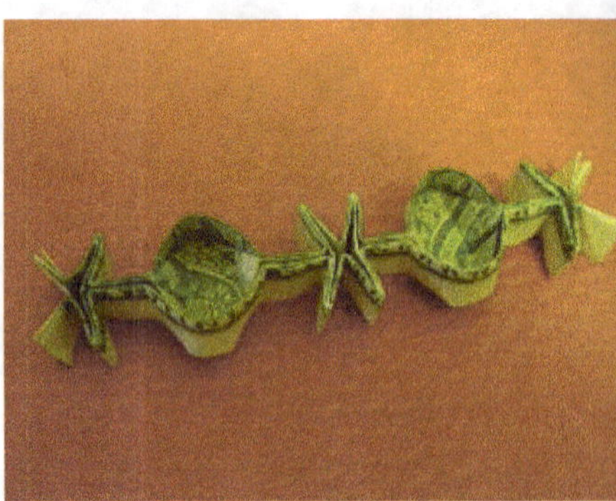

Bank Love Note (Hug$ & Ki$$e$)
One uncut U. S. dollar bill
Unpublished as of 19 Sept. 2017

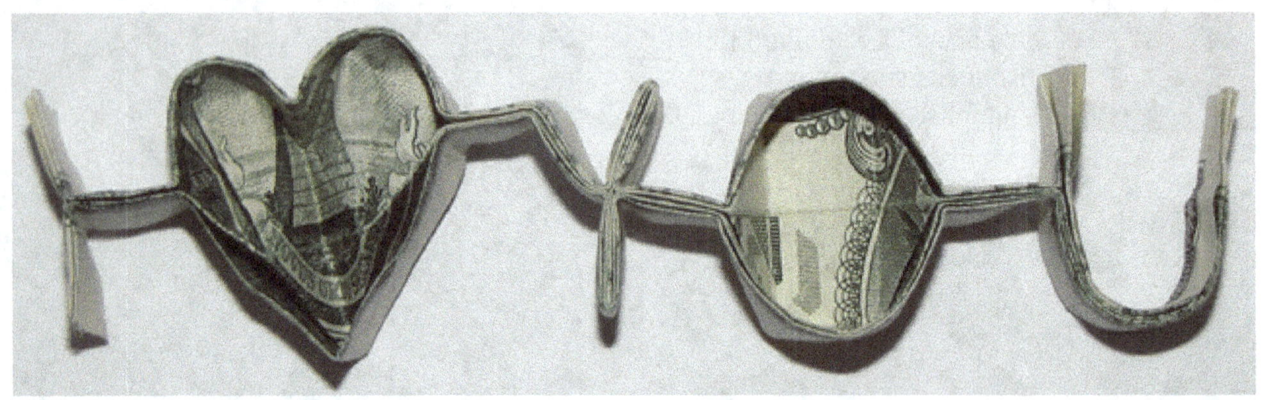

I-♥-You
One uncut U. S. dollar bill
Unpublished as of 19 September 2017

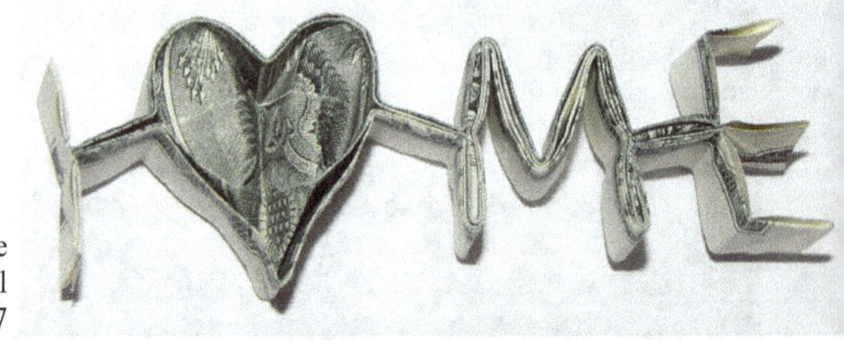

(ME is the U.S. postal code for the state of Maine.)

Ego Trip to Maine
One uncut U. S. dollar bill
Unpublished as of 19 September 2017

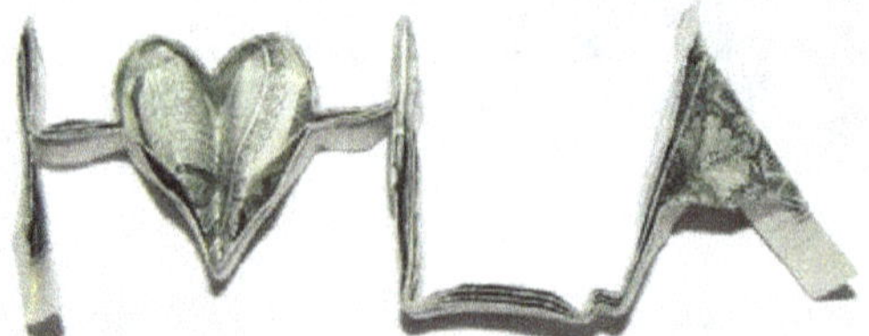

I-♥-LA (Either Louisiana or Los Angeles)
One uncut U. S. dollar bill
Unpublished as of 19 September 2017

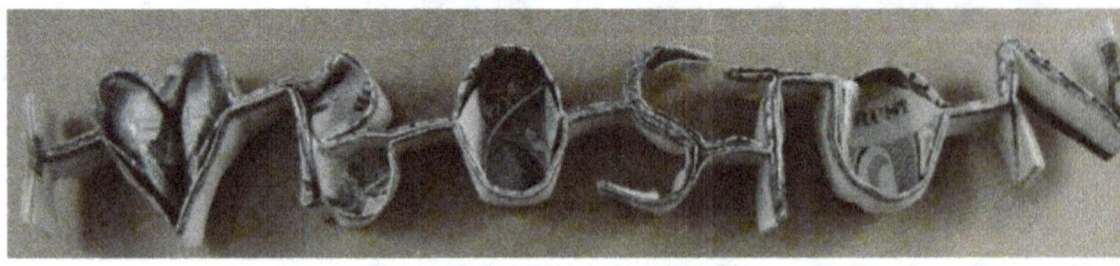

I-♥-Boston
Two uncut U. S. dollar bills, , joined fairly solidly by folding (no glue)
Unpublished as of 19 September 2017

All states.seem possible...
or maybe get the rest of
the road trip quickly...

I-♥-UK.is also feasible.

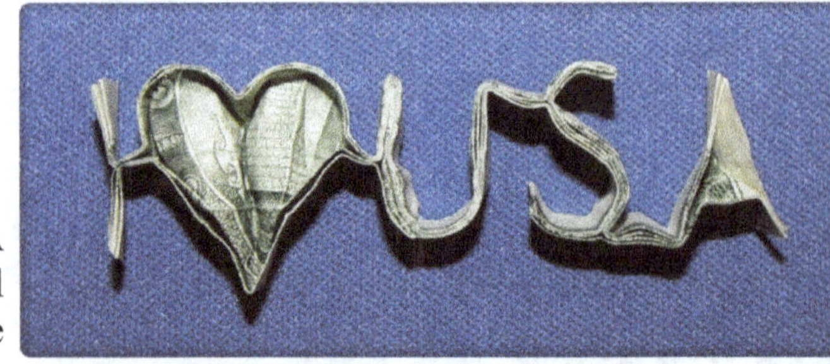

I-♥-USA
One uncut U. S. dollar bill
Published in <u>Election Money Folds 2012</u> on OUSA's website

Dollar Puns
(Orikane)

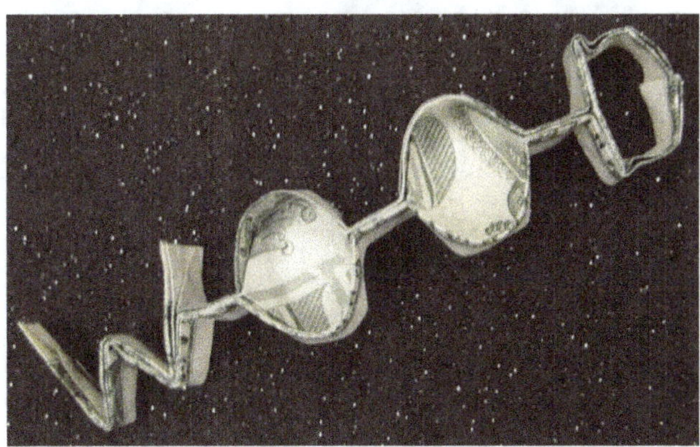

Money to Burn II
One uncut U. S. dollar bill
Unpublished as of 19 September 2017

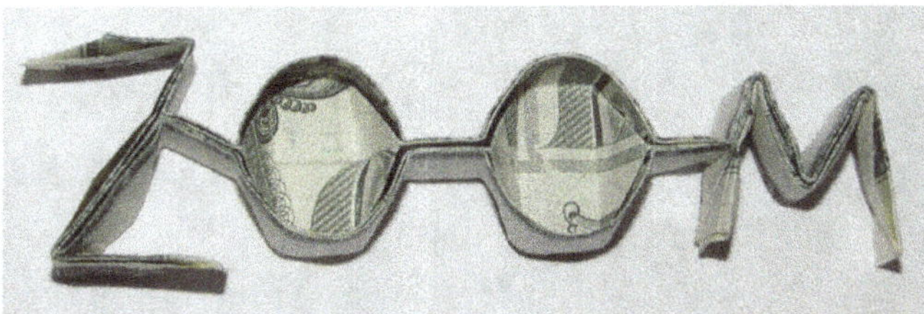

Fast money
One uncut U. S. dollar bill
Unpublished as of 19 September 2017

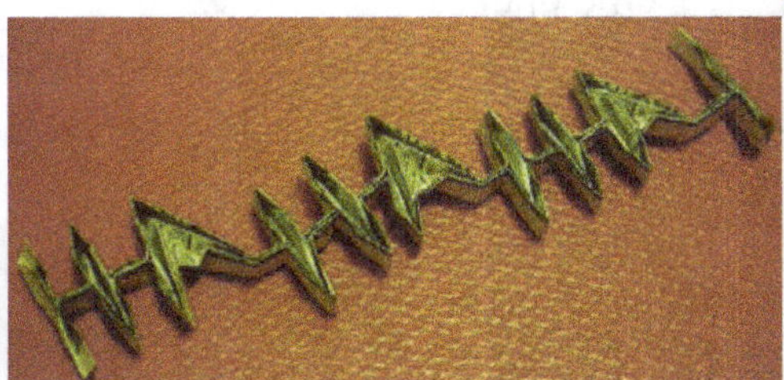

Funny Money
Three uncut U. S. dollar bills
Unpublished as of 19 Sept 2017

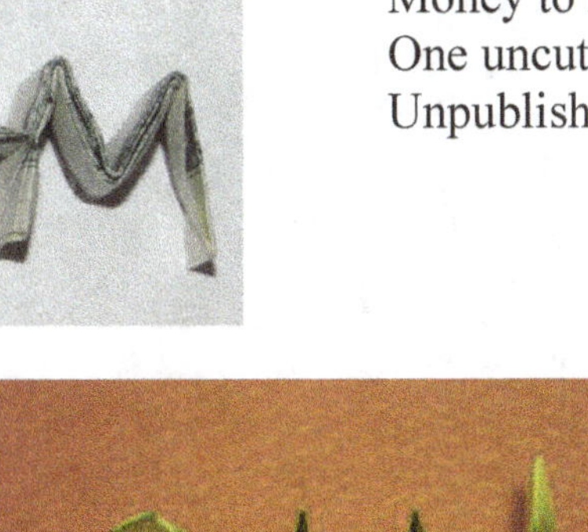

Hush Money
One uncut U. S. dollar bill
Unpublished as of 19 Sept 2017

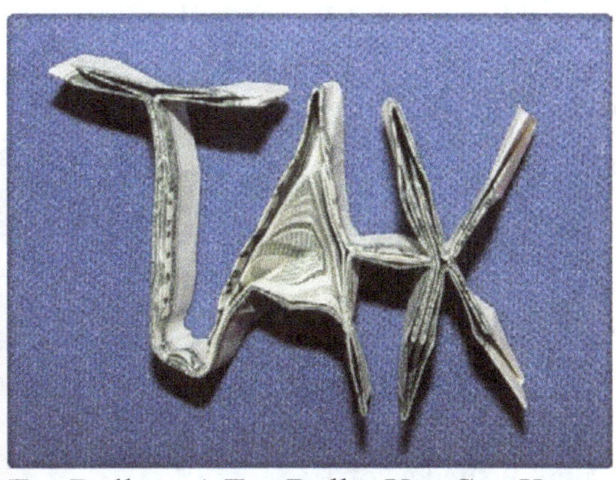

Tax Dollar – A Tax Dollar You Can Keep
One uncut U. S. dollar bill
Published in Election Money Folds 2012
on OrigamiUSA's website.

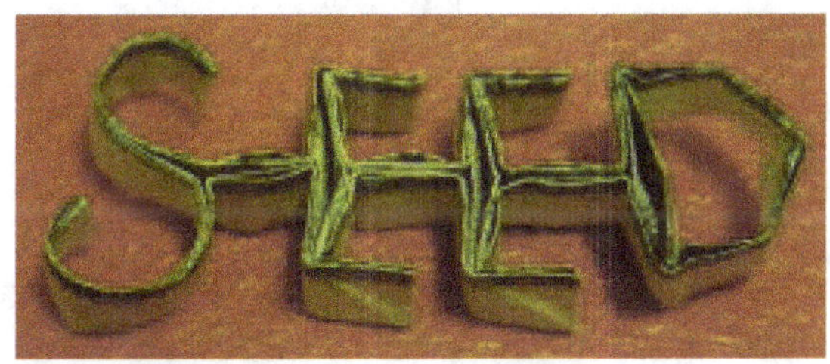

Seed Money
One uncut U. S. dollar bill
Unpublished as of 19 September 2017

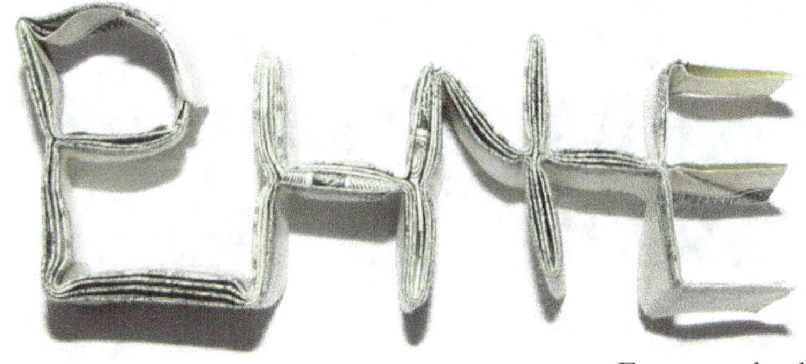

Evergreenback
One uncut U. S. dollar bill
Unpublished as of 19 September 2017

Most words and line-drawings now get wet-folded, but originally I folded them dry and still got reasonable results, as seen in some of these photos.

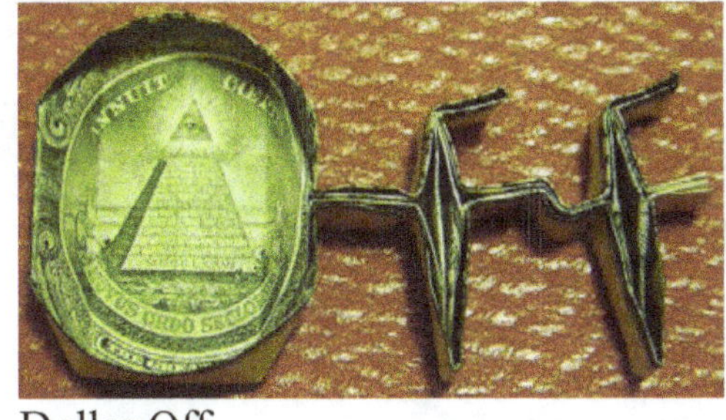

Dollar Off
One uncut U. S. dollar bill
Unpublished as of 19 September 2017

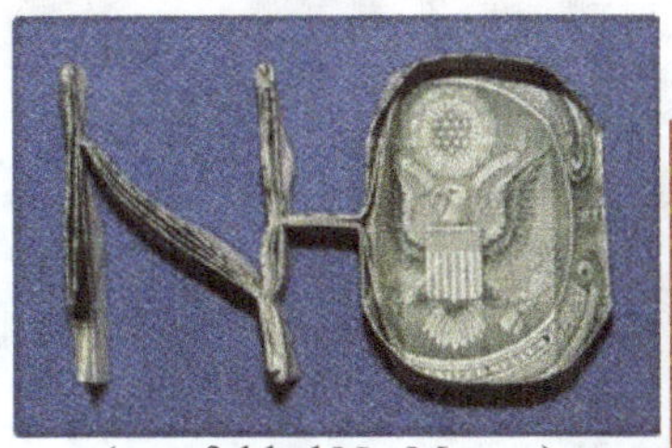

(wet-folded No Money)

(dry-folded On the Money)

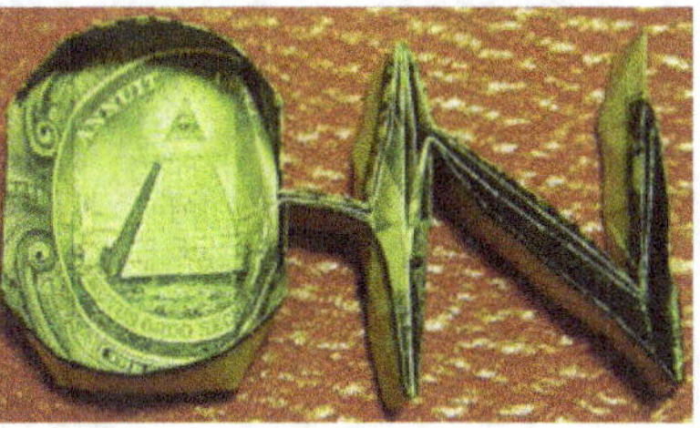

No Money & On the Money
One uncut U. S. dollar bill
Published in Election Money Folds 2012 on OUSA's website

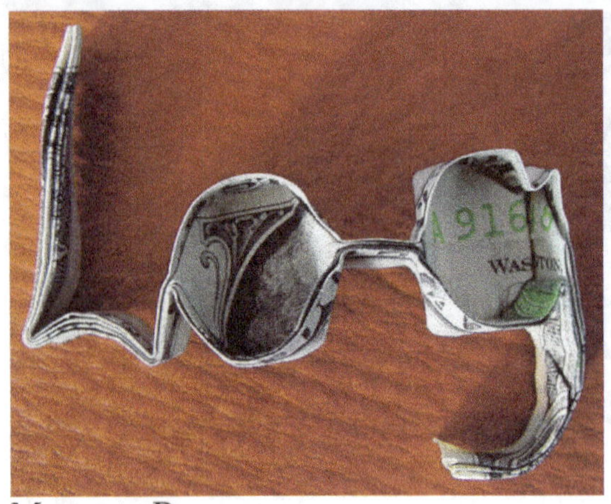

Money to Burn
One uncut U. S. dollar bill
Unpublished as of 19 September 2017

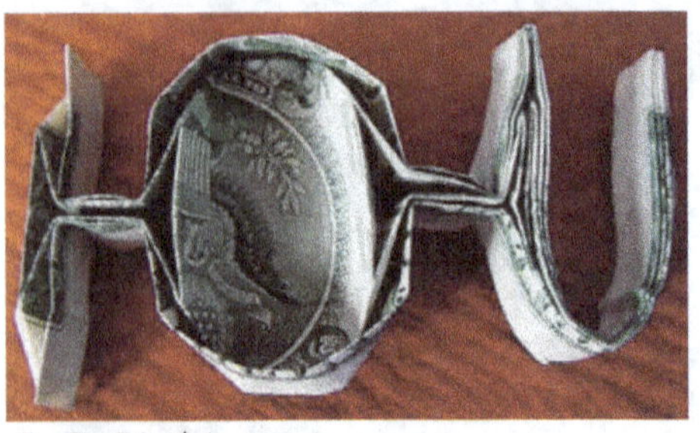

I. O. U. $1
One uncut U. S. dollar bill
Unpublished as of 19 Sept 2017

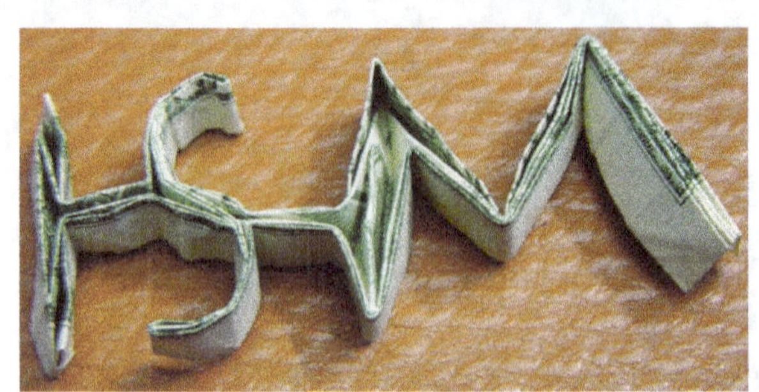

Capitalism
One uncut U. S. dollar bill
Unpublished as of 19 September 2017

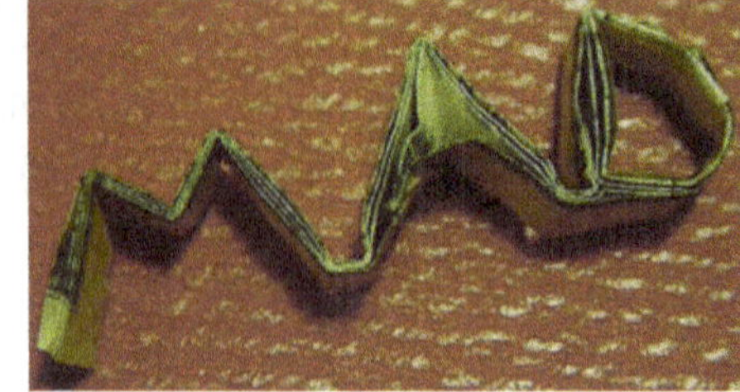

Mad Money
One uncut U. S. dollar bill
Unpublished as of 19 Sept. 2017

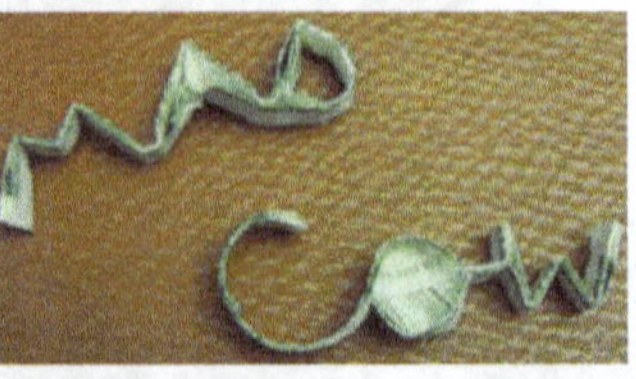

Cash Cow
One uncut U. S. dollar bill
Unpublished as of 19 Sept 2017

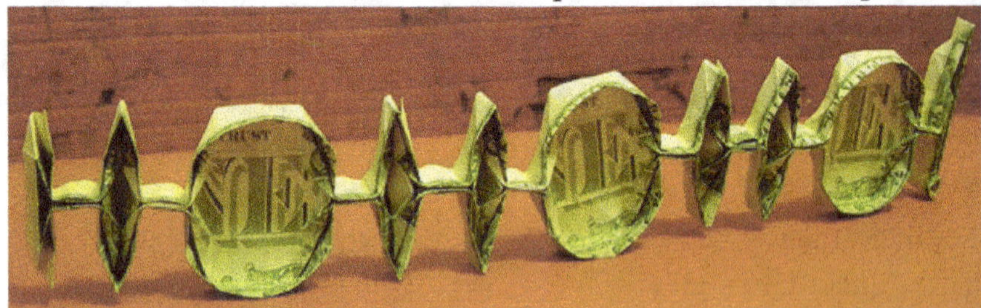

Xmas Money
Three uncut U. S. dollar bills
Unpublished as of 19 Sept 2017

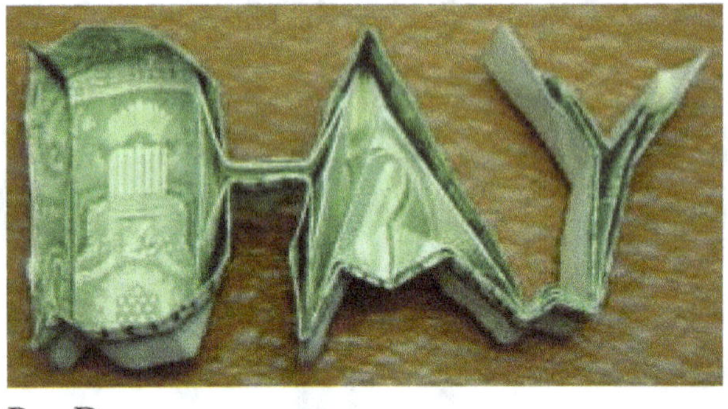

Pay Day
One uncut U. S. dollar bill
Unpublished as of 19 Sept 2017

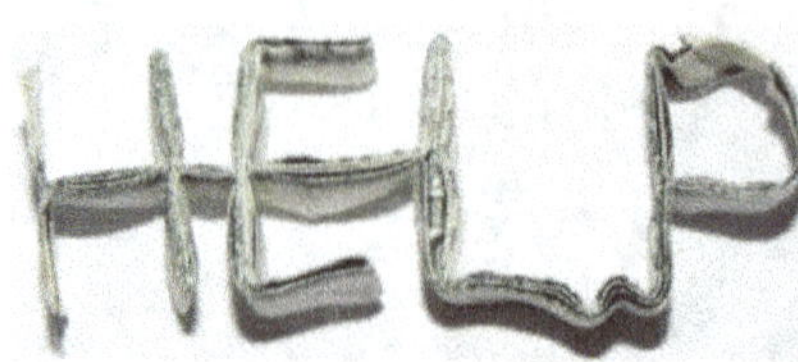

Financial Aid
One uncut U. S. dollar bill
Unpublished as of 19 Sept 2017

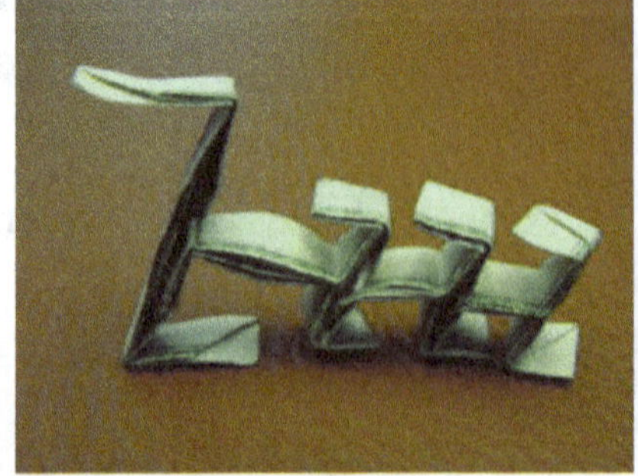

I Fold in my Sleep
One uncut U. S. dollar bill
Unpublished as of 19 Sept 2017

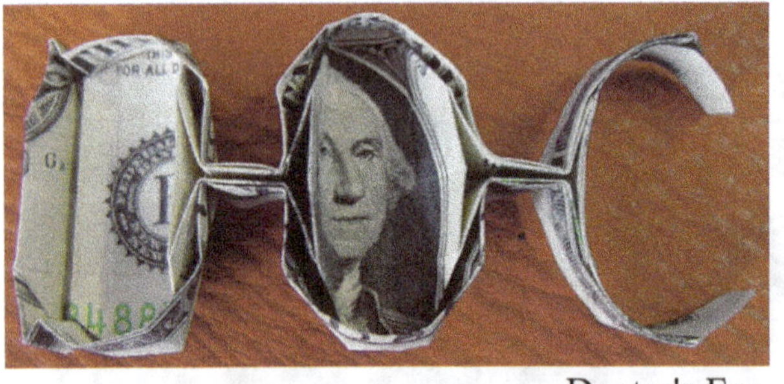

Doctor's Fee
One uncut U. S. dollar bills
Unpublished as of 19 Sept 2017

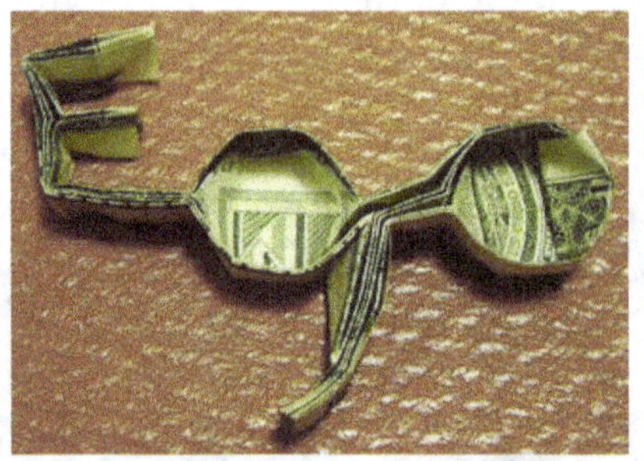

Cents of Self-Worth
One uncut U. S. dollar bill
Unpublished as of 19 Sept 2017

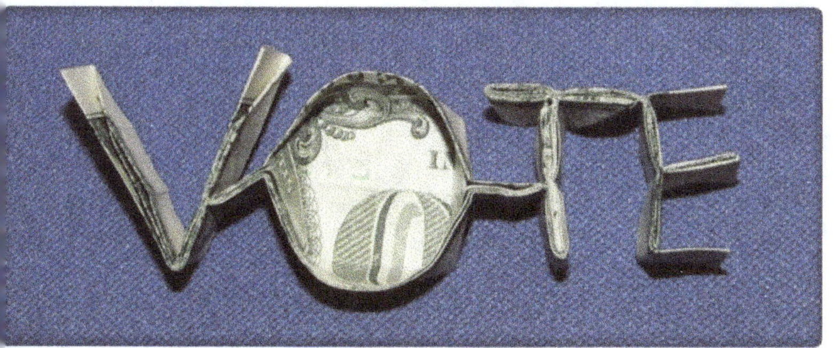

Election Money (Buying Your Vote)
One uncut U. S. dollar bill
Published in Election Money Folds 2012 on OUSA's website

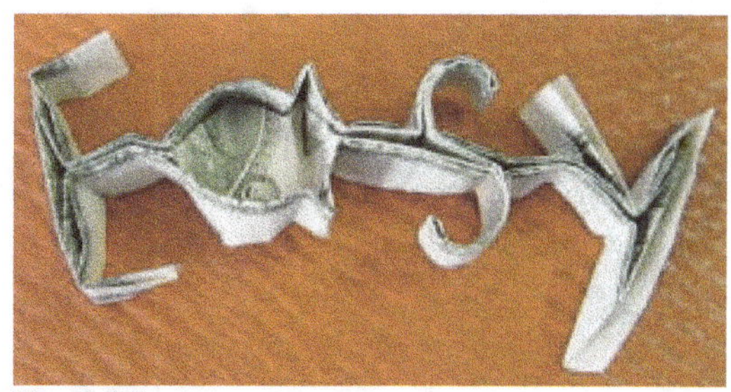

Easy Money
One uncut U. S. dollar bill
Unpublished as of 19 Sept 2017

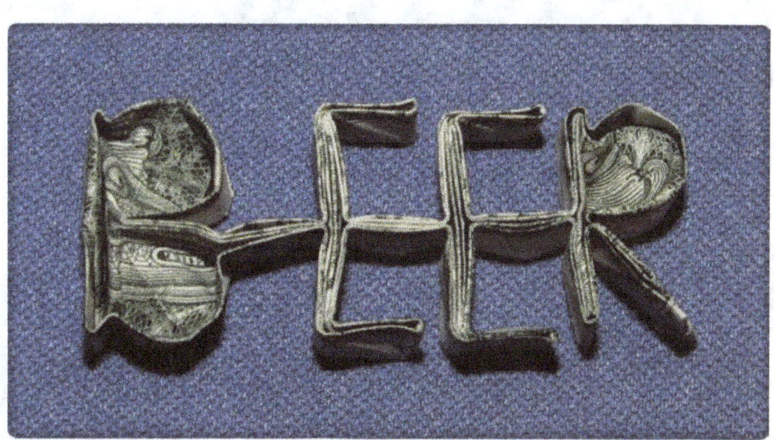

Beer Money
One uncut U. S. dollar bill
Published in Election Money Folds 2012 on OUSA's website

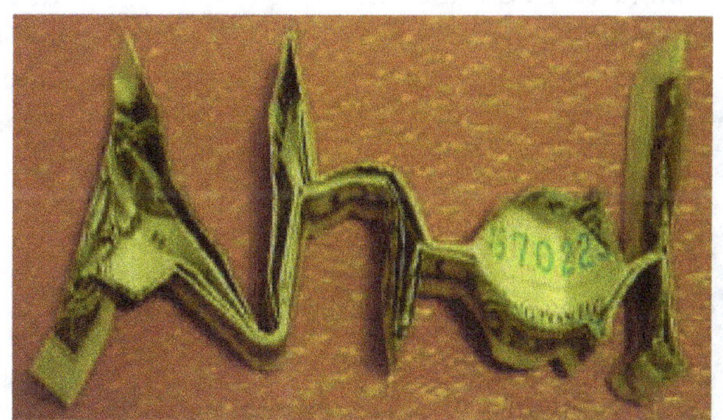

Cents of Discovery
One uncut U. S. dollar bill
Unpublished as of 19 Sept 2017

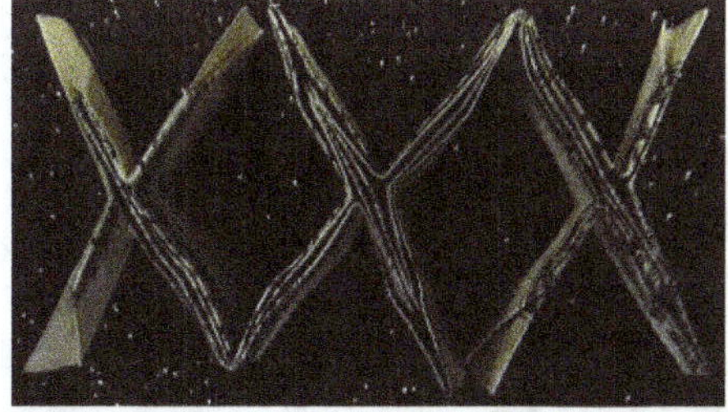

Dirty Money
One uncut U. S. dollar bill
Unpublished as of 19 Sept 2017

Not shown:

The Root of All Evil – EVIL
The Root of All Evil II – DEVIL
Pay Attention – HEED
Cents of Wonder – HOW
Billfold – FOLD
Money to Burn III – COAL
Emergency Funds – SOS
Greenback With Envy – ENVY
Financial Goal – GOAL
Give Money – GIVE
Don't Throw it After Bad – GOOD
Cash in Hand (or Money on Hand) – HAND
Money Can't Buy Happiness – HAPPY
I Already Gave – GAVE
Kiss Your Money Goodbye – KISS
Make Money – MAKE
Turn One into Many – MANY
Money is Power – WATT
Money Talks – CHAT
Save Money – SAVE
Sawbuck – SAW
Silver Dollar – Ag
Price Spike – SPIKE
Greenbackbone – SPINE
Tip Money – TIP
Double Your Money – two
OrigamiUSA – USA
Ohio Paper Folders – OHIO
Christmas Money II – XMAS

Dollar Amounts (Orikane)

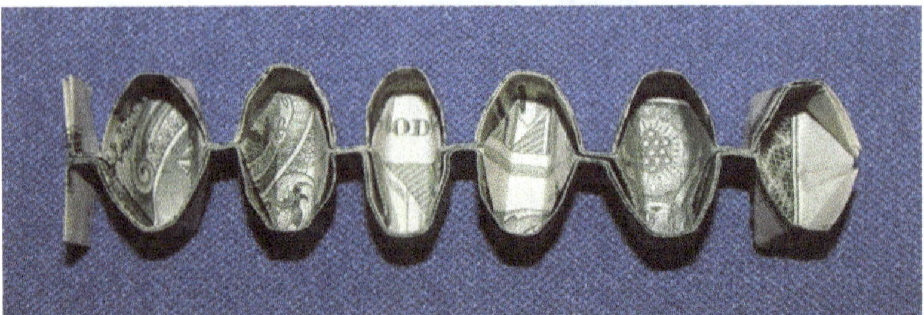

Million in One (also a Small Contribution to a SuperPAC)
One uncut U. S. dollar bill
Published in Election Money Folds 2012 on OUSA's website

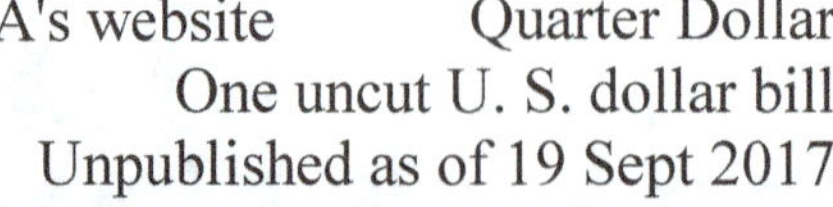

For Pennies on the Dollar
One uncut U. S. dollar bill
Unpublished as of 19 Sept 2017

Quarter Dollar
One uncut U. S. dollar bill
Unpublished as of 19 Sept 2017

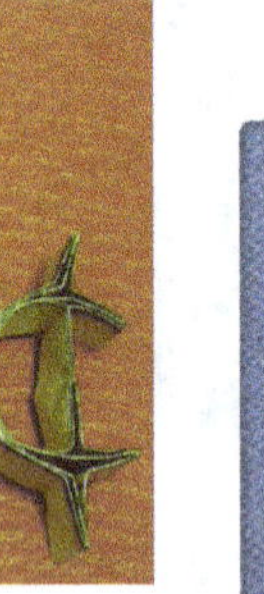

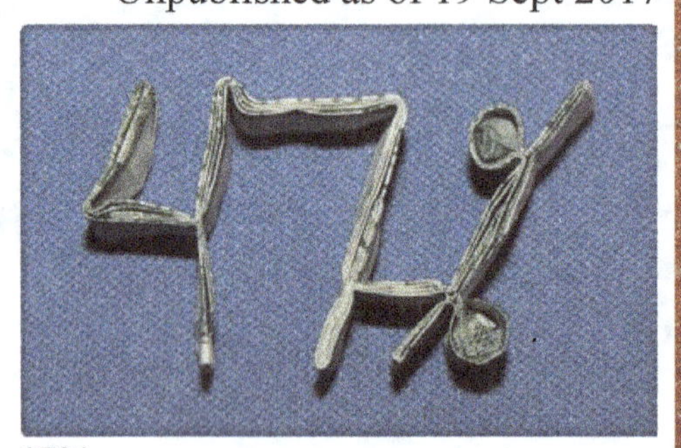

Five and Dime (or Nickel and Dime)
One uncut U. S. dollar bill
Unpublished as of 19 Sept 2017

47%
One uncut U. S. dollar bill
Published in Election Money Folds 2012 on OUSA's website

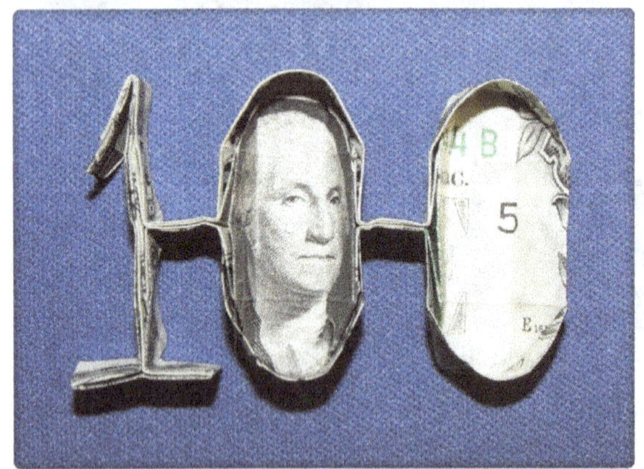

Washington on the 100 (Romney's Smallest Bill)
One uncut U. S. dollar bill
Published in Election Money Folds 2012 on OUSA's website

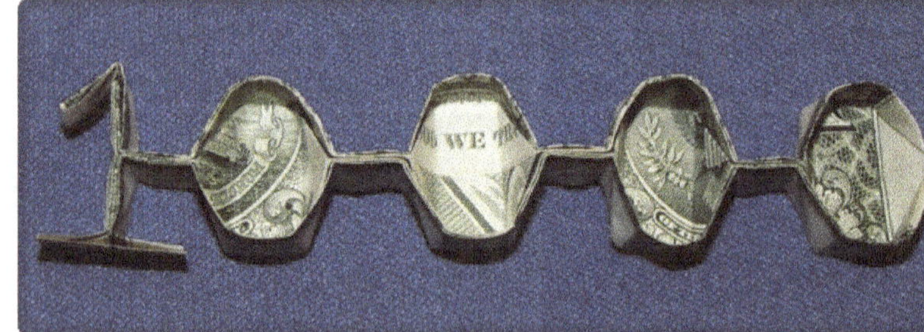

10,000 (Romney's Bet)
One uncut U. S. dollar bill
Published in Election Money Folds 2012 on OUSA's website

One Grand
One uncut U. S. dollar bill
Unpublished as of 19 Sept 2017

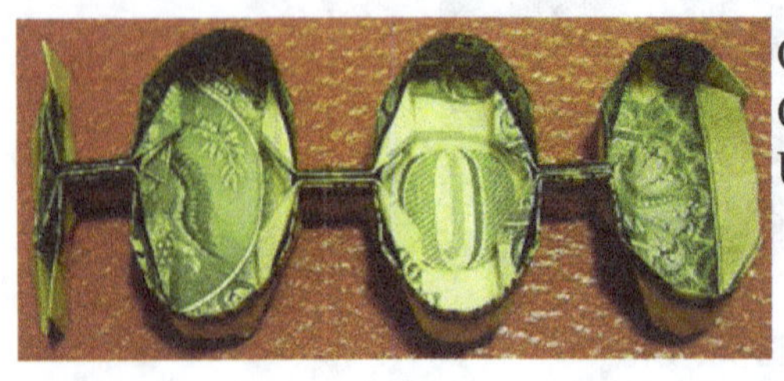

Lincoln on the Half Dollar
One uncut U. S. dollar bill
Unpublished as of 19 Sept 2017

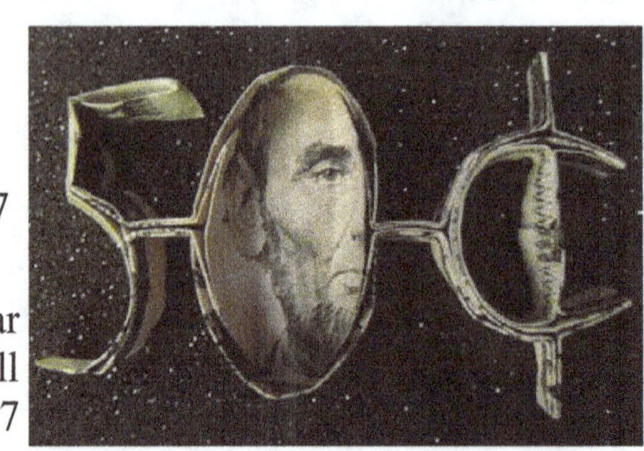

Dollar Symbols (Orikane)

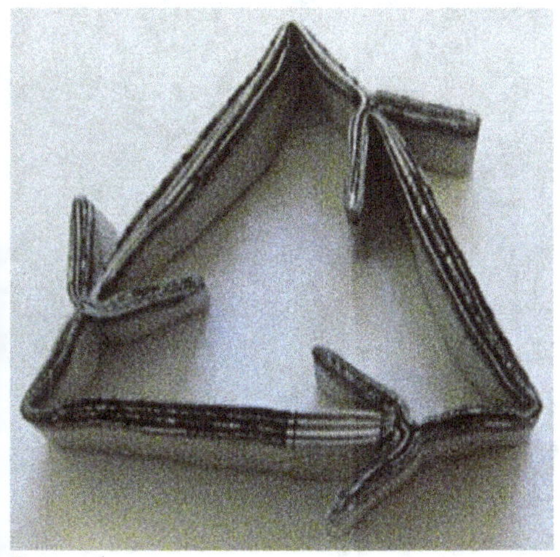

Recycle
One uncut U. S. dollar bill
Unpublished as of 19 Sept 2017

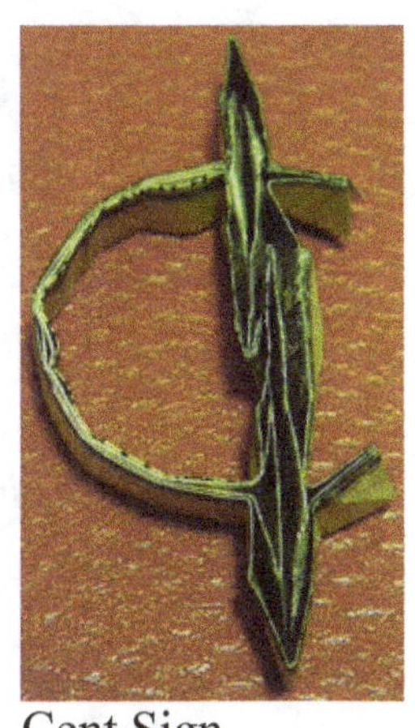

Cent Sign
One uncut U. S. dollar bill
Unpublished as of 19 Sept 2017

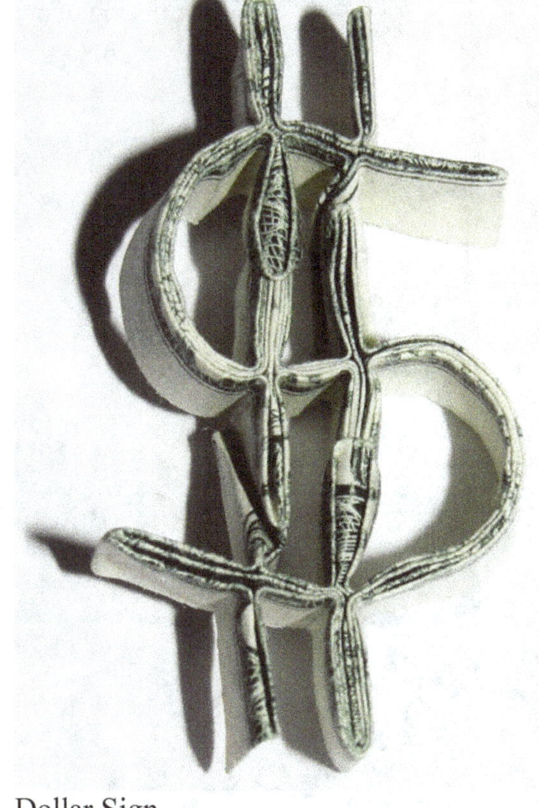

Dollar Sign
One uncut U. S. dollar bill
Unpublished as of 19 Sept 2017

Euro Sign
One uncut U. S. dollar bill
Unpublished as of 19 Sept 2017

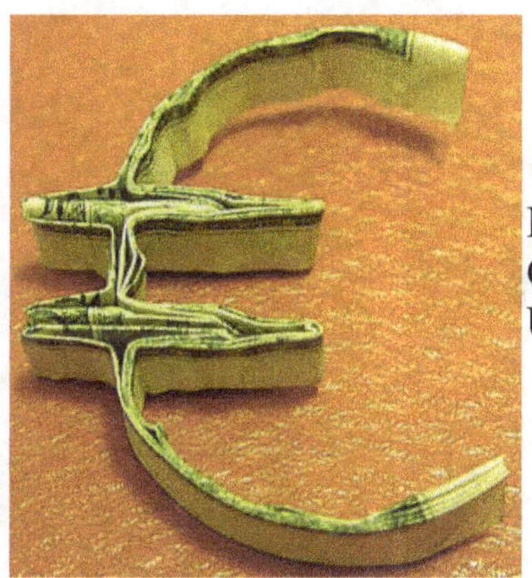

Price of Peace
One uncut U. S. dollar bill
Unpublished as of 19 Sept 2017

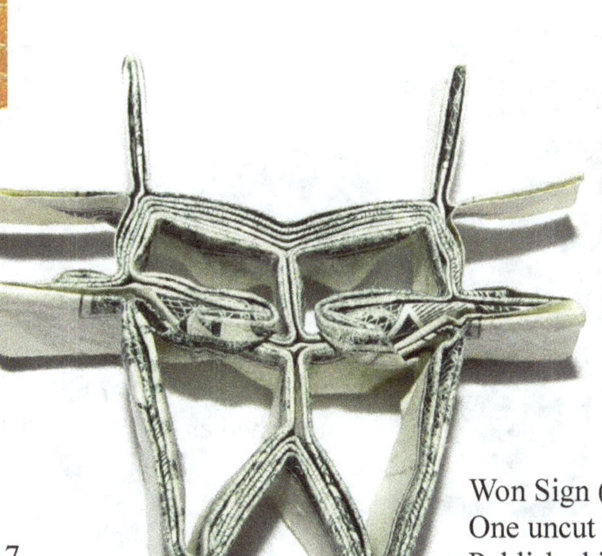

Yen Sign
One uncut U. S. dollar bill
Unpublished as of 19 Sept 2017

Won Sign (South Korean money)
One uncut U. S. dollar bill
Published in OrigaMIT Convention Book 2016.

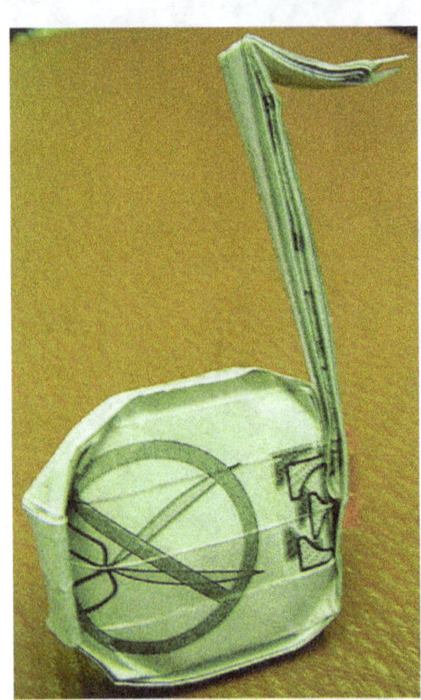

Musical Banknote
One uncut origami-themed pretend U. S. dollar bill
Unpublished as of 19 Sept 2017

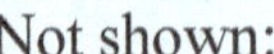

Not shown:

(British) Pound Sign
Mercury
Pluto

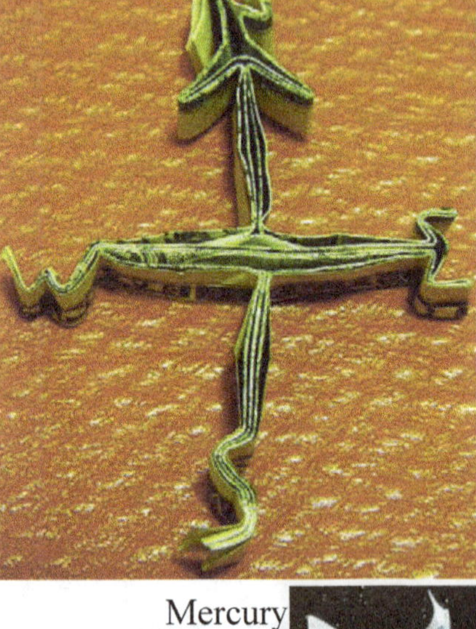

Double Happiness
Two uncut U. S. dollar bills
Unpublished as of 19 Sept 2017

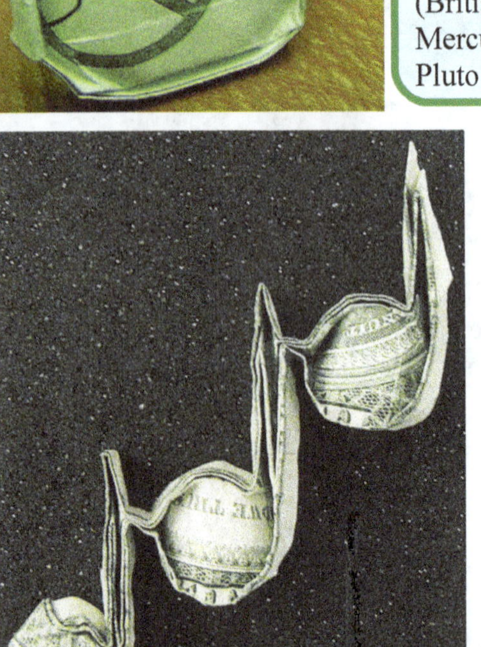

Cents of Direction
One uncut U. S. dollar bill
Unpublished as of 19 Sept 2017

(Show Me the) Do-Re-Mi
One uncut U. S. dollar bill
Unpublished as of 19 Sept 2017

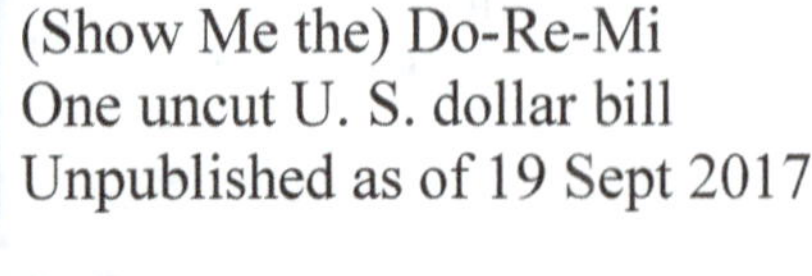

Venus
One uncut U. S. dollar bill
Unpublished as of 19 Sept 2017

Mercury
One uncut U. S. dollar bill
Unpublished as of 19 Sept 2017

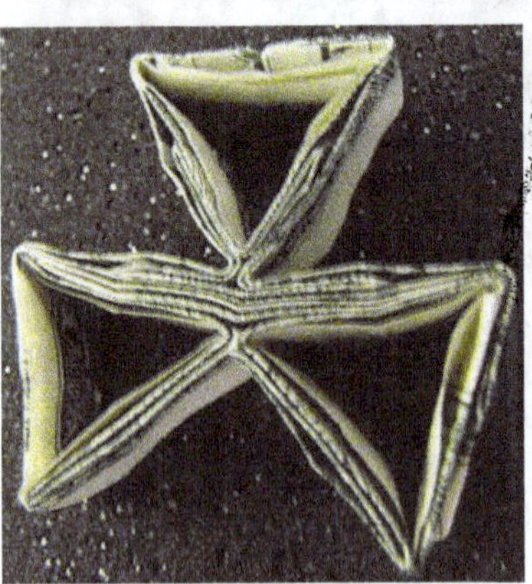

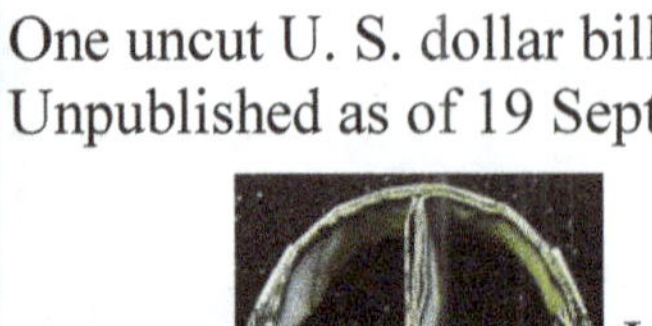

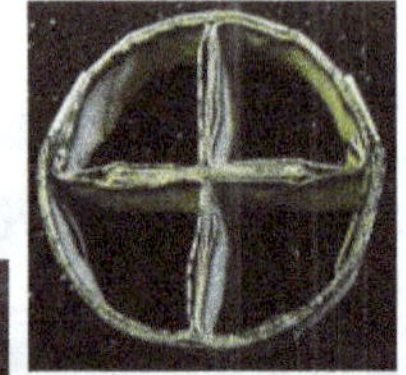

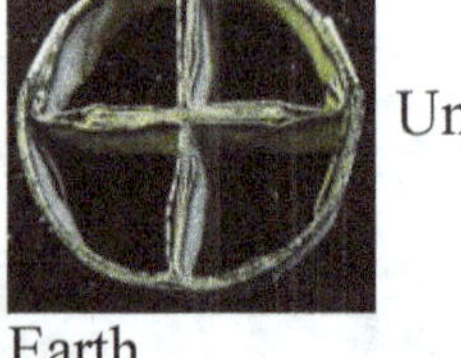

Earth
One uncut U. S. dollar bill
Unpublished as of 19 Sept 2017

Radiation Symbol
One uncut U. S. dollar bill
Unpublished as of 19 Sept 2017

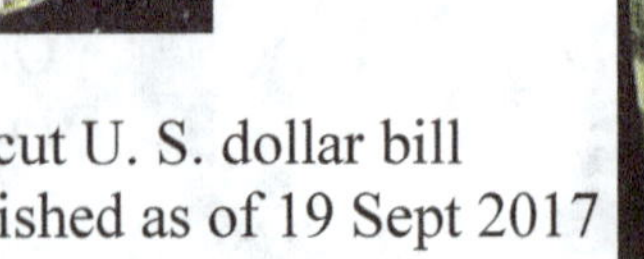

Pluto
One uncut U. S. dollar bill
Unpublished as of 19 Sept 2017

Mars
One uncut U. S. dollar bill
Unpublished as of 19 Sept 2017

Fantasy Origami

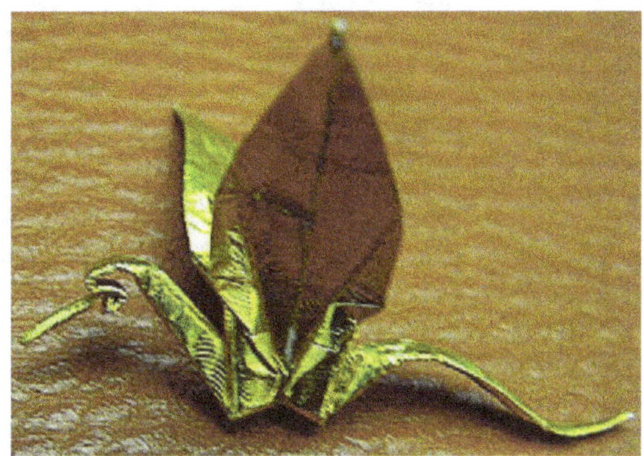
Candy Wrapper Dragon
One uncut square of foil-backed paper
Variation on the traditional Crane
Unpublished as of 19 September 2017

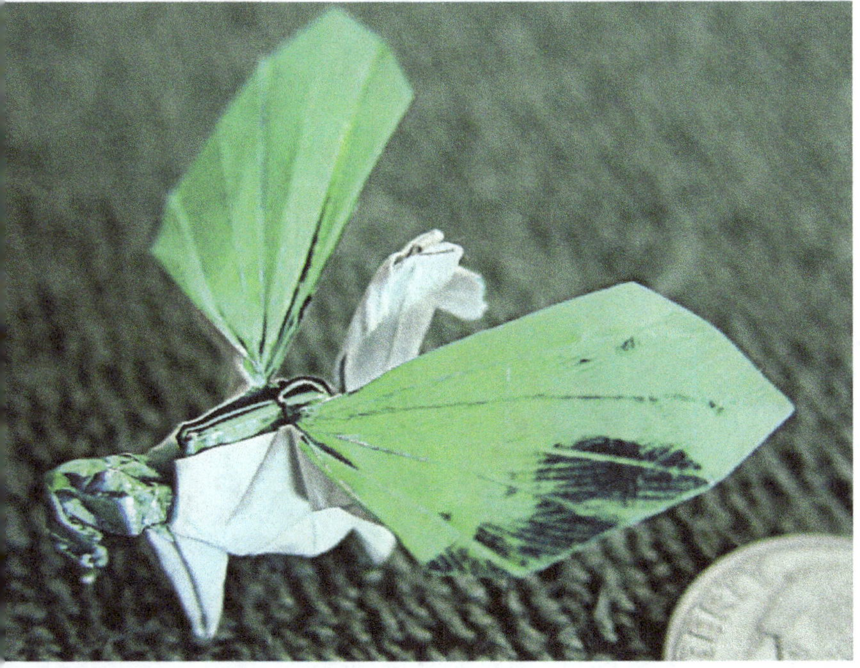

Pegasus (Harry Potter: Thestral)
One uncut square of foil-backed paper
Optionally twist a wing backward for a helicopter-style action model
Unpublished as of 19 September 2017

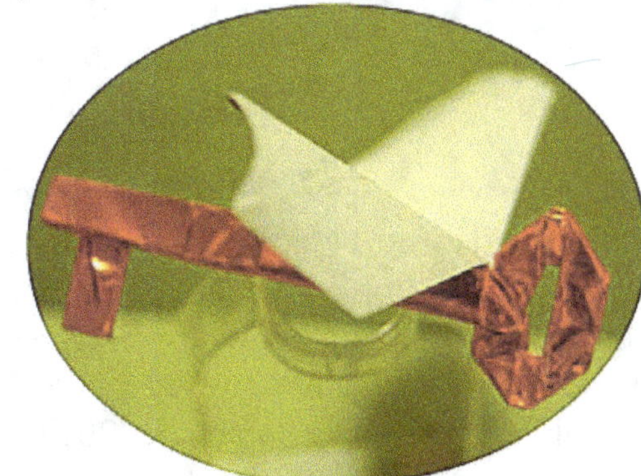
Winged Key (Harry Potter)
One uncut square of foil-backed paper
Action Model: spins when dropped
Unpublished as of 19 September 2017

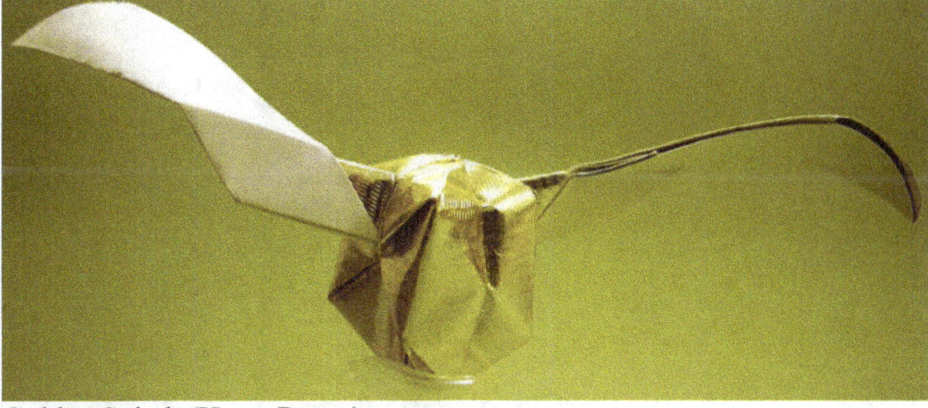
Golden Snitch (Harry Potter)
One uncut square of foil-backed paper
Variation on the traditional Waterbomb
Action Model: spins when dropped or pulled through the air on a string
Unpublished as of 19 September 2017

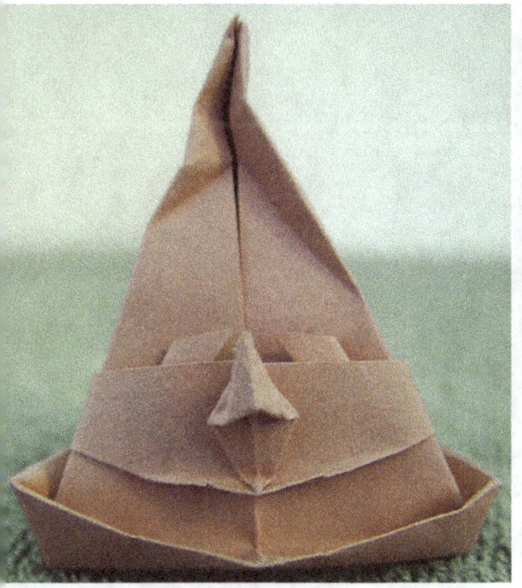
Sorting Hat (Harry Potter)
Three uncut squares
Unpublished as of 19 September 2017

A handful of these fantasy-inspired are specific to the Harry Potter series, but many others are general to myth and fantasy even though they have echos in Harry Potter. A few have mundane counterparts instead of imaginary ones. No rights to Harry Potter here, just respect, appreciation and a bit of fan art.

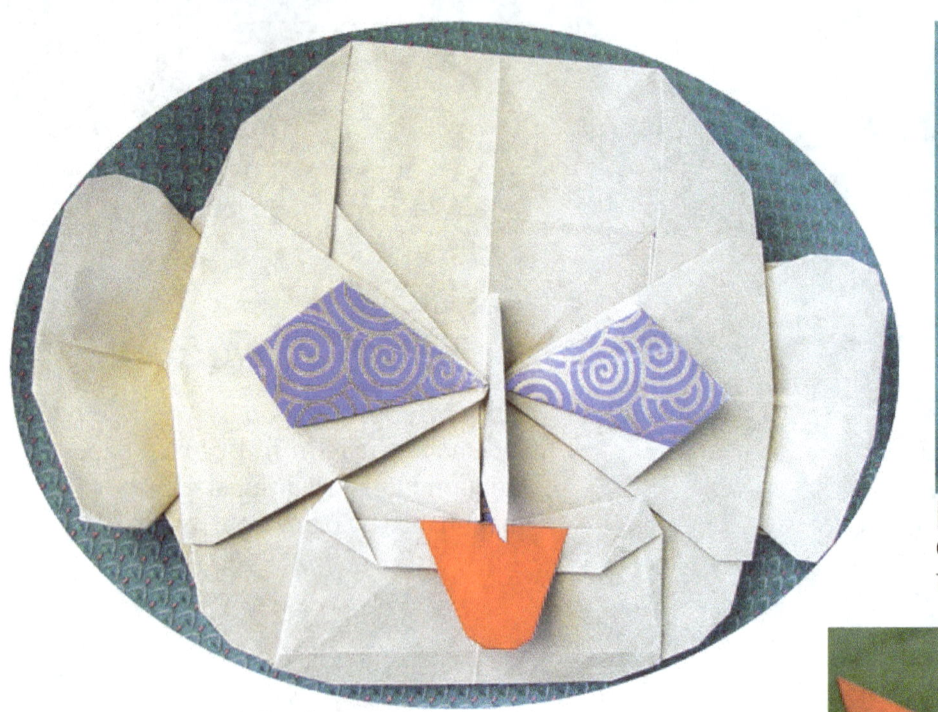

My Uncle Howard Getting His Picture Taken
    (Harry Potter: Peeves Blowing a Raspberry)
One uncut square of gift wrap with a red laminated corner
Appeared in "OrigamiNow!" at the Peabody Essex Museum
Unpublished as of 19 September 2017

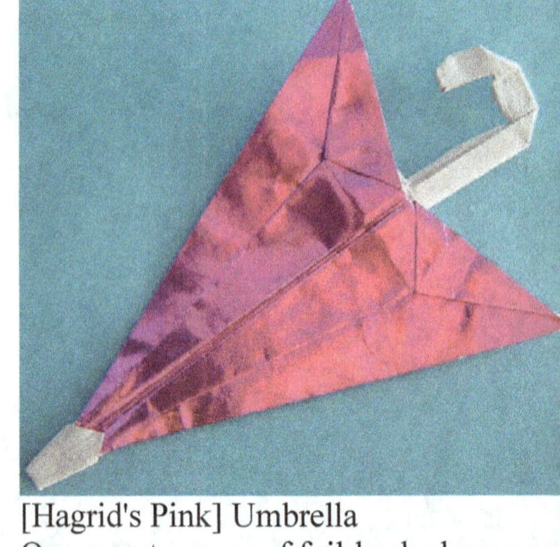

[Hagrid's Pink] Umbrella
One uncut square of foil-backed paper
Unpublished as of 19 September 2017

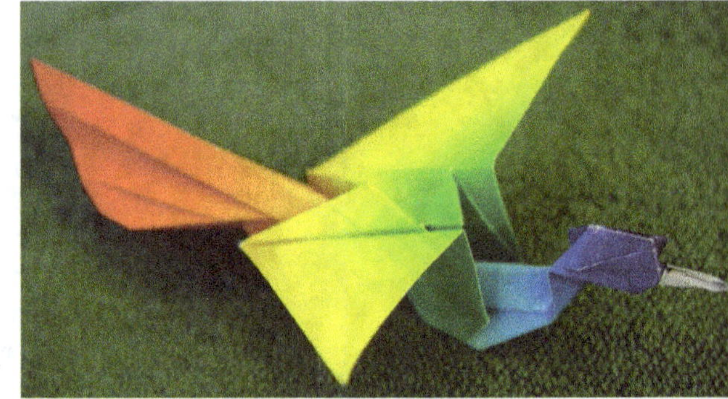

Flapping Phoenix
One uncut square
Variation on the traditional Flapping Bird
Action model: Pull the tail to flap the wings.
Unpublished as of 19 September 2017

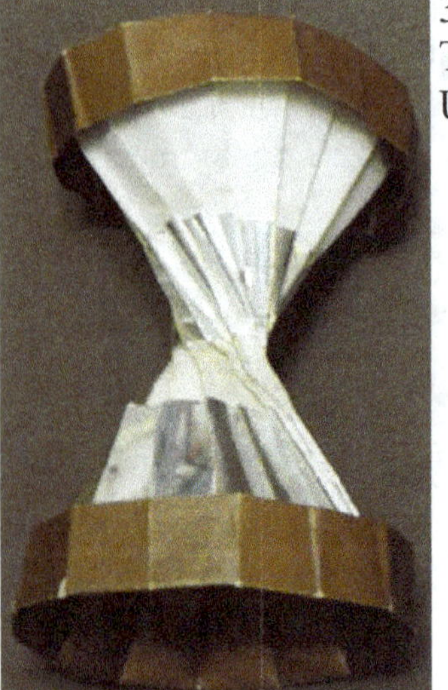

3D Hour Glass (HP: Time Turner)
Two uncut rectangles
Unpublished as of 19 Sept. 2017

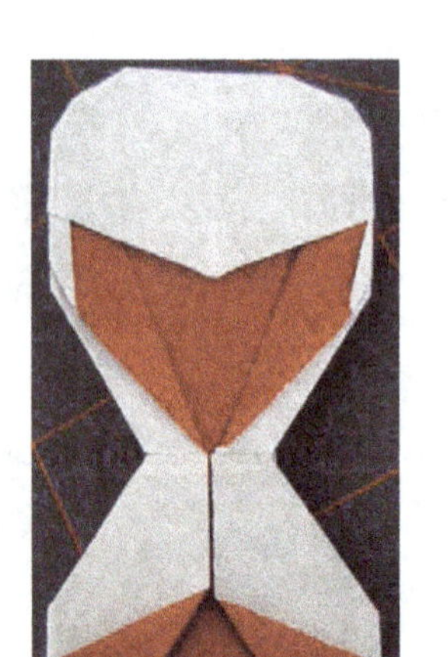
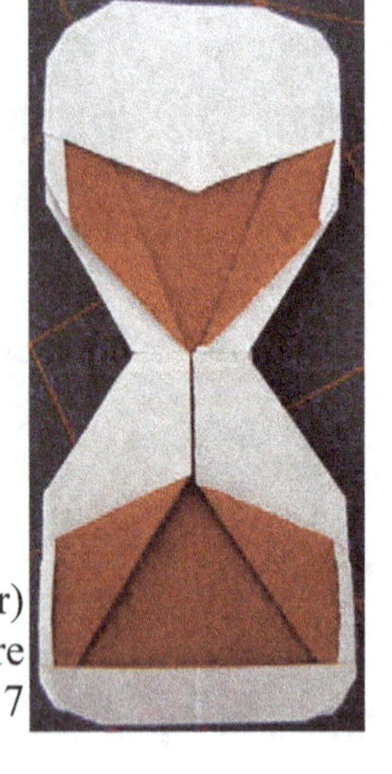

2D Hour Glass (HP: Time Turner)
One uncut square
Unpublished as of 19 Sept.2017

Wizard Hat
Three uncut squares
Unpublished as of 19 Sept. 2017

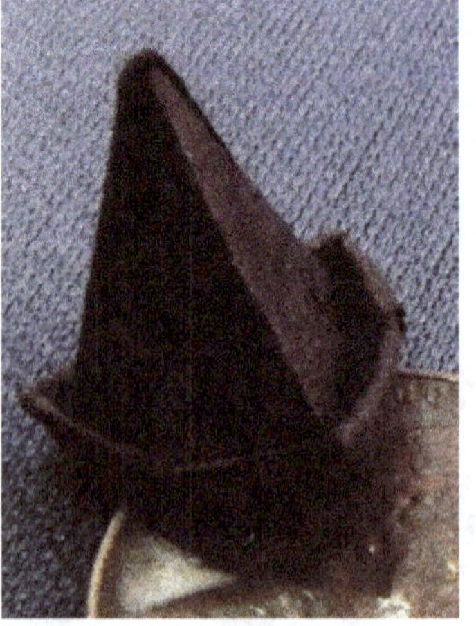

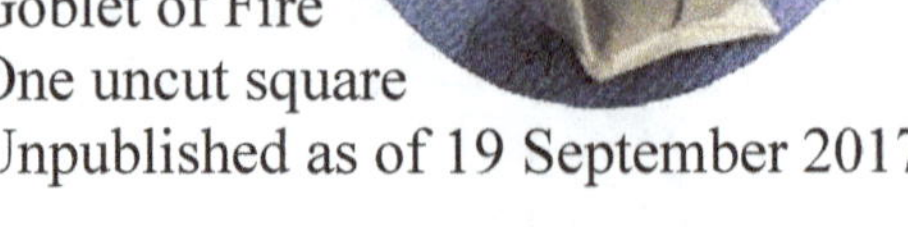

Goblet of Fire
One uncut square
Unpublished as of 19 September 2017

Perched Phoenix
One uncut square
Unpublished as of 19 September 2017

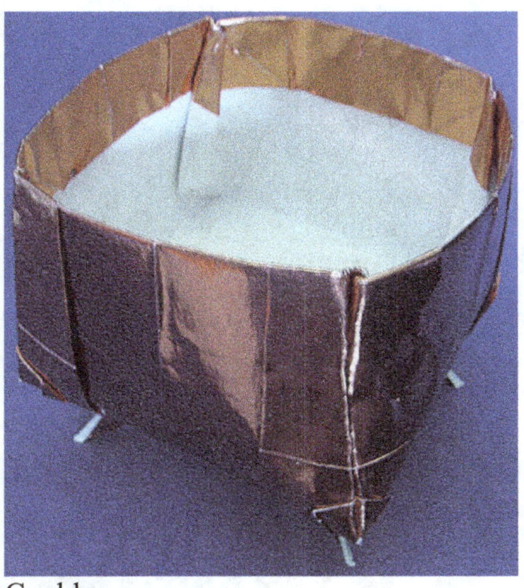

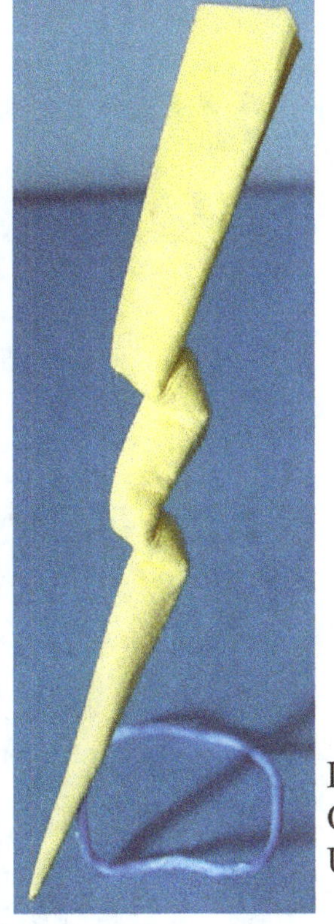

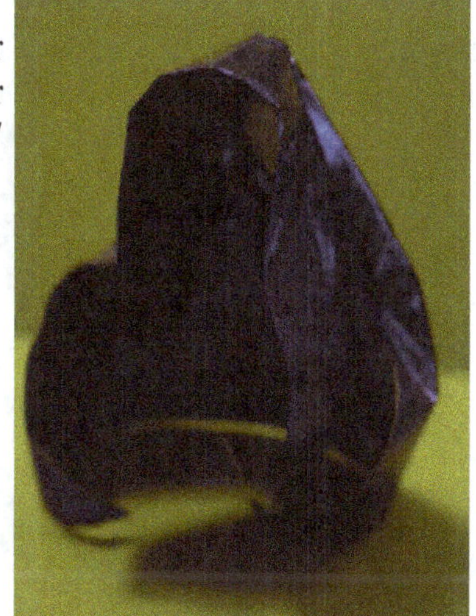

Troll with a Wand Up its Nose
One uncut square of foil-backed paper
Unpublished as of 19 September 2017

Cauldron
One uncut square of foil-backed paper
Unpublished as of 19 September 2017

Lightning Bolt (HP: Lightning Shaped Scar)
One uncut square
Unpublished as of 19 September 2017

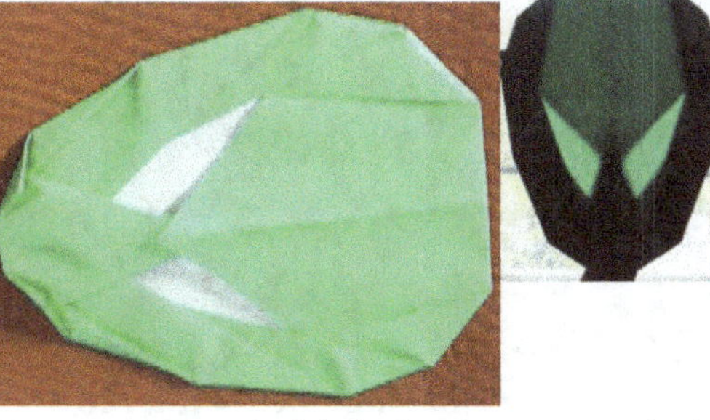

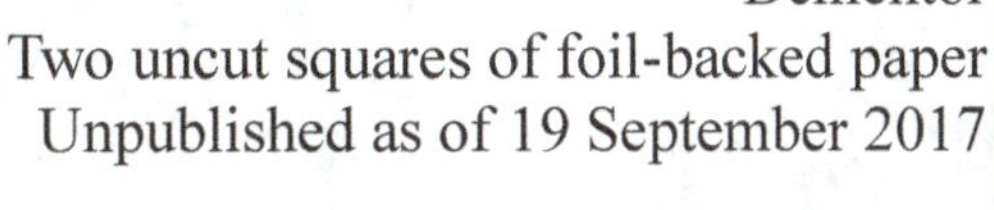

Dementor
Two uncut squares of foil-backed paper
Unpublished as of 19 September 2017

Dragon's Egg (with baby dragon curled up inside) and
        Alien with Glowing Eyes (when held up to the light)
One uncut square of kami (origami paper)
Unpublished as of 19 September 2017

Not shown:

Candy (Ton-Tongue Toffee)
Caramel Cream (HP: Canary Cream)
Jelly Bean (HP: Every Flavor Bean)
More Spinning Tops (HP: Sneakoscopes)
School Trunk
Spell Book
Nose with Wand Up It
...and upwards of a dozen more..

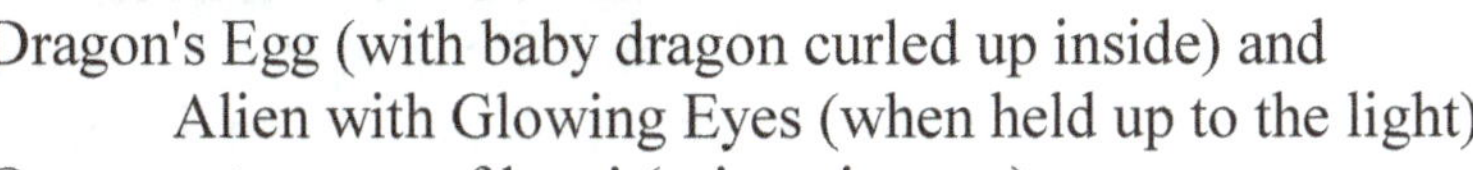

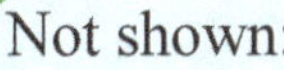

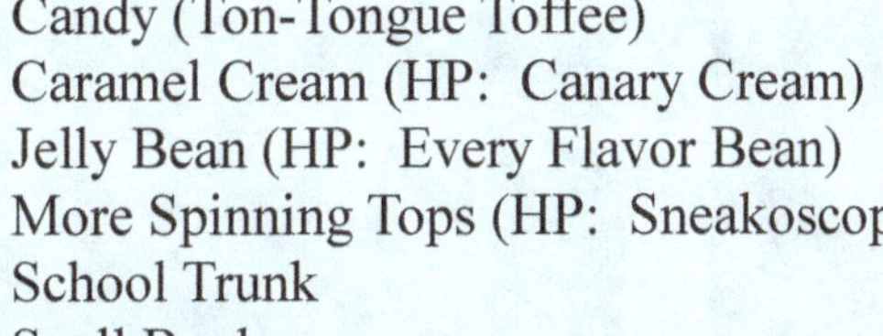

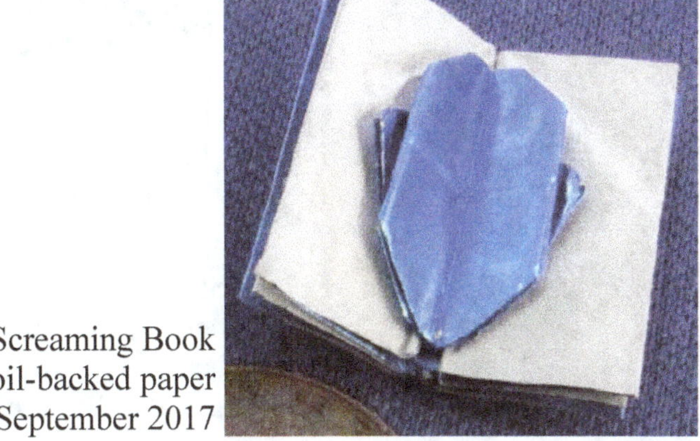

Spinning Top (HP: Sneakoscope)
Nine uncut squares of foil-backed paper
Unpublished as of 19 September 2017

Screaming Book
One uncut square of foil-backed paper
Unpublished as of 19 September 2017

Modular Origami

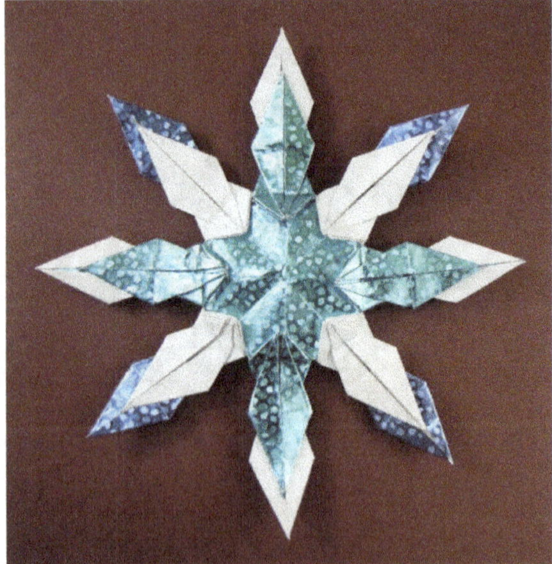

Flutterby Cube
Six uncut squares of kami (origami paper)
The wings can optionally be fastened down.
Unpublished as of 19 September 2017

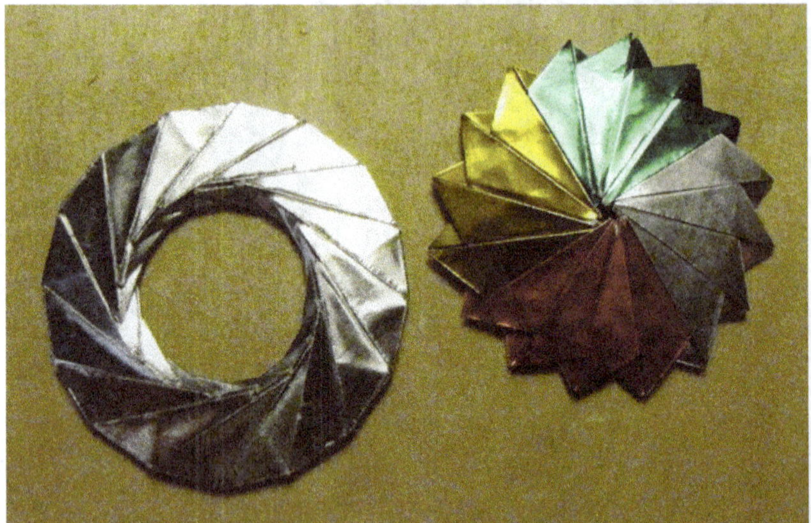

Iris (as in Camera, Eye or Stargate, Not a Flower)
Two uncut squares of foil-backed paper
Action model: It slides open and closed.
Unpublished as of 19 September 2017

Flaky Star
Two uncut squares of foil-backed paper
Published in Not Quite Traditional Origami
on OrigamiUSA's website

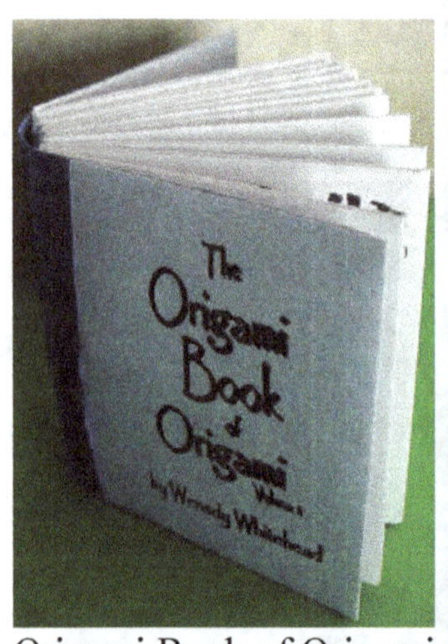

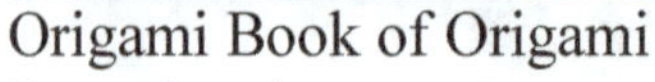

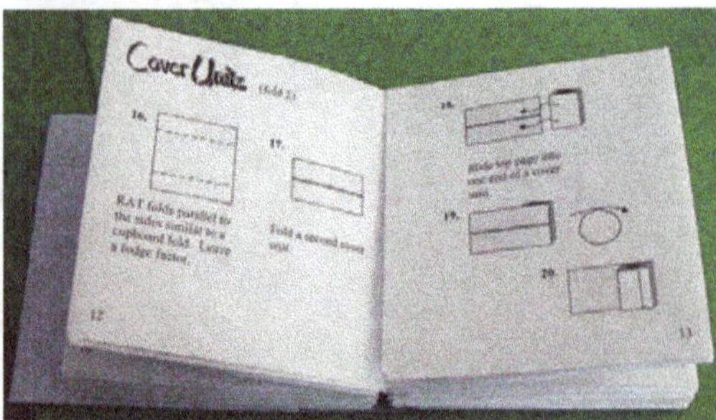

Origami Book of Origami
Pre-printed pages, cover and spine for my plain Modular Book
Unpublished as of 19 September 2017

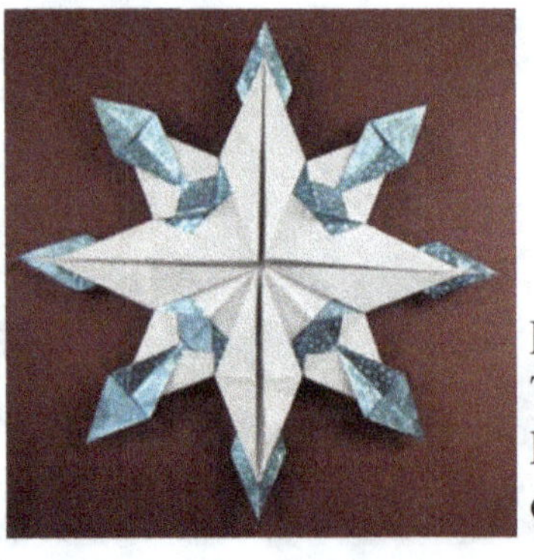

Flaky Star
Two uncut squares of foil-backed paper
Published in Not Quite Traditional Origami
on OrigamiUSA's website

Emojis, Etc. From One Versatile Unit

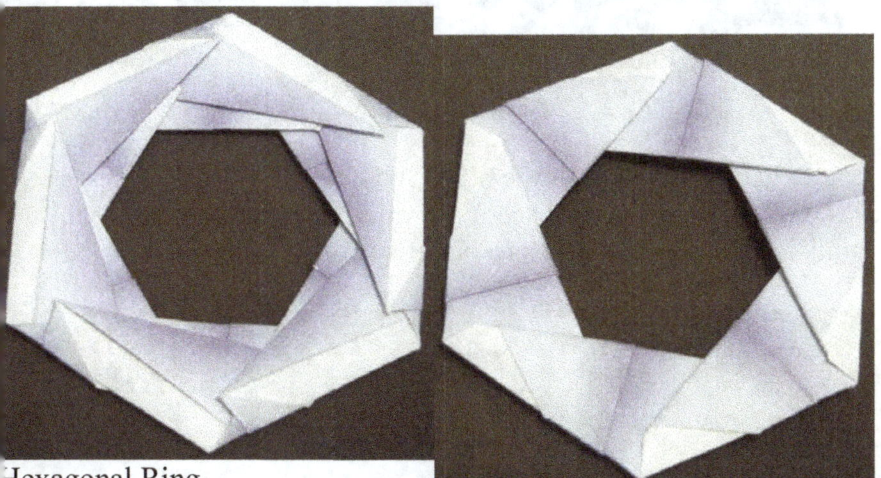

Hexagonal Ring
Six uncut squares of kami (origami paper)
This is the basic version that links up into the Ring of Rings, Chaos
Theory and Ringed Planet. Front and back can be a matter of opinion.

This Hexagonal unit is extremely versatile. A corner is free to form variations. There is enough play in the joints that multiple layers of paper may be used in a kasane technique and units can link to slightly larger and smaller units. More importantly, the hexagonal rings formed from the basic unit link together in interesting, stable ways. Careful color choice of each unit makes the assemblages even more interesting, with patterns and simple drawings such as smiley faces, mushrooms and hearts. The hexagons can also nest one inside another larger one to form various level of Nestagons. This unit and all its variants and assemblages remain unpublished as of 19 September 2017. The draft instructions are around 100 pages (U. S. letter) and describe how to make everything in these six pages..

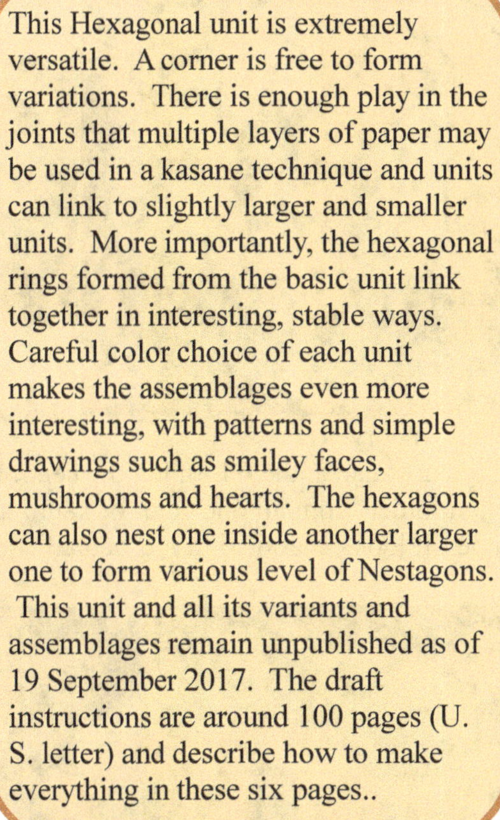

Starry Space
Six uncut squares

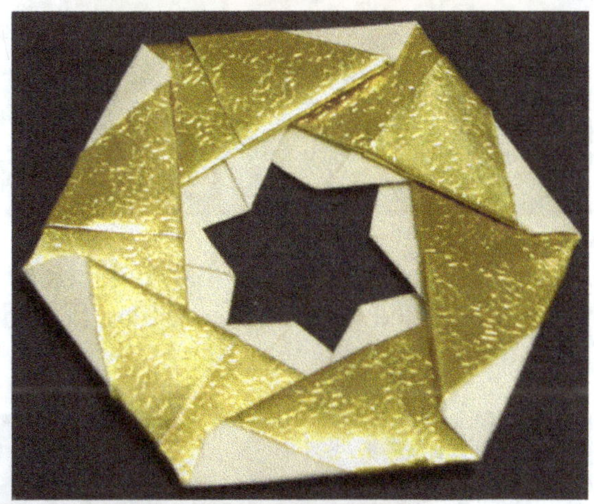

Triple Hex
Six uncut squares

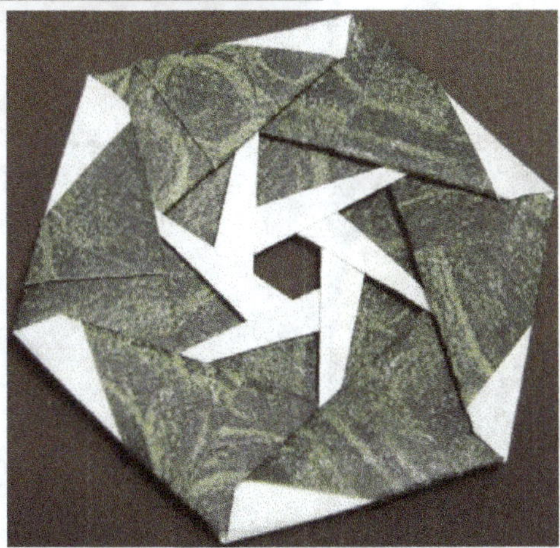

Hex Vortex
Six uncut squares

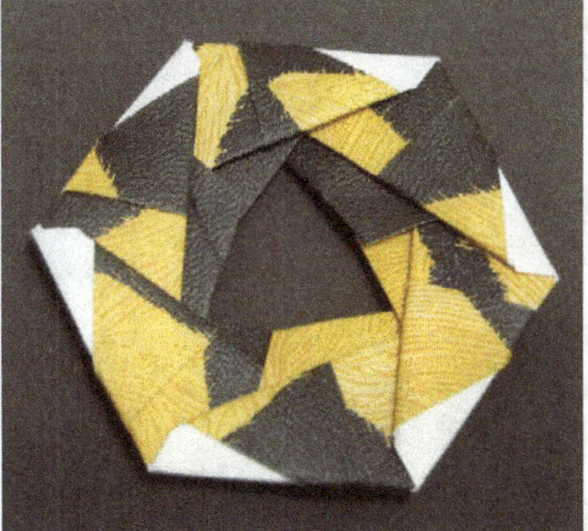

Triangle in a Hexagon
Six uncut squares
The various versions of the unit can link
together for more interesting effects.

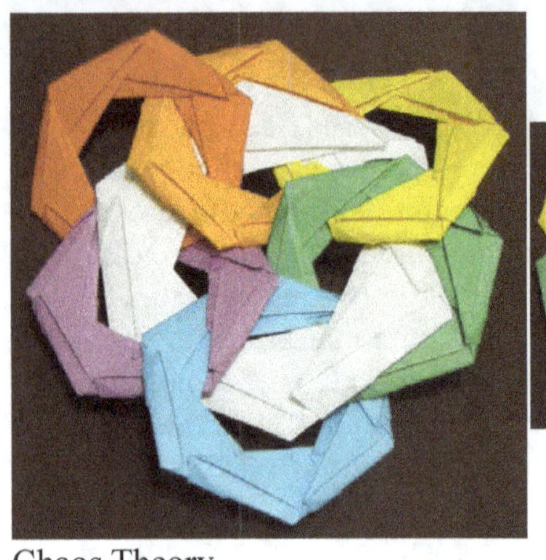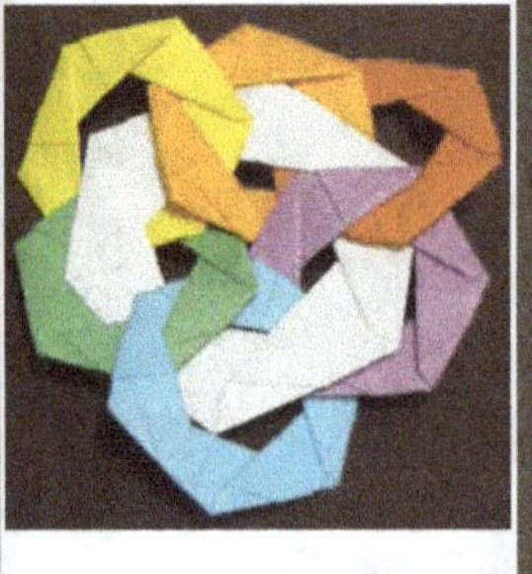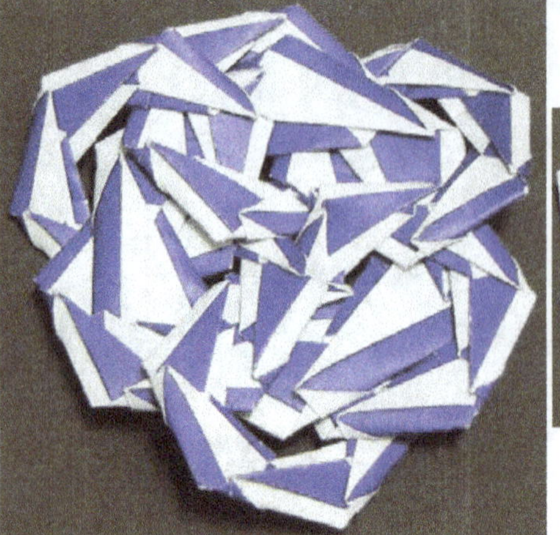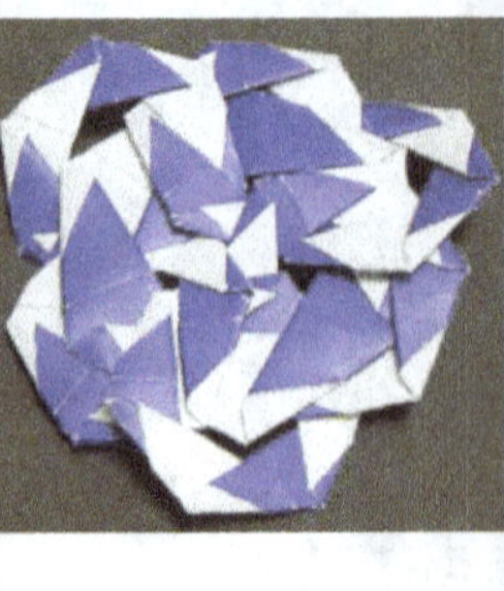

Chaos Theory
42 uncut squares, the 6 forming the central ring are 1½ times as large as the other 36
When folded from all one color of kami, the eyes have great difficulty discerning which ring is which, hence the name. It looks chaotic, but it is actually deterministic, even though it lacks a butterfly effect.

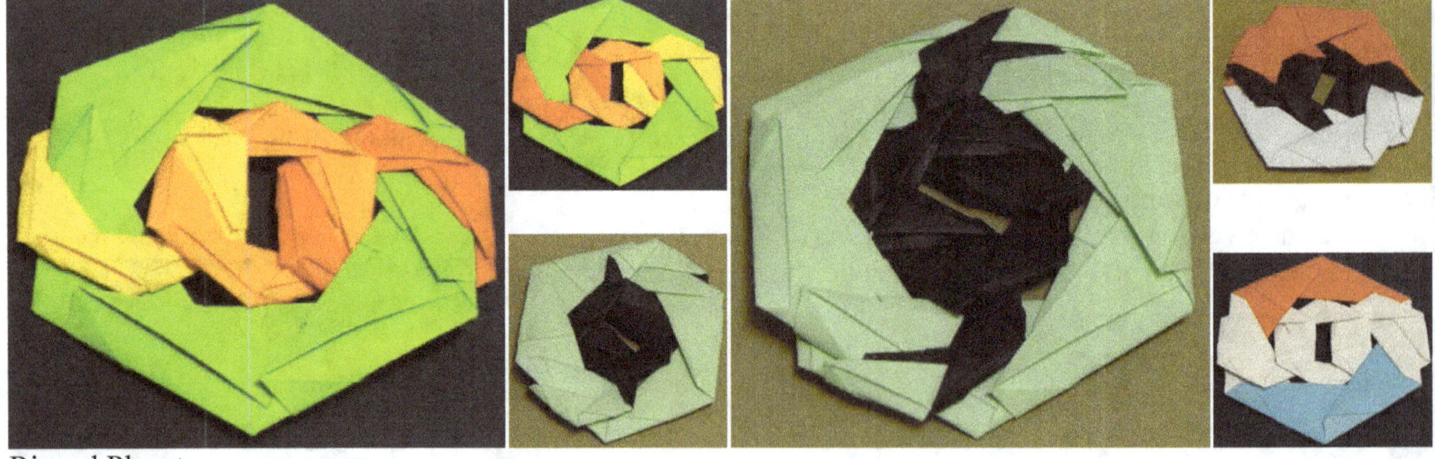

Ringed Planet
24 uncut squares, 6 (center ring) twice as large as the other 18
A couple related assemblages remain to be documented; the belt can bend rather than go straight across. It can also fork and bend both ways.

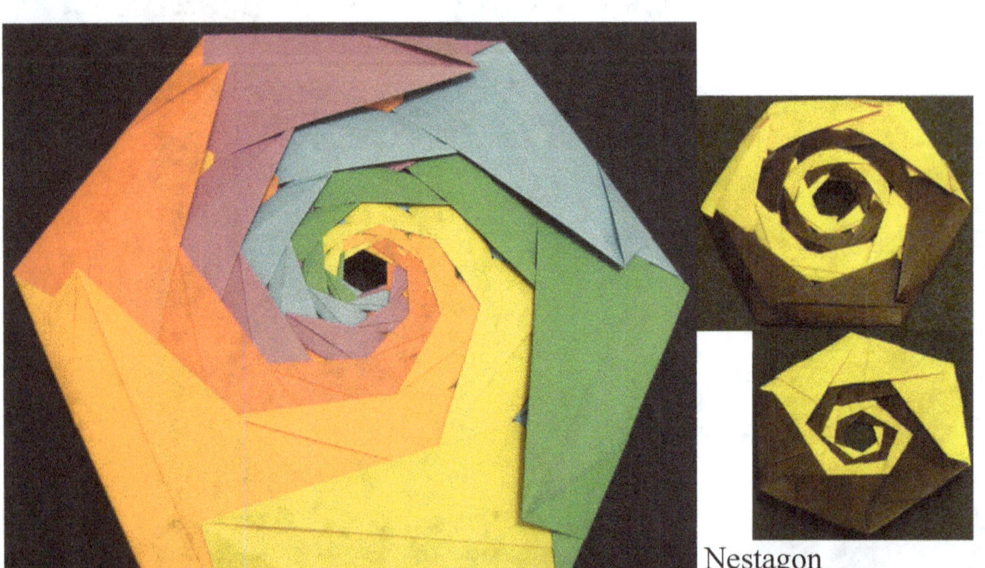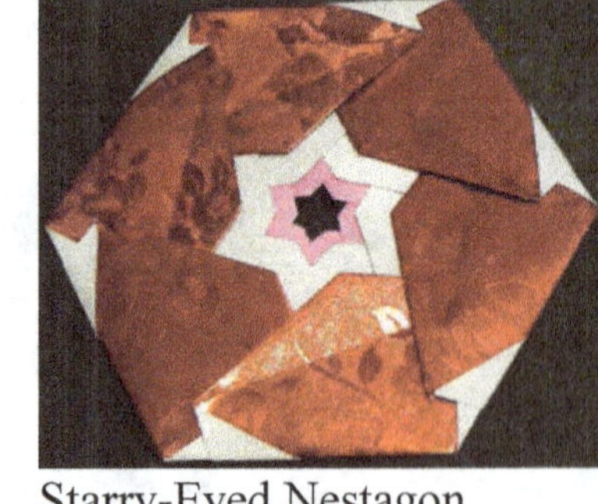

Starry-Eyed Nestagon
6 units per hexagon, 18 total

Nestagon
6 units per hexagon, in this case 36 total

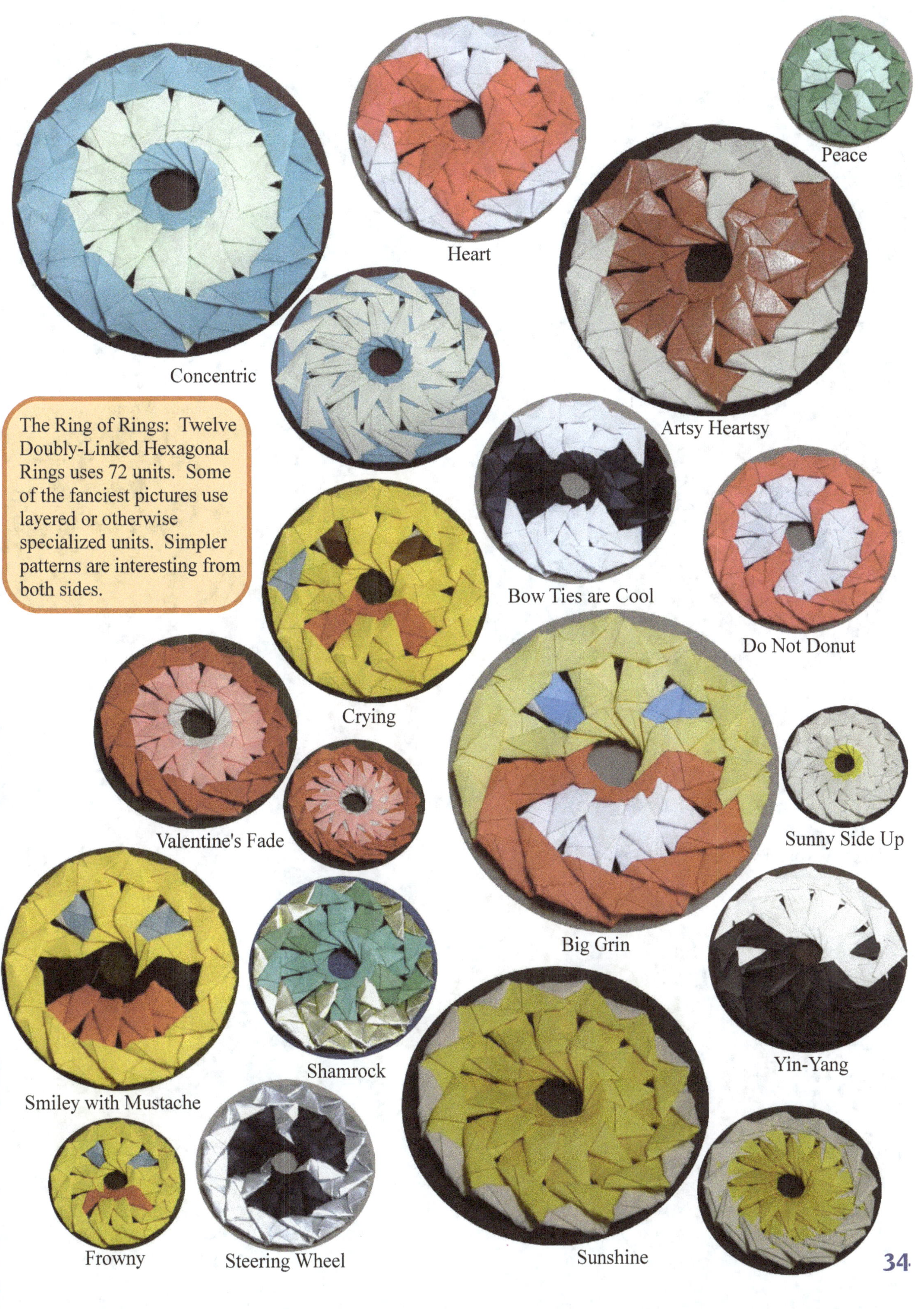

Peace

Heart

Concentric

Artsy Heartsy

The Ring of Rings: Twelve Doubly-Linked Hexagonal Rings uses 72 units. Some of the fanciest pictures use layered or otherwise specialized units. Simpler patterns are interesting from both sides.

Bow Ties are Cool

Do Not Donut

Crying

Valentine's Fade

Big Grin

Sunny Side Up

Smiley with Mustache

Shamrock

Yin-Yang

Frowny

Steering Wheel

Sunshine

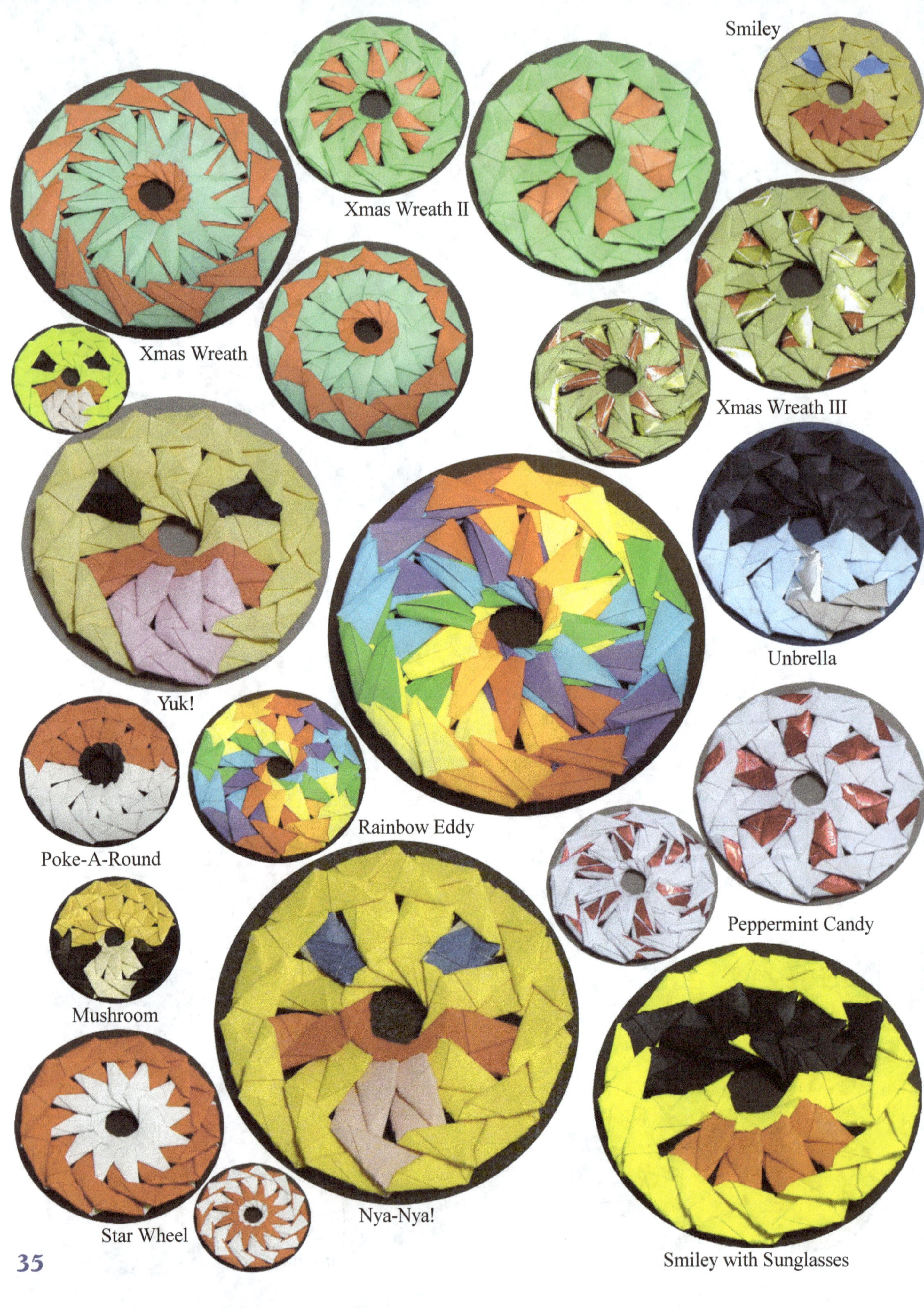

Smiley
Xmas Wreath II
Xmas Wreath
Xmas Wreath III
Yuk!
Unbrella
Poke-A-Round
Rainbow Eddy
Peppermint Candy
Mushroom
Star Wheel
Nya-Nya!
Smiley with Sunglasses

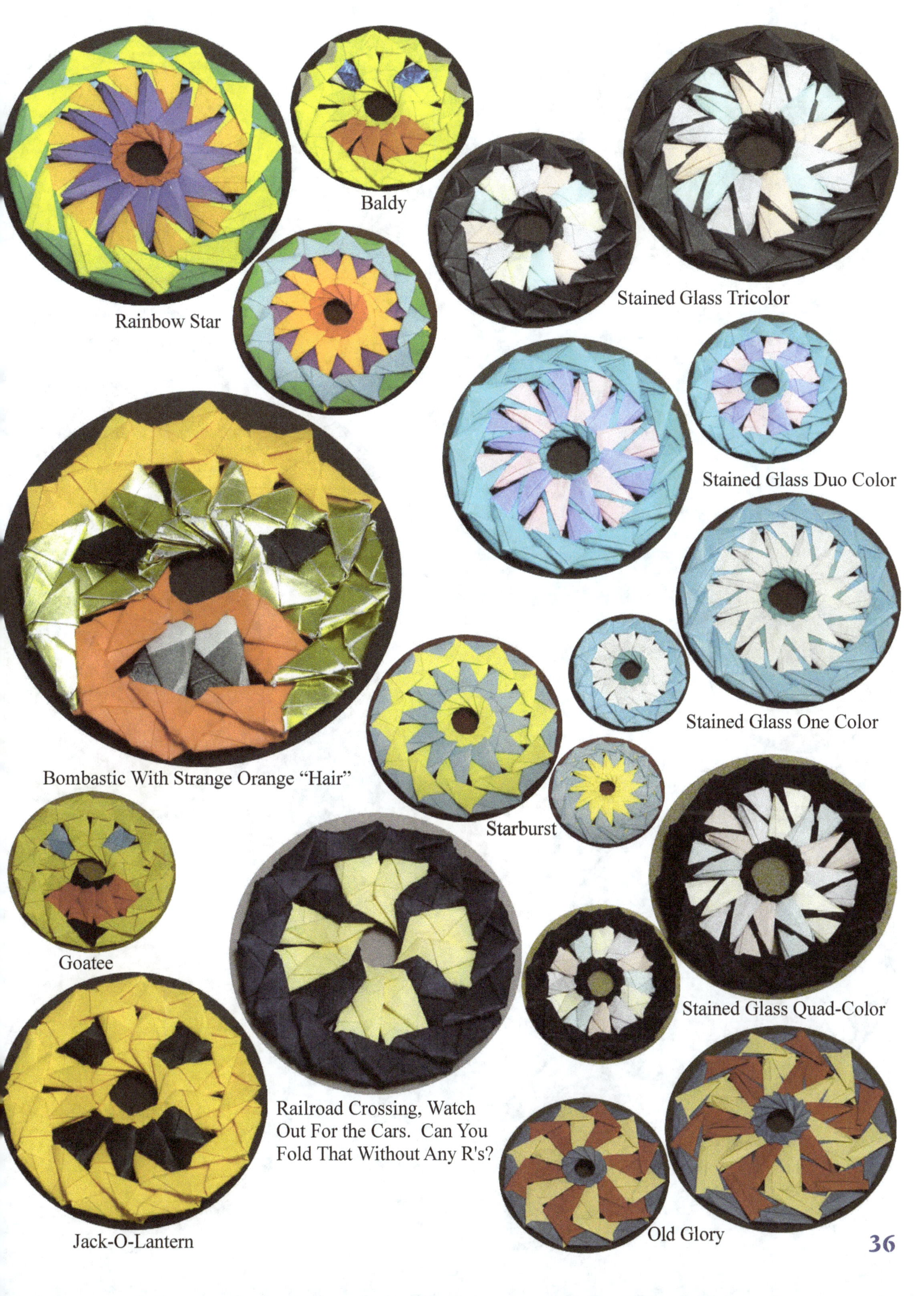

Rainbow Star

Baldy

Stained Glass Tricolor

Stained Glass Duo Color

Stained Glass One Color

Bombastic With Strange Orange "Hair"

Starburst

Goatee

Railroad Crossing, Watch Out For the Cars. Can You Fold That Without Any R's?

Stained Glass Quad-Color

Jack-O-Lantern

Old Glory

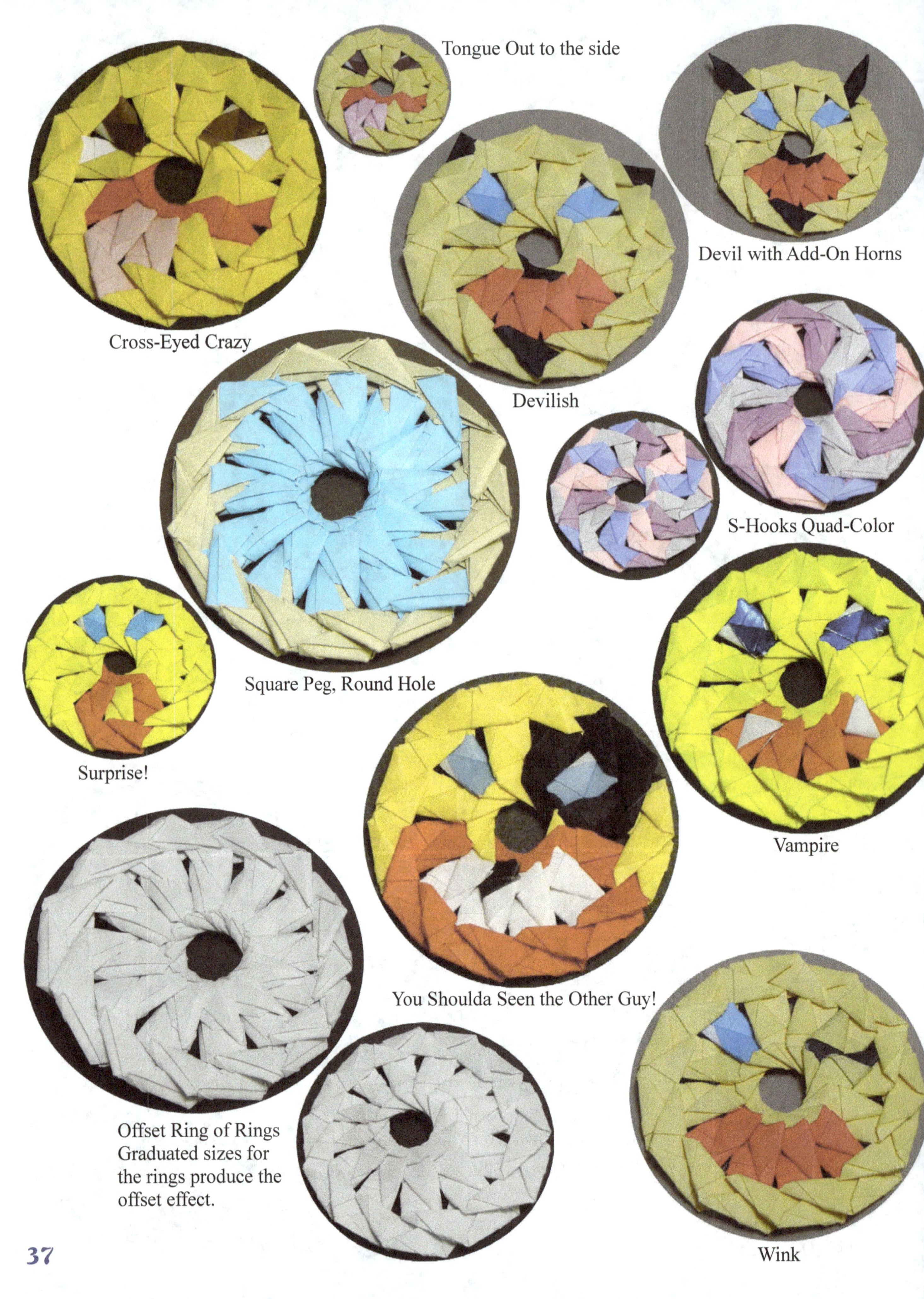

Tongue Out to the side
Cross-Eyed Crazy
Devil with Add-On Horns
Devilish
S-Hooks Quad-Color
Square Peg, Round Hole
Surprise!
Vampire
You Shoulda Seen the Other Guy!
Offset Ring of Rings
Graduated sizes for
the rings produce the
offset effect.
Wink

Variations on Traditional Origami

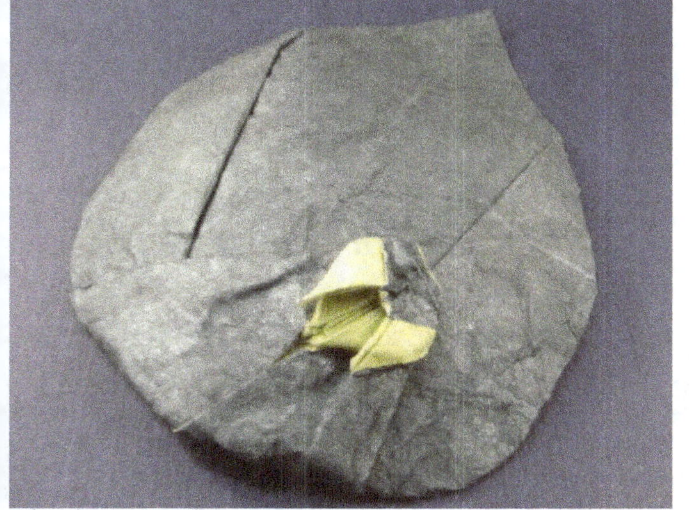

Cicada on Leaf
One uncut square of tissue foil
Variation on the traditional Cicada
Unpublished as of 19 September 2017

Cicada Longwings
One uncut square of memo cube
Variation on the traditional Cicada
Unpublished as of 19 September 2017

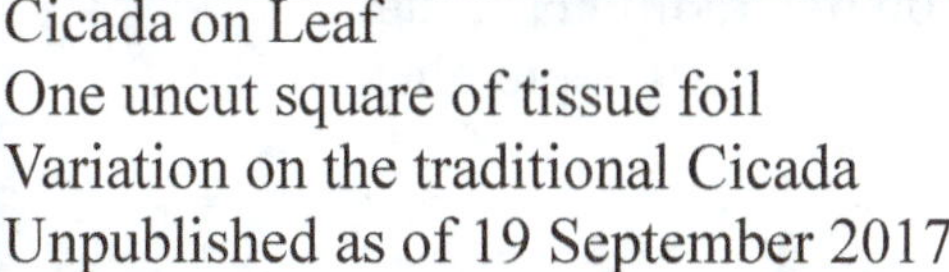

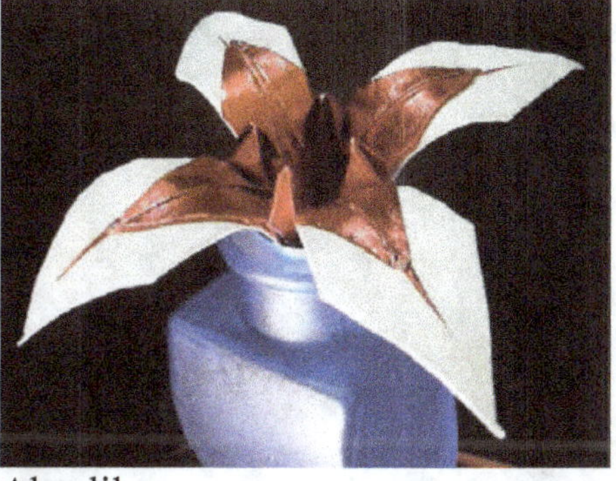

Absolily
One uncut square of foil-backed paper
Variation on the traditional Lily or Iris
Published in Not Quite Traditional Origami
on OrigamiUSA's website

Flapping Bird Wearing a Crane Costume
One uncut square of kami (origami paper)
Variation on the traditional Crane and Flapping Bird models
Action model! Pull the tail to flap the wings as per the Flapping Bird.
Published as promotional item, individual download and part of
Not Quite Traditional Origami on OrigamiUSA's website

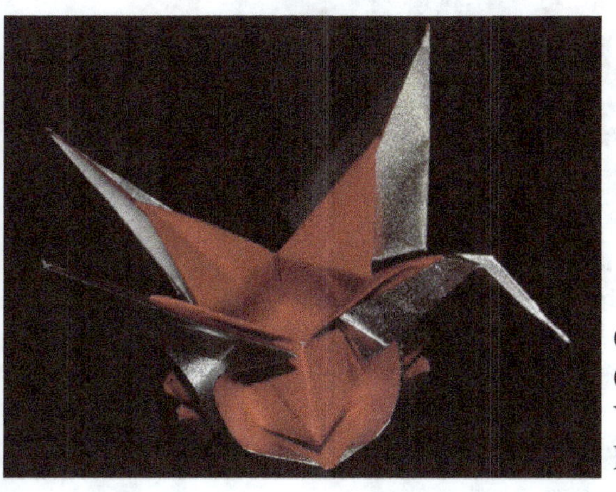

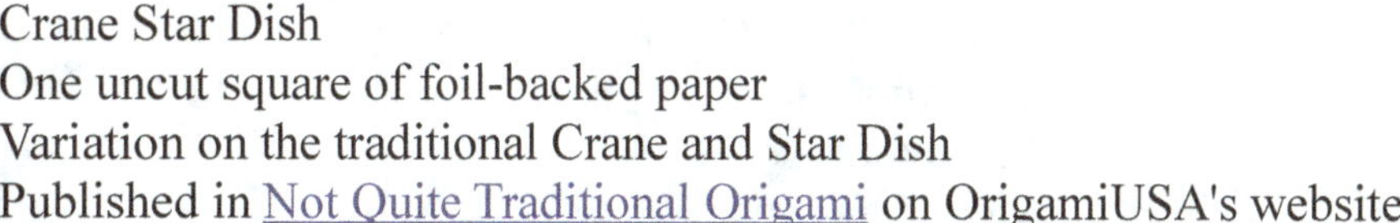

Crane Star Dish
One uncut square of foil-backed paper
Variation on the traditional Crane and Star Dish
Published in Not Quite Traditional Origami on OrigamiUSA's website

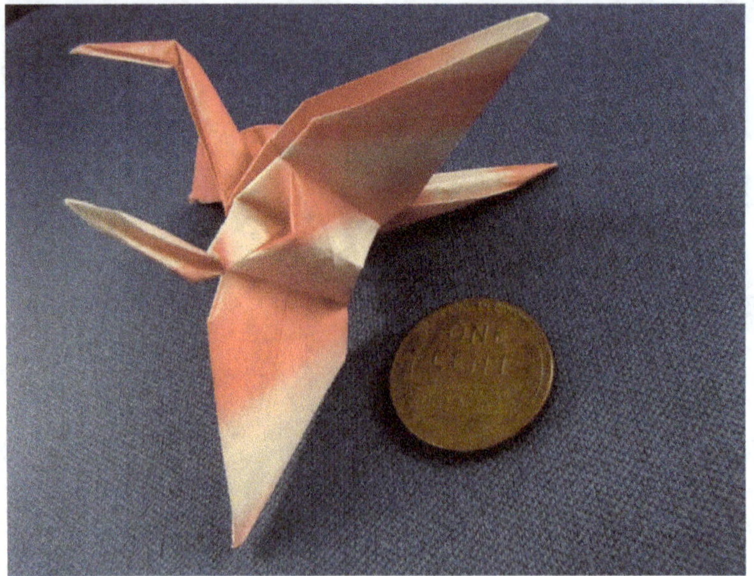
Mitosis Crane
One uncut 1:2 rectangle of harmony origami paper
Variation on the traditional Crane as if reproducing like a
single cell by mitosis starting at the heads; this falls into
the popular category of "mutant cranes" and relates to the
traditional thousand cranes technique
Unpublished as of 19 September 2017

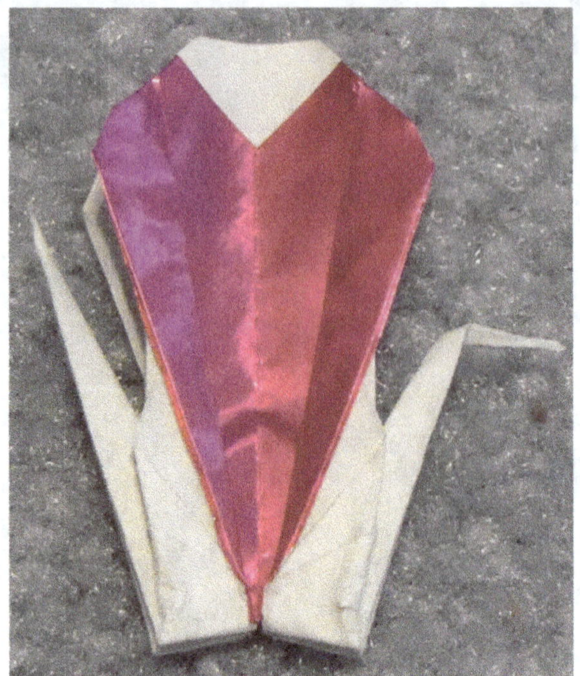
Diamond Heart Crane
One uncut square of foil-backed paper
Variation on the traditional Crane
Unpublished as of 19 September 2017

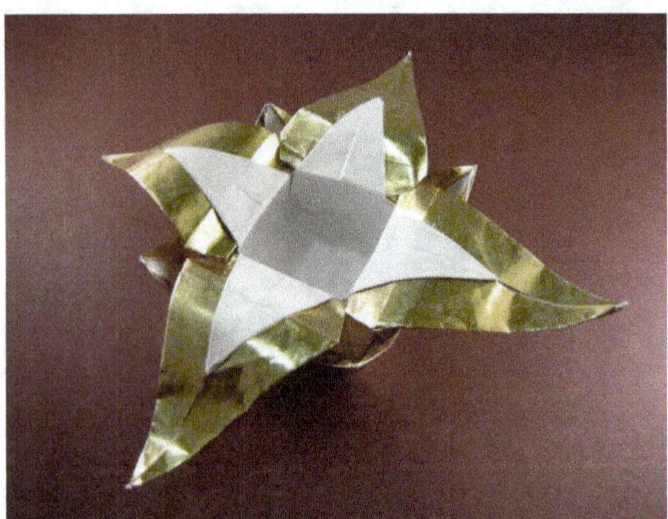
Starburst Dish
One uncut square of foil-backed paper
Variation on the traditional Star Dish
Published in Not Quite Traditional Origami on
OrigamiUSA's website

More variations can be found in the
Heart Transplant section.

Not shown:
    Hatching Crane (action model)
    Checkerboard Crane
    Wingtip Crane
    Crested Crane
    More crane variations
    Better, Sturdier Tulip

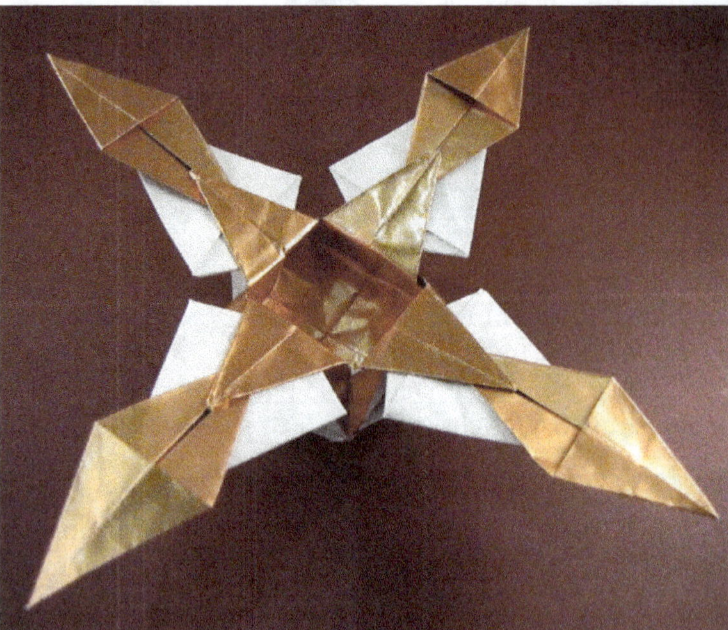
Supernova Dish
One uncut square of foil-backed paper
Variation on the traditional Star Dish
Published in Not Quite Traditional Origami on
OrigamiUSA's website

Tools and Such

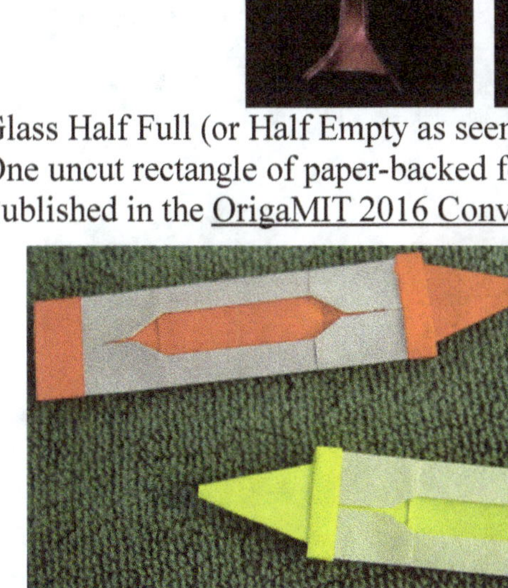

Glass Half Full (or Half Empty as seen from the back)
One uncut rectangle of paper-backed foil
Published in the OrigaMIT 2016 Convention Book.

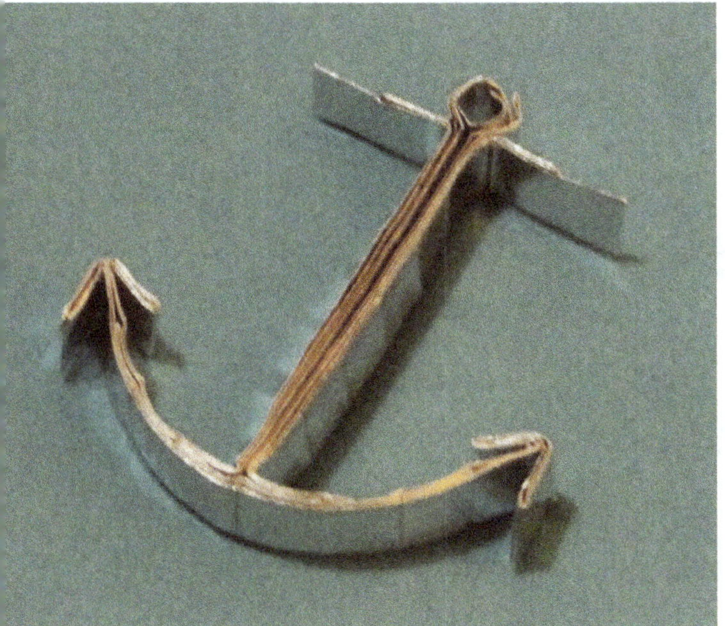

Anchor
One uncut square of paper-backed foil
Published in Techno Origami (Polish convention
collection, ISBN: 978-83-942177-1-6) and the
OrigaMIT 2014 Convention Book.

Crayon
One uncut rectangle each
Unpublished as of 19 September 2017

Campfire
Squares plus shreds for steam
Fire and Logs unpublished as of 19
Sept. 2017
Stewpot published in BOS issue 240

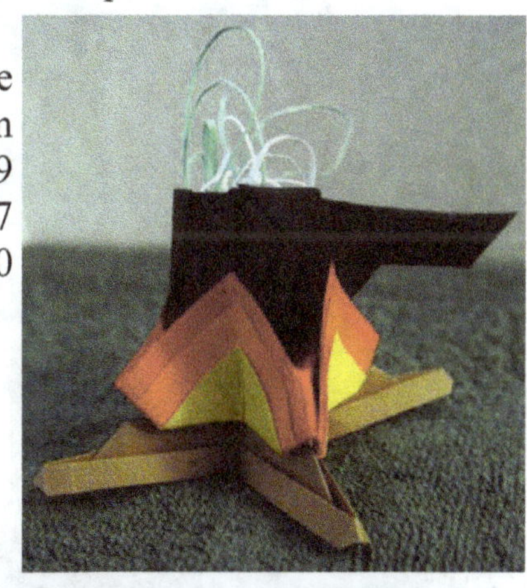

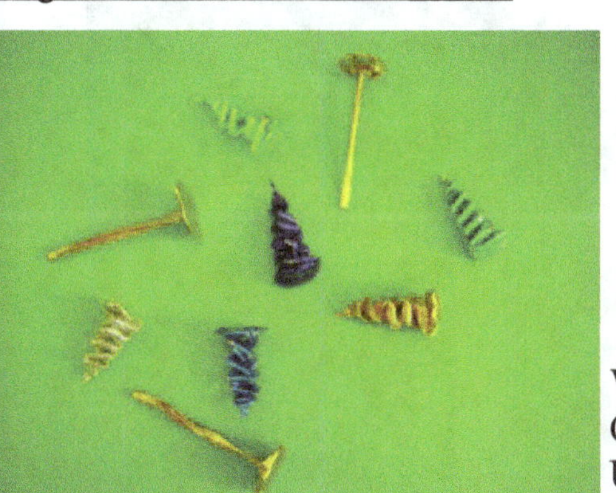

Wood Screws and Nails
One uncut square each
Unpublished as of 19 Sept. 2017

Not shown:

Adze
Hot Air Balloon (published in Techno Origami)
Stop Sign
Hoe
Railroad Spike (published in Techno Origami)
Saw
Shovel

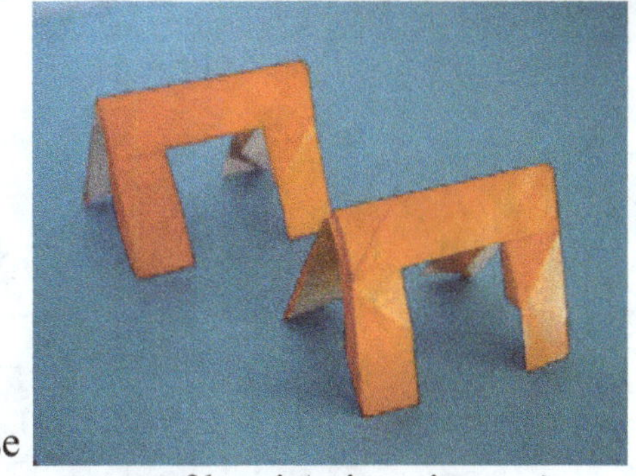

Sawhorse
One uncut square of kami (origami paper)
Unpublished as of 19 September 2017

Origami States of America

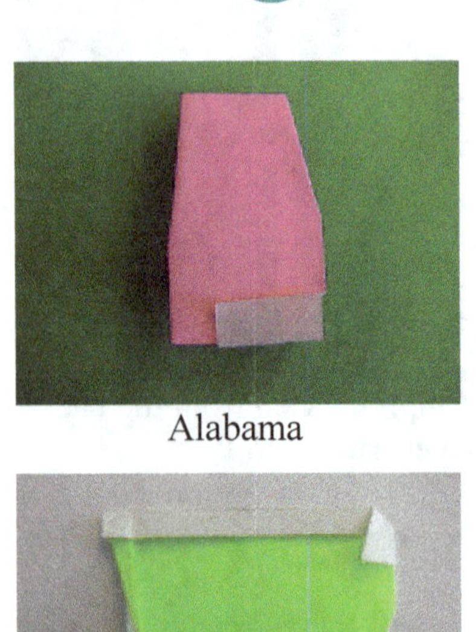
Alabama

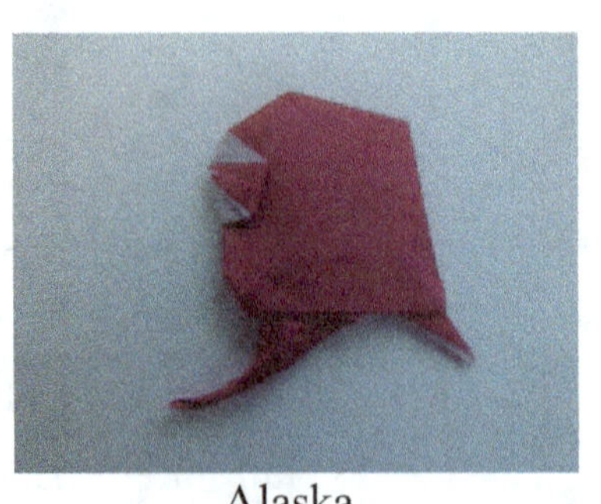
Alaska

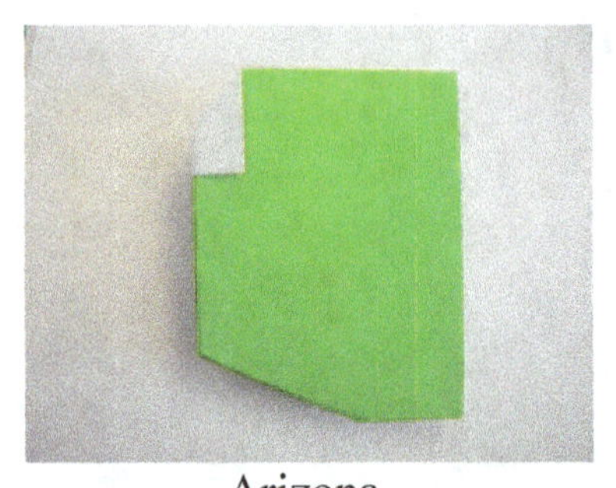
Arizona

All origami states remain unpublished as of 19 September 2017.

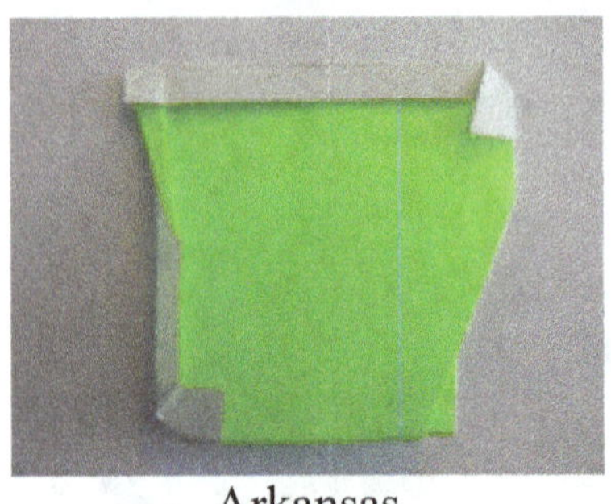
Arkansas

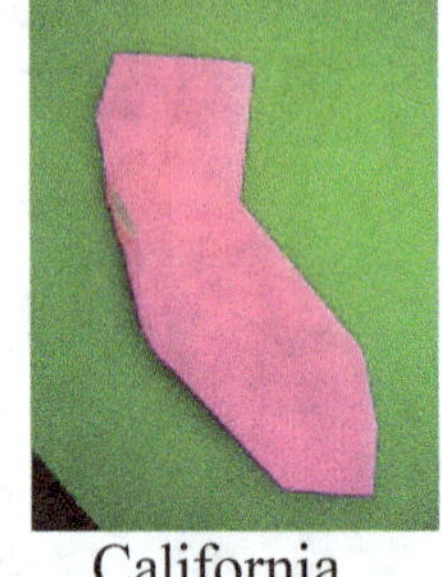
California

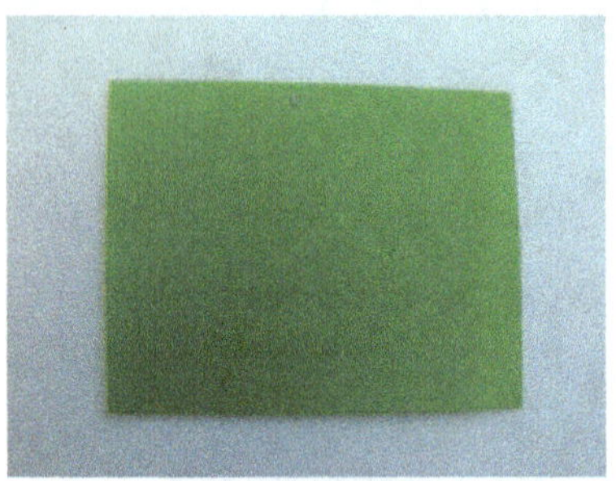
Colorado

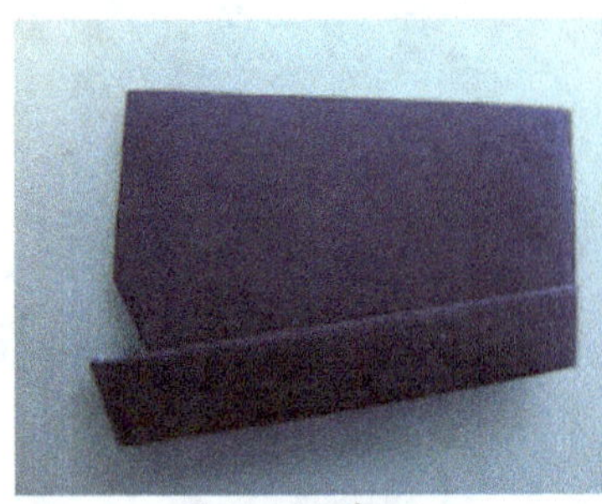
Connecticut

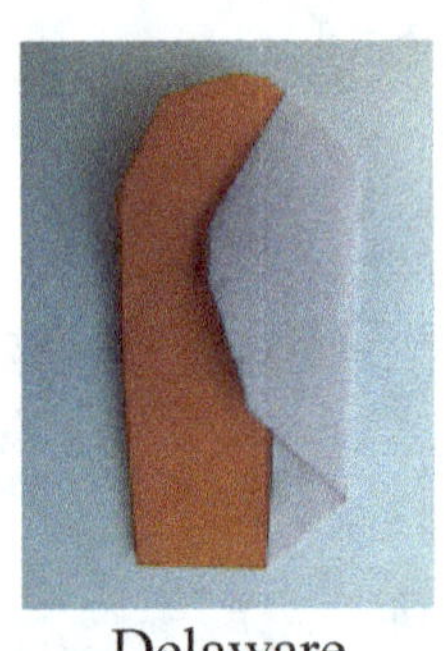
Delaware

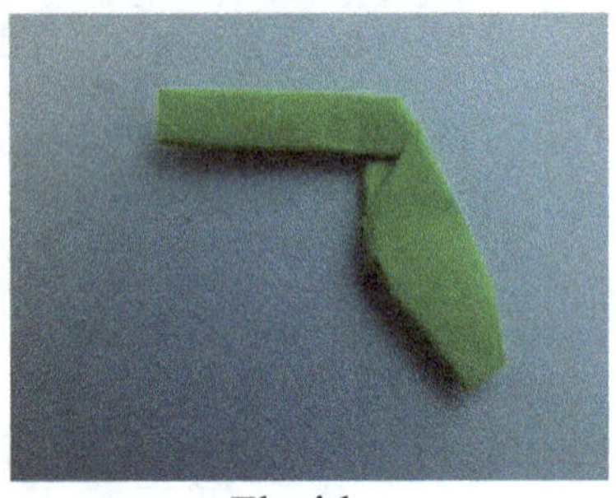
Florida

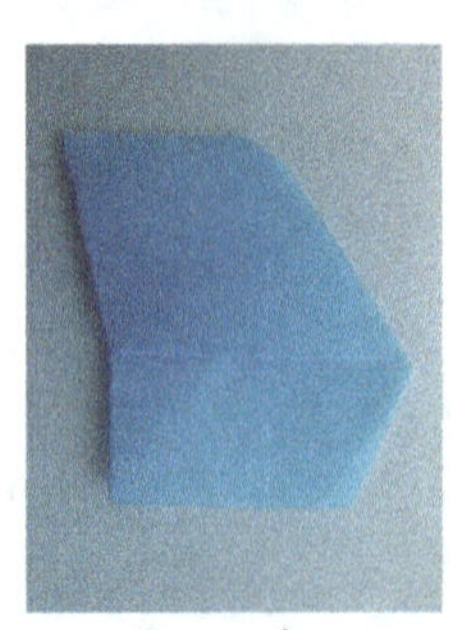
Georgia

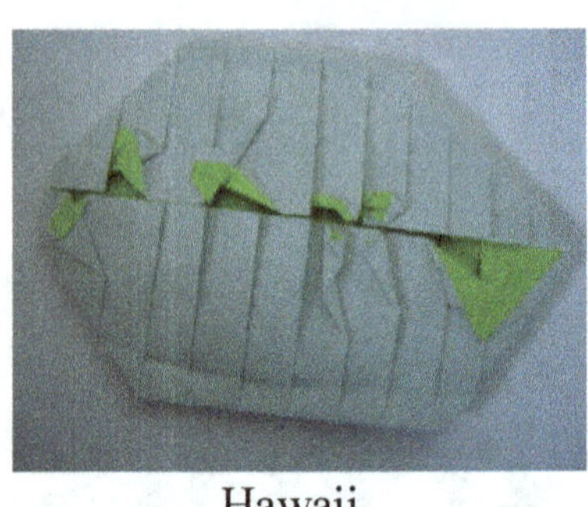
Hawaii

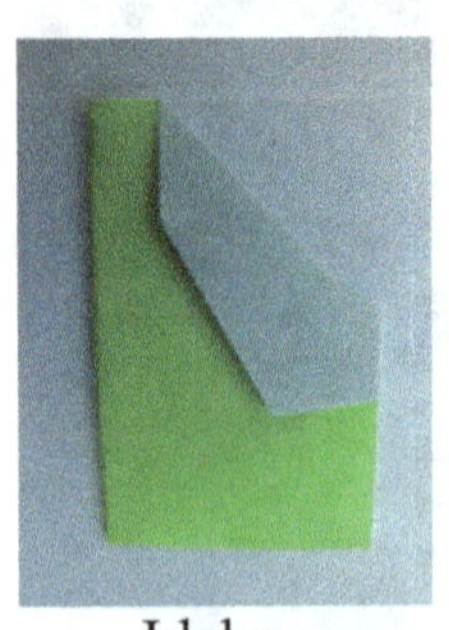
Idaho

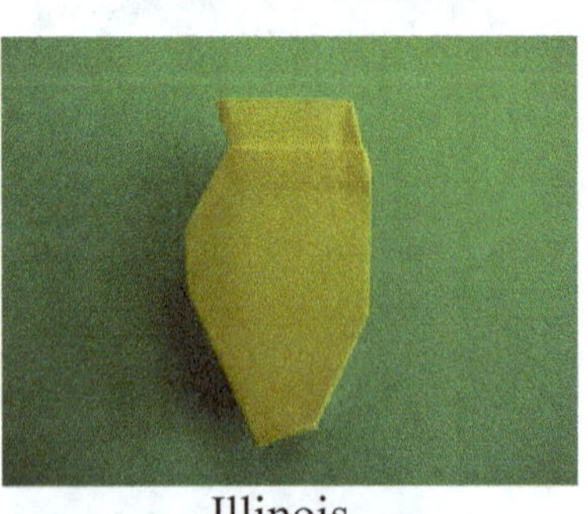
Illinois

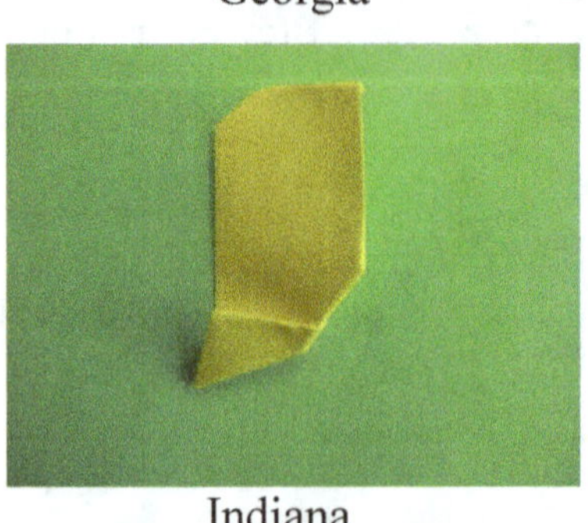
Indiana

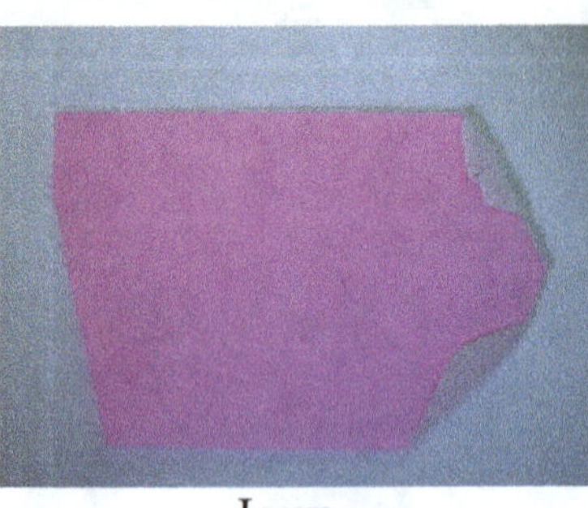
Iowa

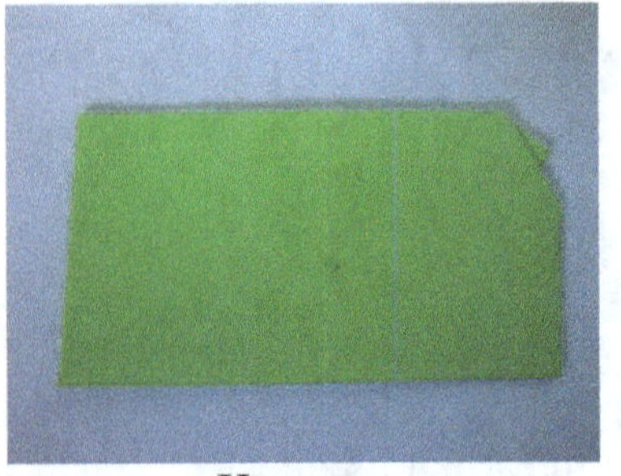
Kansas

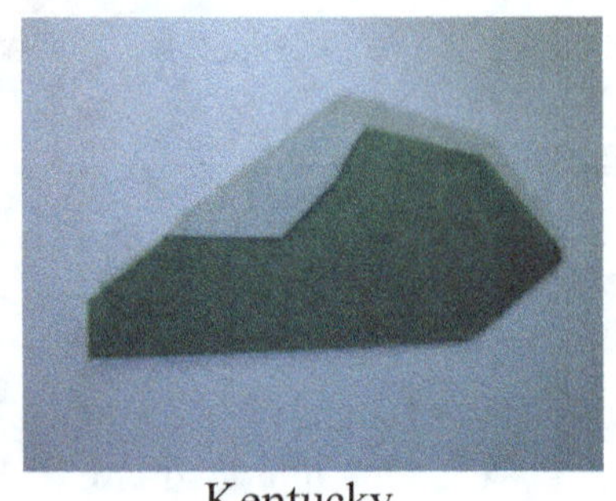
Kentucky

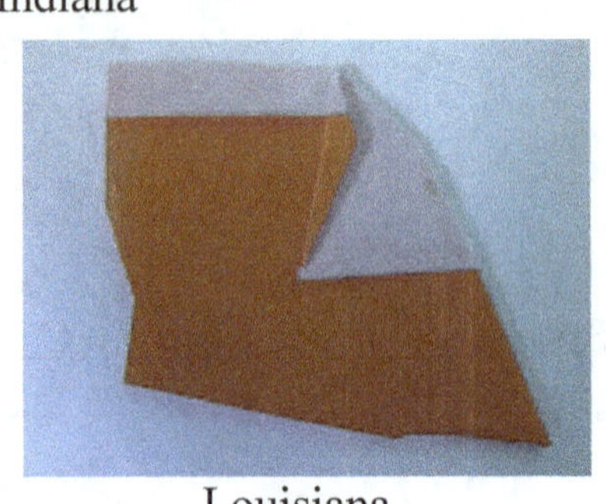
Louisiana

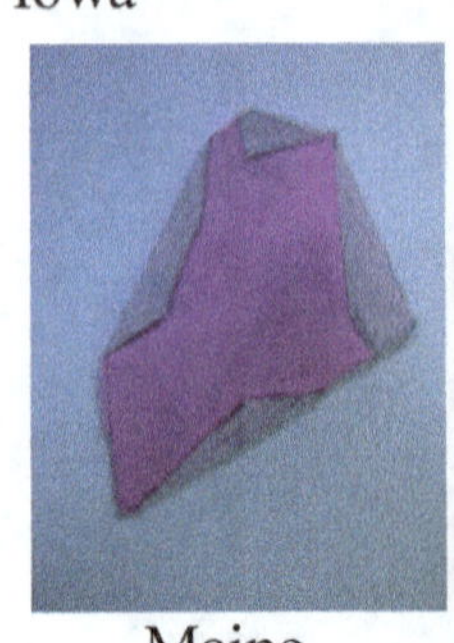
Maine

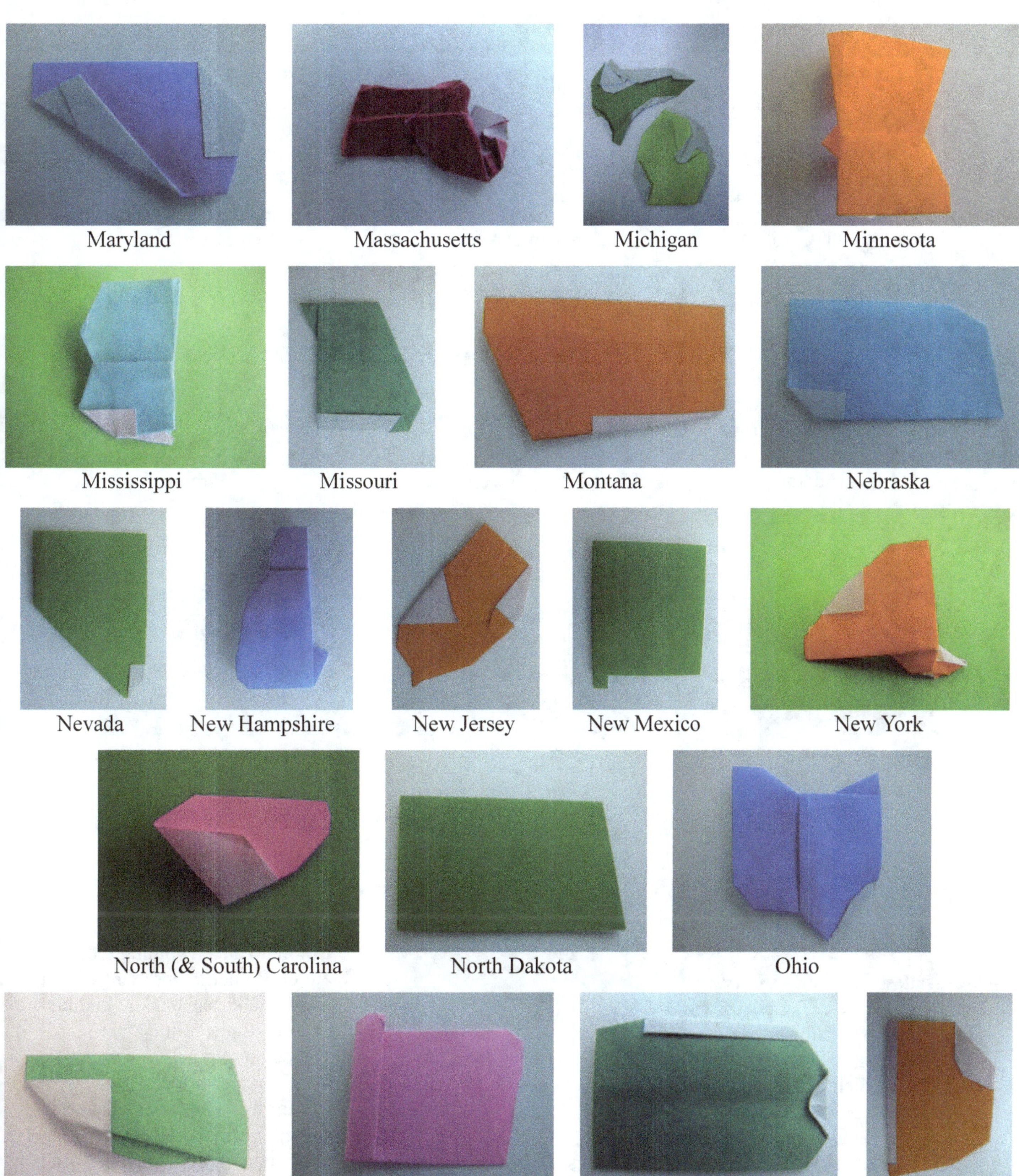

Maryland | Massachusetts | Michigan | Minnesota

Mississippi | Missouri | Montana | Nebraska

Nevada | New Hampshire | New Jersey | New Mexico | New York

North (& South) Carolina | North Dakota | Ohio

Oklahoma | Oregon | Pennsylvania | Rhode Island

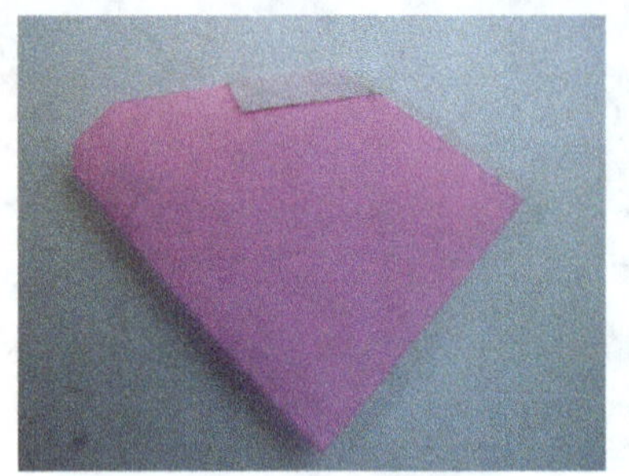

South Carolina

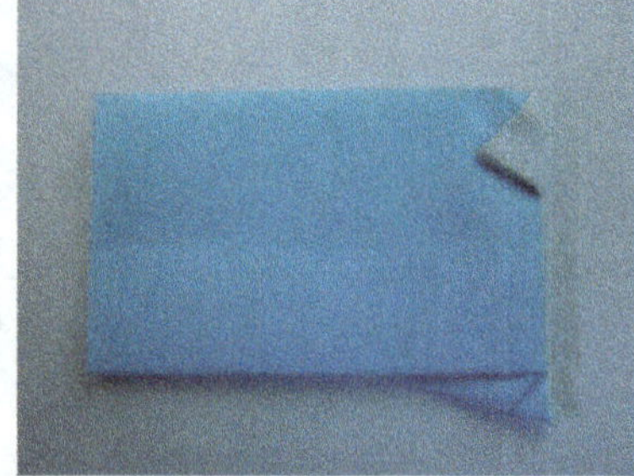

South Dakota

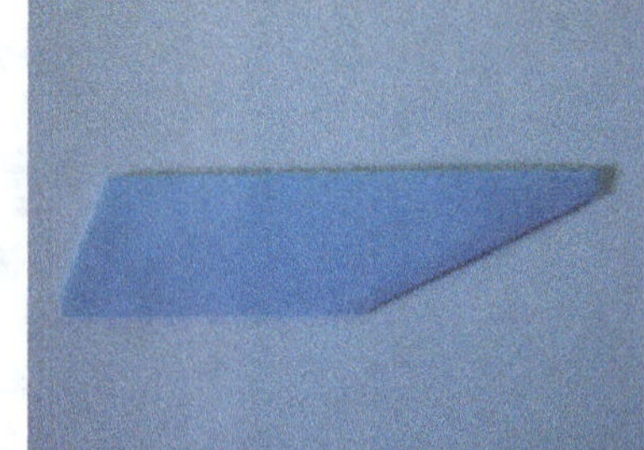

Tennessee

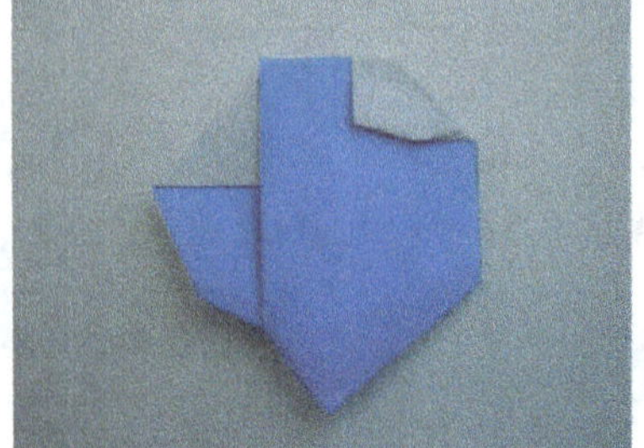

Texas Fold 'Em

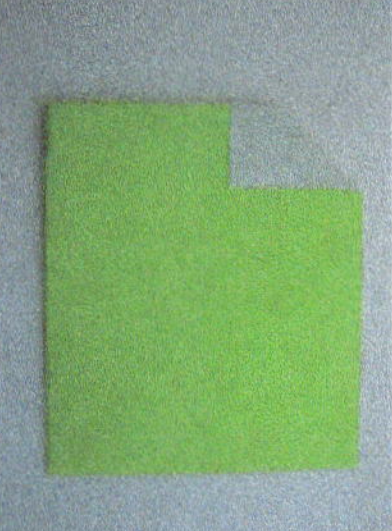

Utah

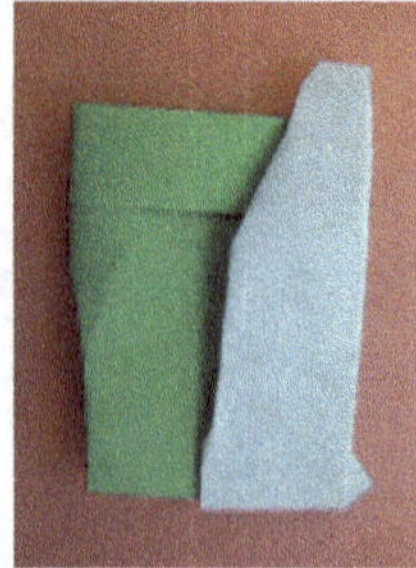

Vermont (and
New Hampshire)

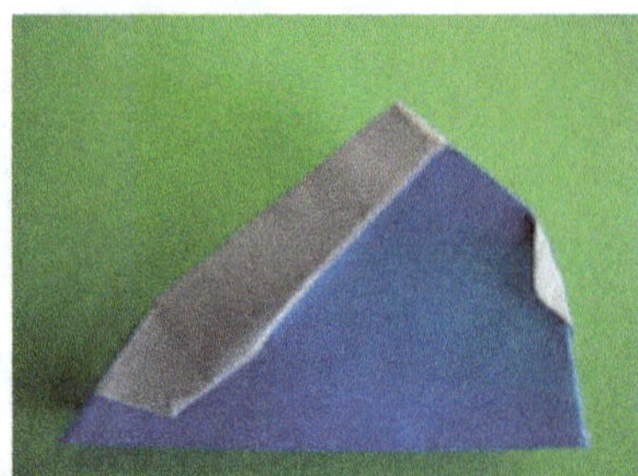

Virginia

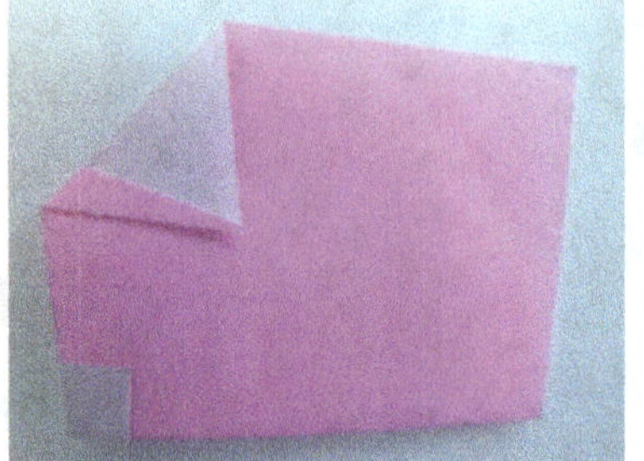

Washington

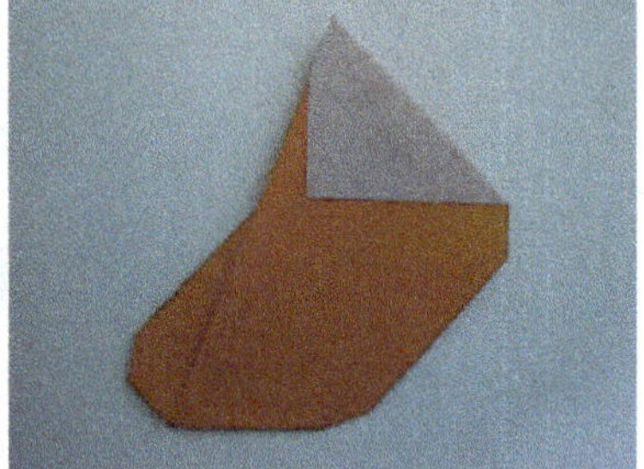

West Virginia

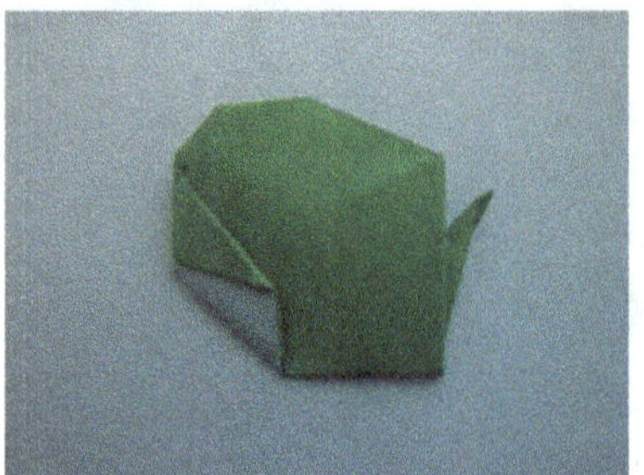

Wisconsin

Wyoming

Most states use a fairly short folding sequences. Rough drafts fitted one state per page of graph paper, with the Hawaii and Michigan as the only two exceptions. These geographic shapes do often require judgment folds.

The states all use kami (standard origami paper with one side colorful and the other side plain white). The featured state is always the colorful part of the paper. In two cases, the white part forms a neighbor!

Colorado and Wyoming look alike! Rather than relying on natural features, lines of latitude and longitude define them. Notice San Francisco Bay detail on the western side of California. The series of states started with Texas Fold 'Em, the only State model with a play on word. Notice also the two pairs of states where one state shows as one color and a neighbor shows as the other color.

Acorn

Recommended Paper: Any small square such as 1.5-6" (40-150mm) kami or memo cube.

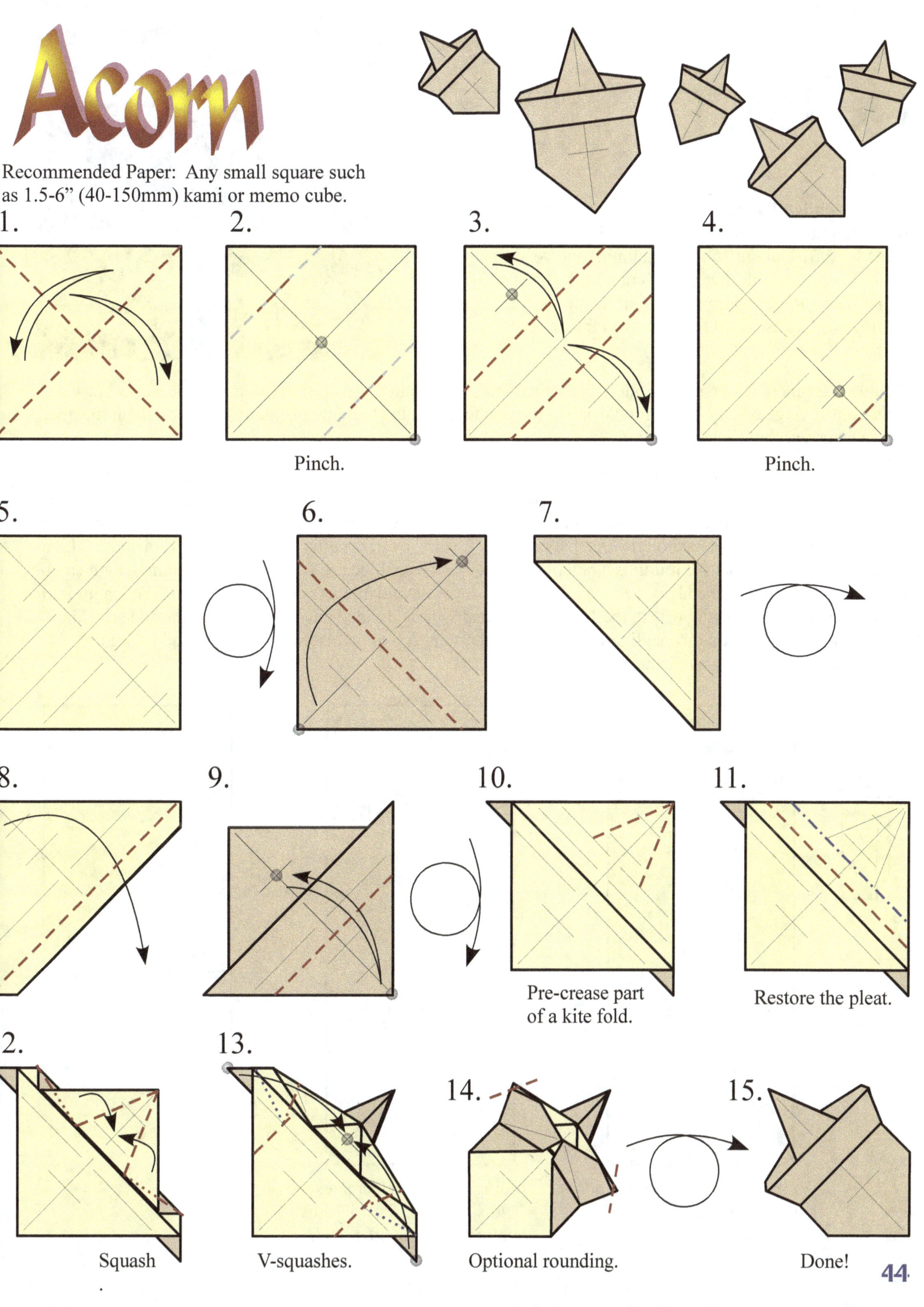

Double Happine$$

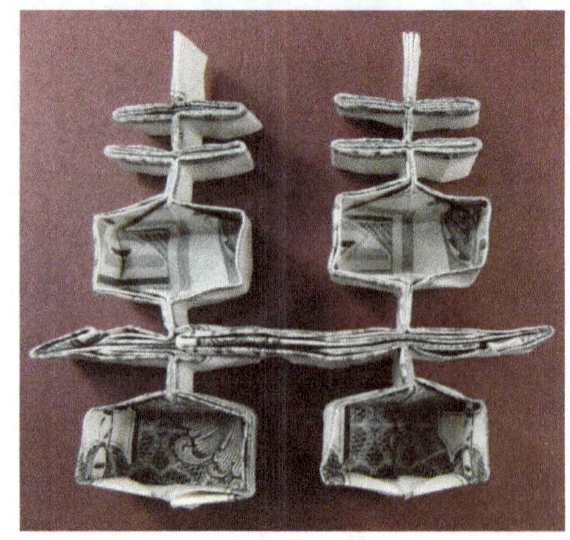

Recommended Paper: Two U.S. dollar bills or play money with accurate proportions (close to 8:19). A real dollar bill is 6.14 x 2.61" (about 156.0 x 66.3 mm) and *very* close to 8:19. If you cut your own paper, cut it to the 8:19 ratio rather than another approximation of the dollar bill. Wet-folding works best. Red for luck, gold for riches.

Double Happiness is two similar but not identical units or modules. *Most* of the steps are the same, but directions diverge briefly in the middle and at the end to create the locking mechanism to hook them together. These steps will be labeled as *Left* or *Right*.

There is more than one way to grid a dollar bill into 8x19 squares. It is intuitive to fold diagonals to measure off a 1:2 rectangle for a 8x16 grid, then replicate the sixteenths for the remaining lengthwise divisions. Even with quite precise folding, any tiny, imperceptible inaccuracies accumulate until they gather and become evident in the 19th division. This method inverts that process. It starts by generating four of the 19th divisions. Three are needed, not four, but the fourth is a practical necessity. Once three are known, the remaining length can be treated as a 1:2 rectangle and divided into sixteenths. Any unavoidable inaccuracy in dividing the length into a 1:2 rectangle and the rest now is in the 1:2 rectangle and will be divided among the sixteenths and should be imperceptible and thoroughly negligible. It is still important to fold precisely, but this method is slightly forgiving whereas the intuitive one forgives nothing.

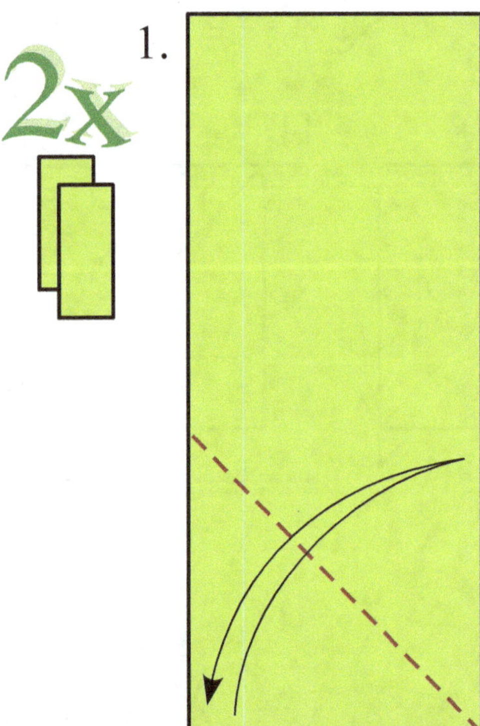

1.

A pinch would suffice, but a complete diagonal is harmless and usually more accurate.

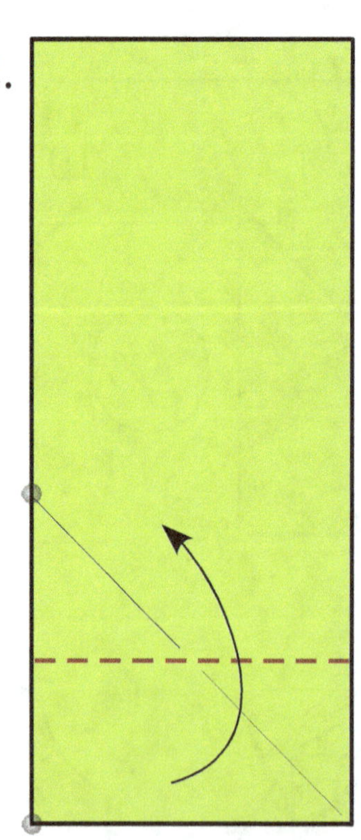

2.

Folding to the pinch creates the 4/19ths line -- or the 15/19ths counting from the other end.

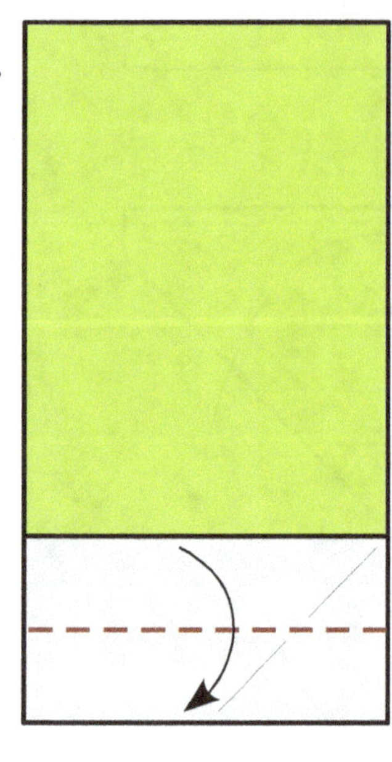

3.

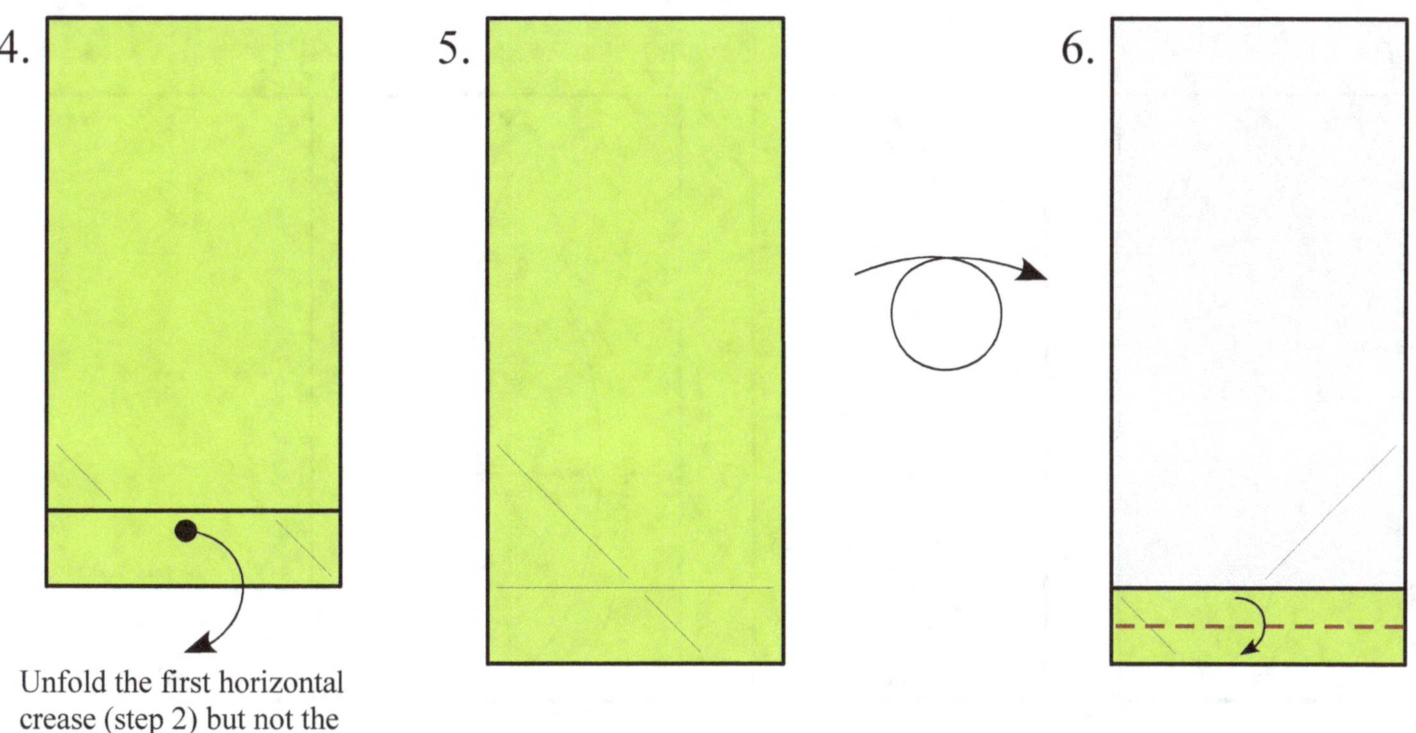

4.

Unfold the first horizontal
crease (step 2) but not the
second (step 3).

5.

6.

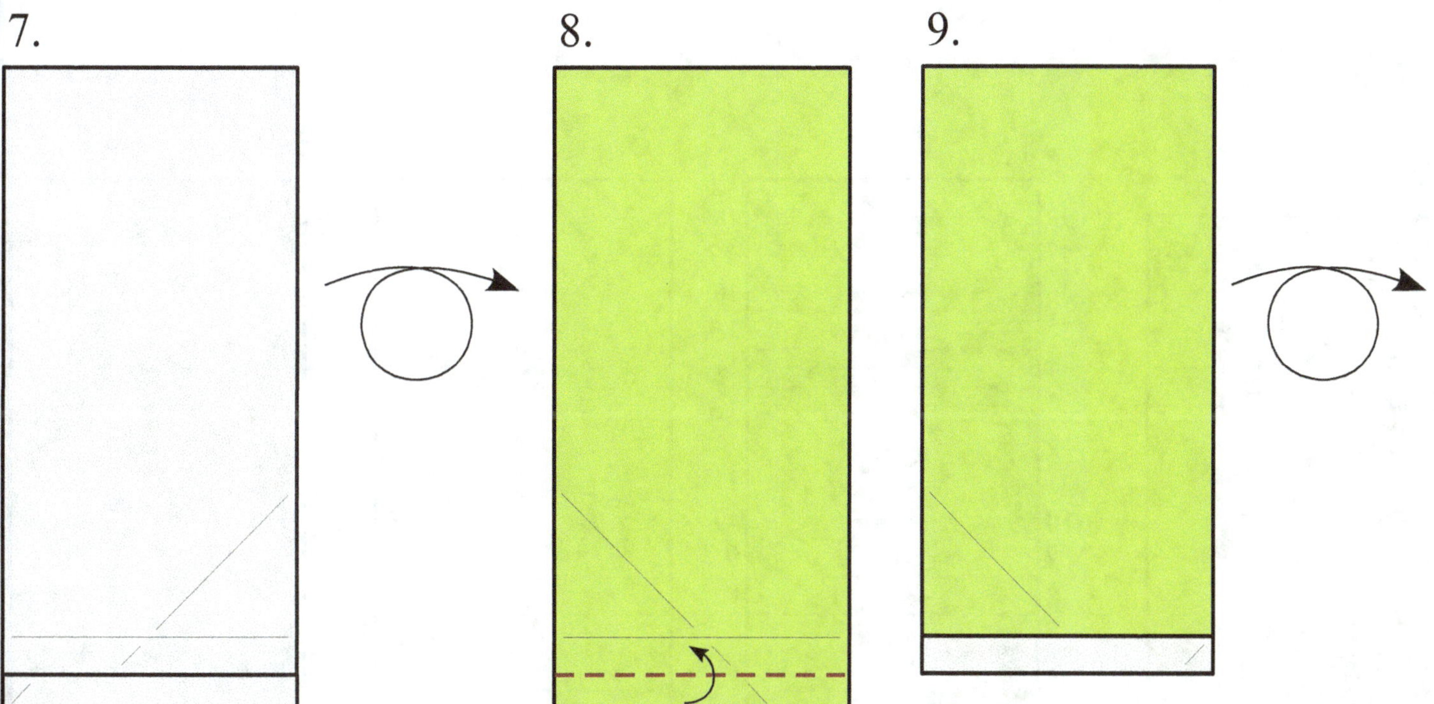

7.

8.

9.

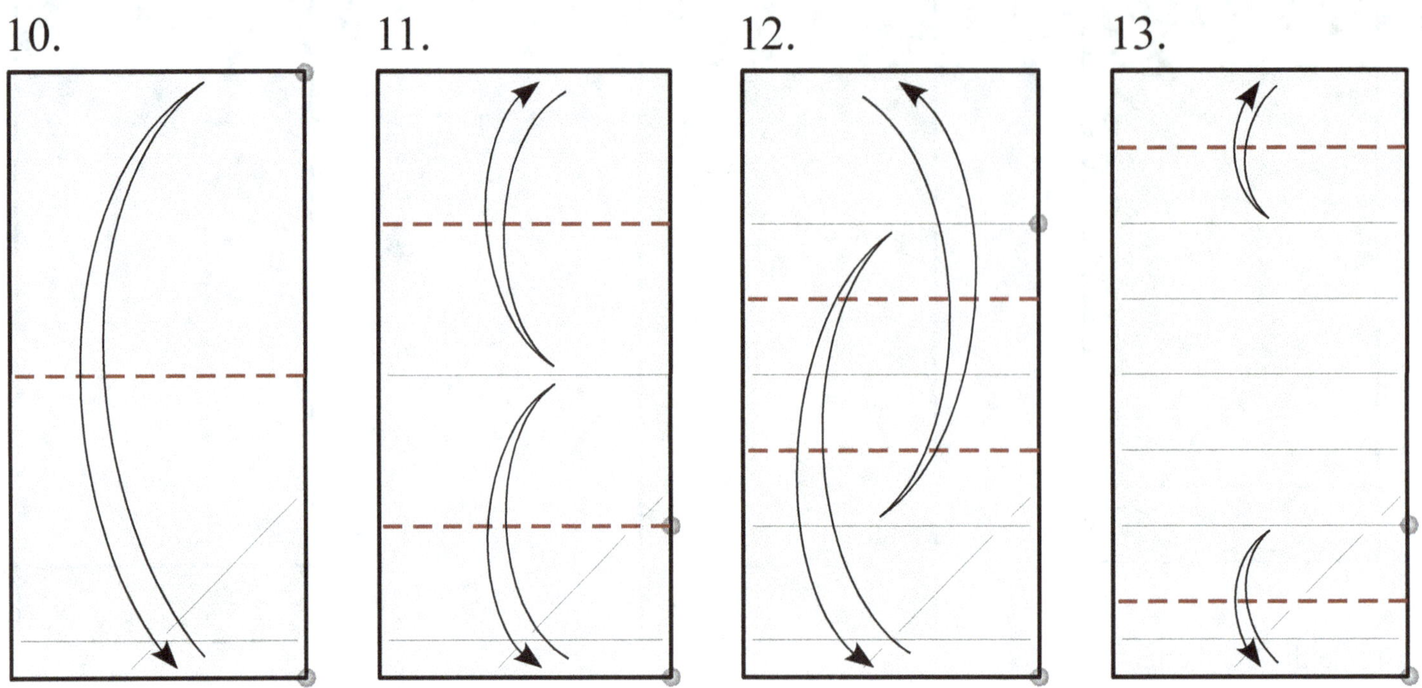

10.

The visible rectangle is 1:2, with the first three (3) 19ths folded behind.

11.

12.

13.

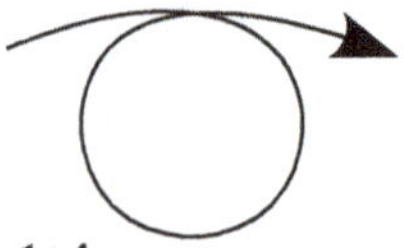

14.

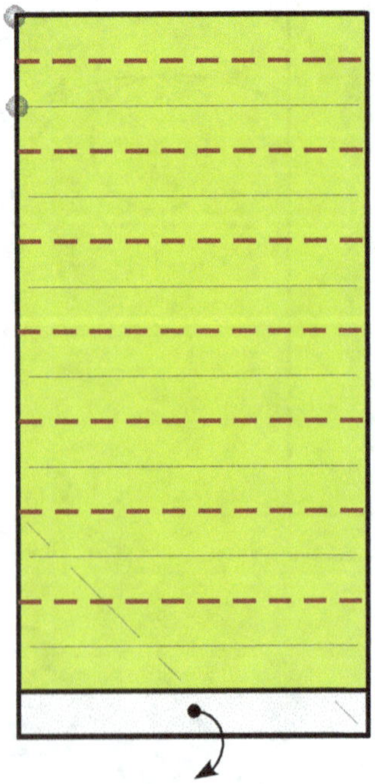

For the remaining divisions, it is best to fan-fold. Unfold completely.

15.

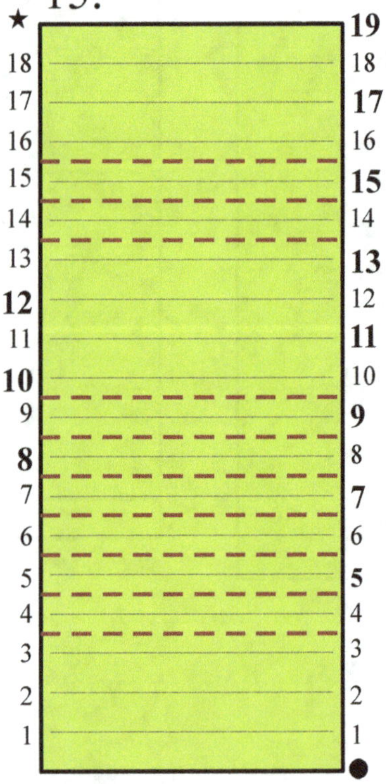

Pre-crease. Fold the near end to lines 7, 9, 11, 13, 15, 17 and 19 (the far end). Fold the far end to lines 8, 10 and 12.

16.

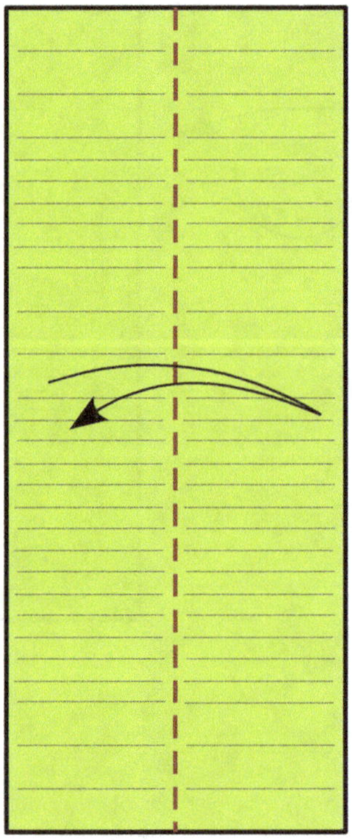

17.

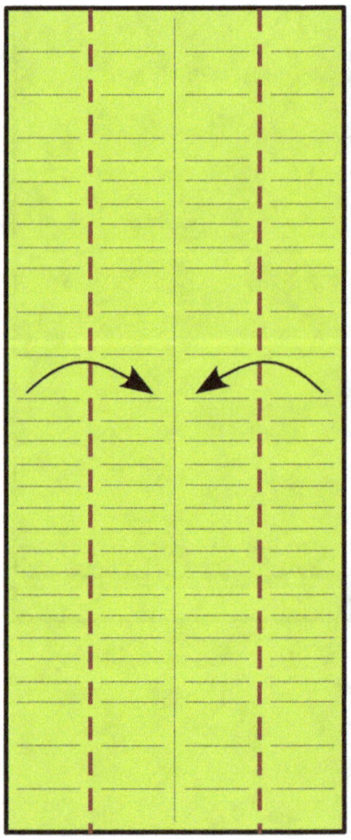

Cupboard fold.

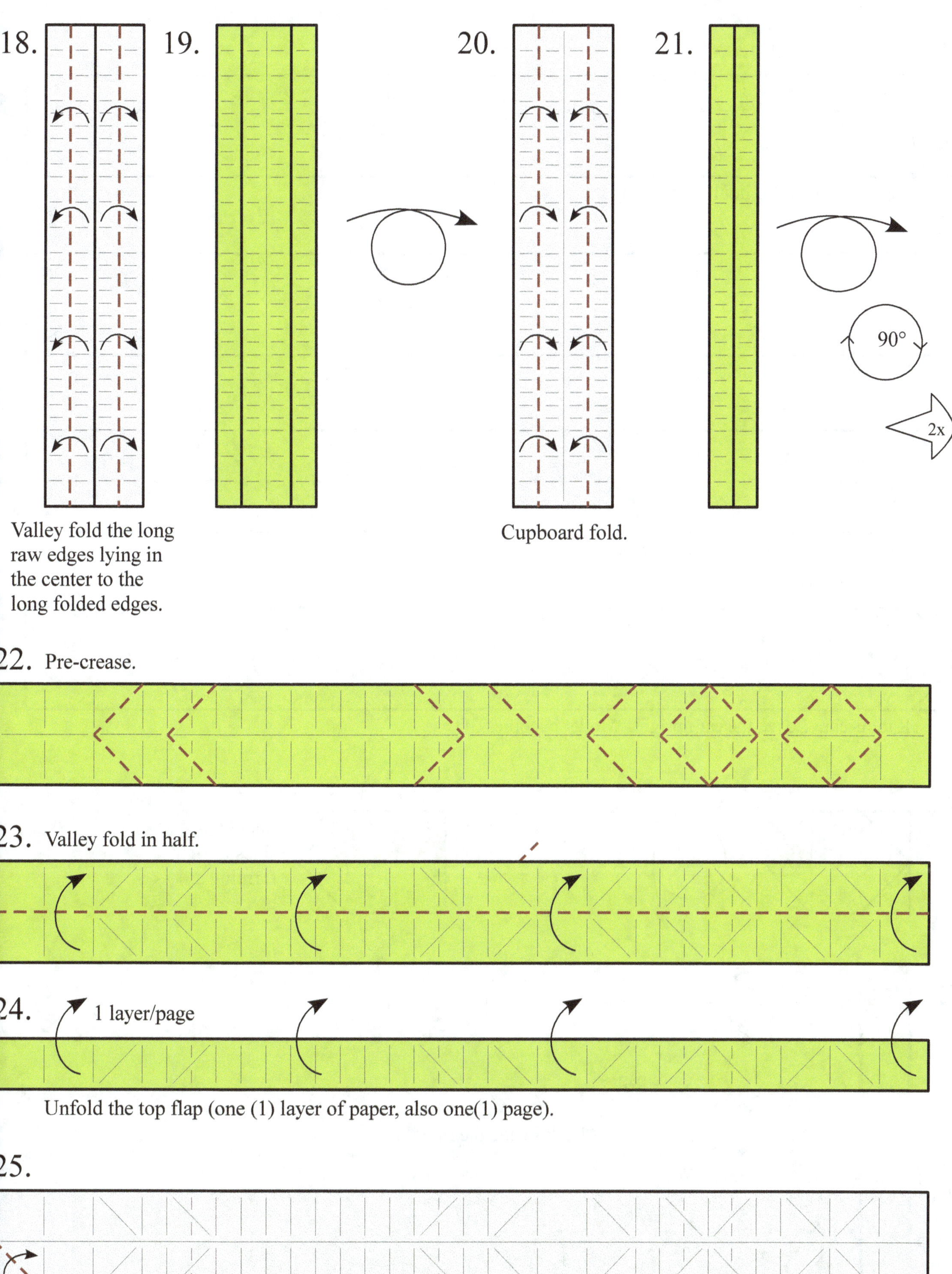

18.

19.

20.

21.

Valley fold the long raw edges lying in the center to the long folded edges.

Cupboard fold.

22. Pre-crease.

23. Valley fold in half.

24. 1 layer/page

Unfold the top flap (one (1) layer of paper, also one(1) page).

25.

Dog-ear two (2) double-thick pages.

26.

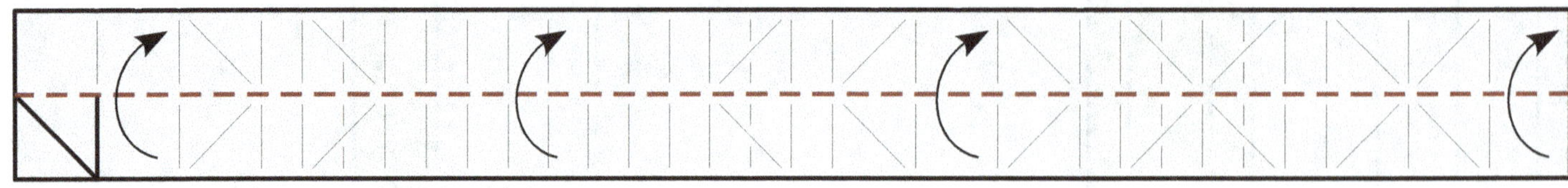

Page-turn three (3) double-thick pages.

27.

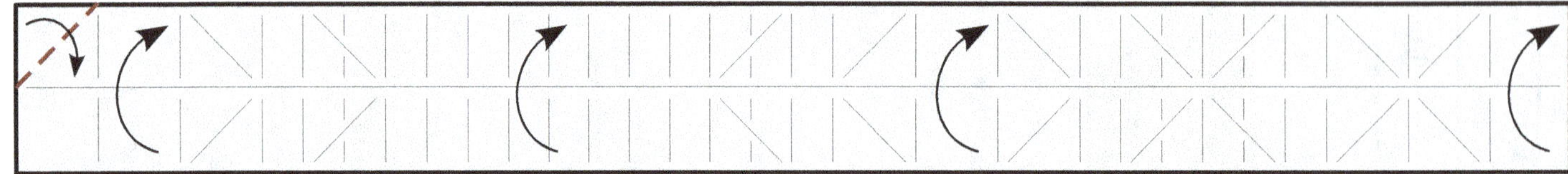

Dog-ear one (1) double-thick page.

28.

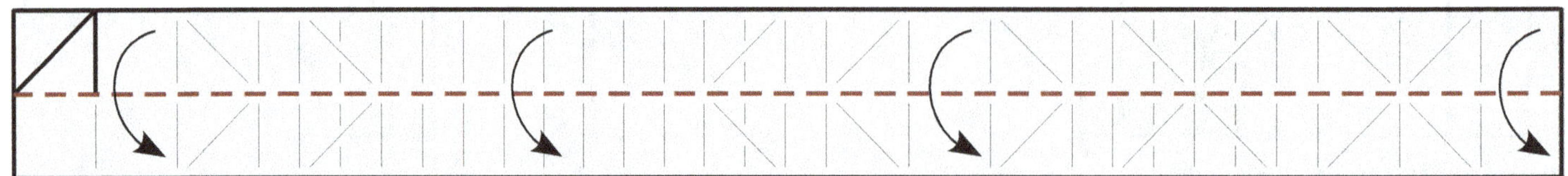

Page-turn one (1) double-thick page.

29.

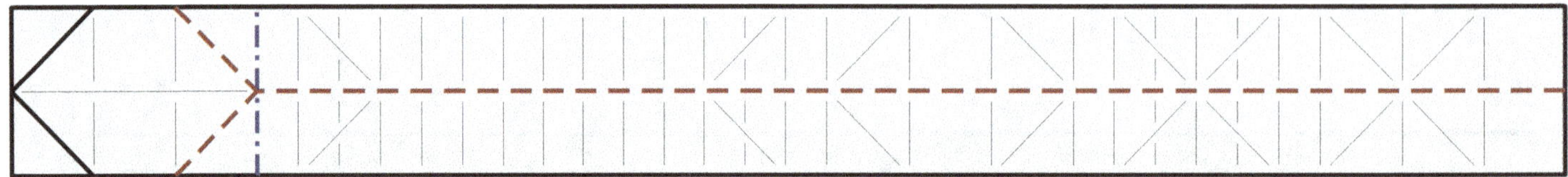

Rabbit-ear. Leave the ear upright. Model becomes 3D.

30. **31.**
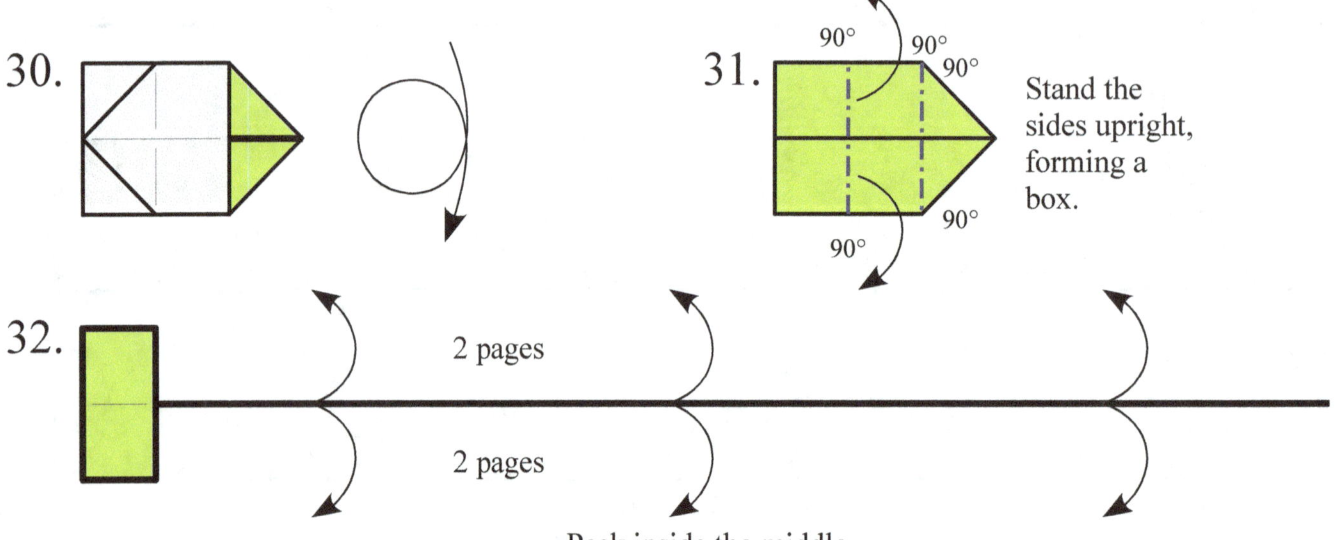

32.
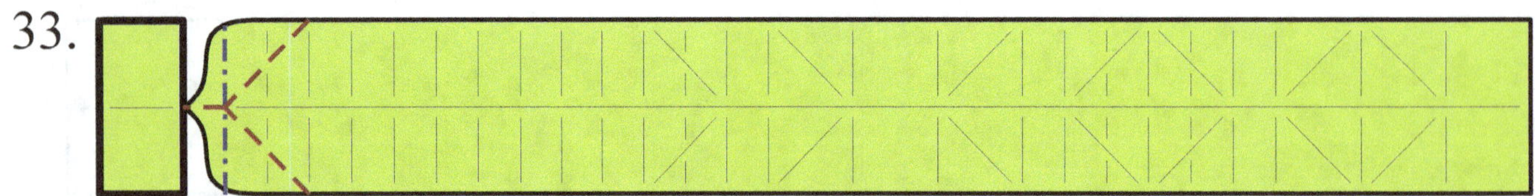

Peek inside the middle.

33.

Rabbit-ear. Leave the ear upright.

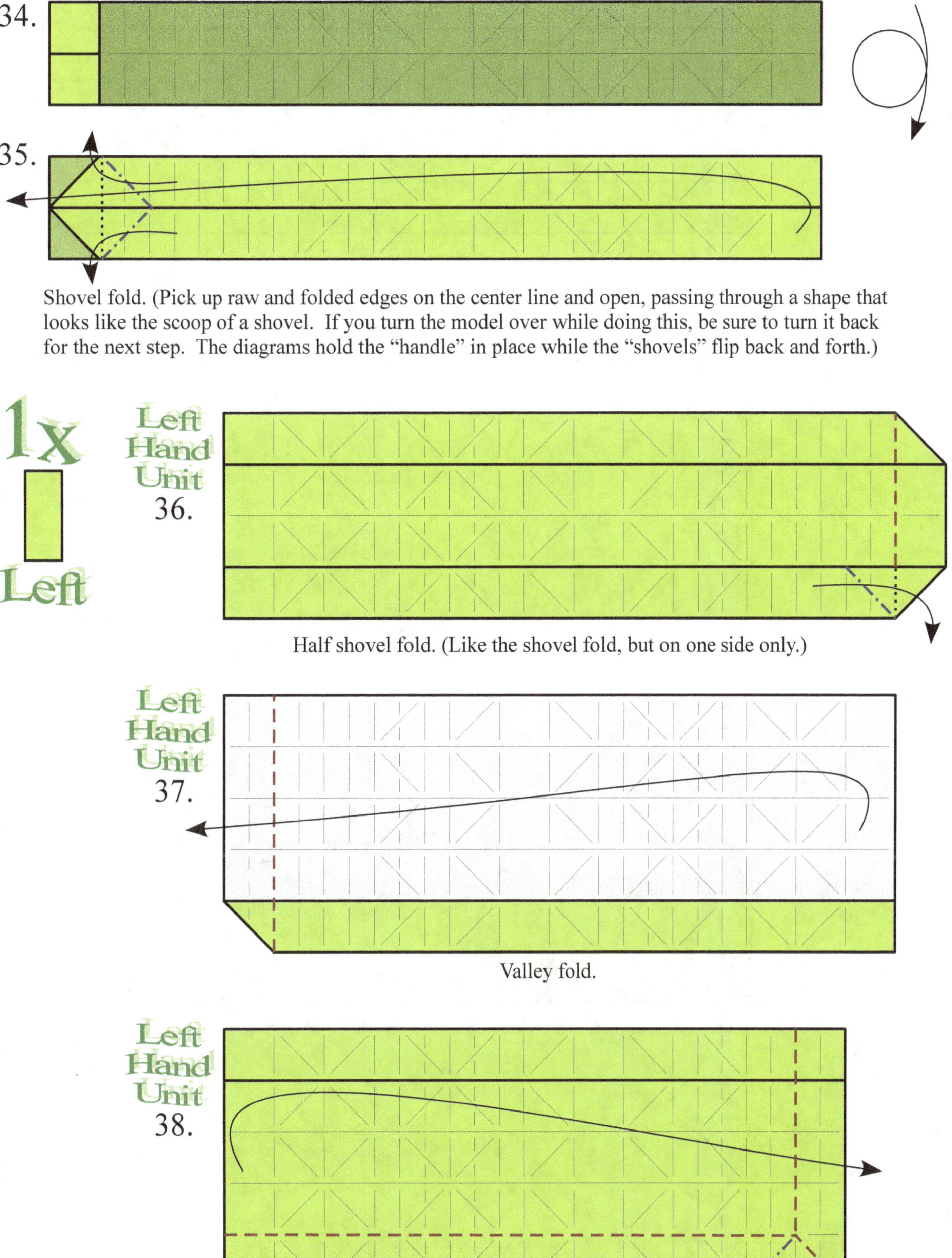

34.

35.

Shovel fold. (Pick up raw and folded edges on the center line and open, passing through a shape that looks like the scoop of a shovel. If you turn the model over while doing this, be sure to turn it back for the next step. The diagrams hold the "handle" in place while the "shovels" flip back and forth.)

1x

Left

Left Hand Unit

36.

Half shovel fold. (Like the shovel fold, but on one side only.)

Left Hand Unit

37.

Valley fold.

Left Hand Unit

38.

Half inverse shovel fold. Essentially, this is a half shovel fold performed in reverse

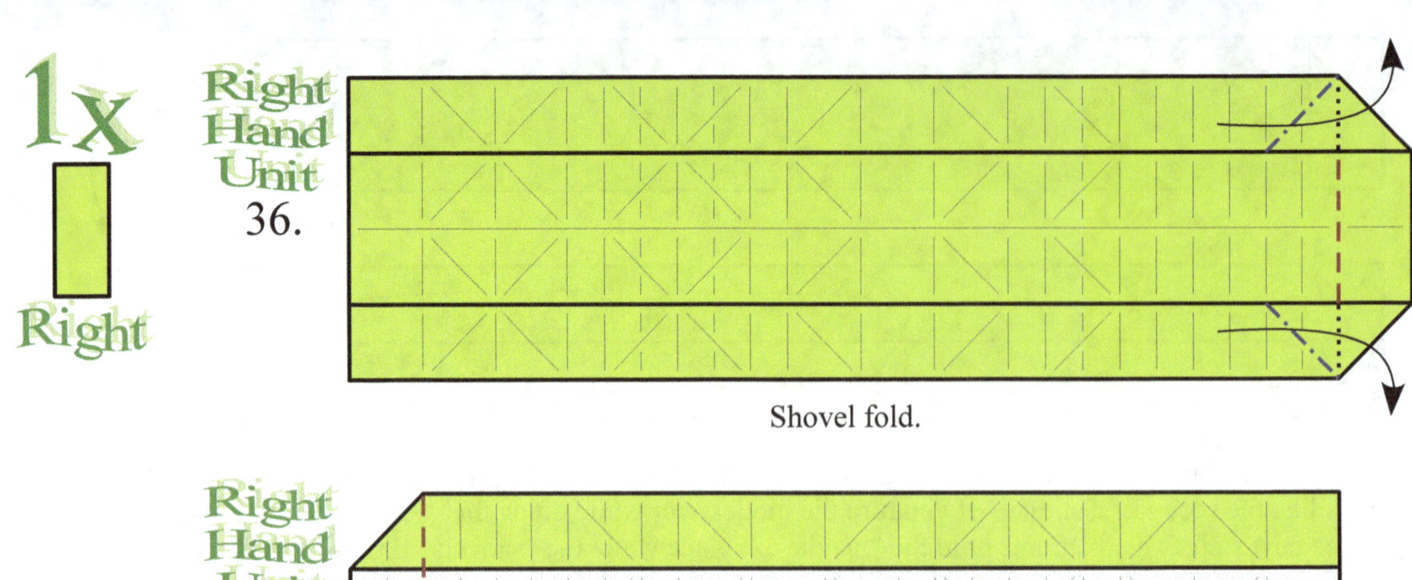

Shovel fold.

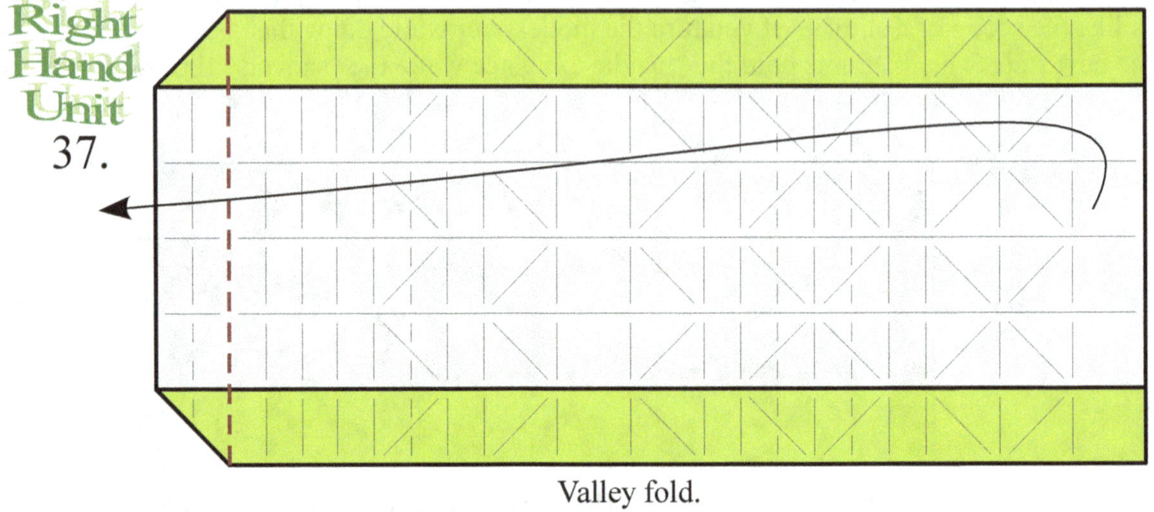

Valley fold.

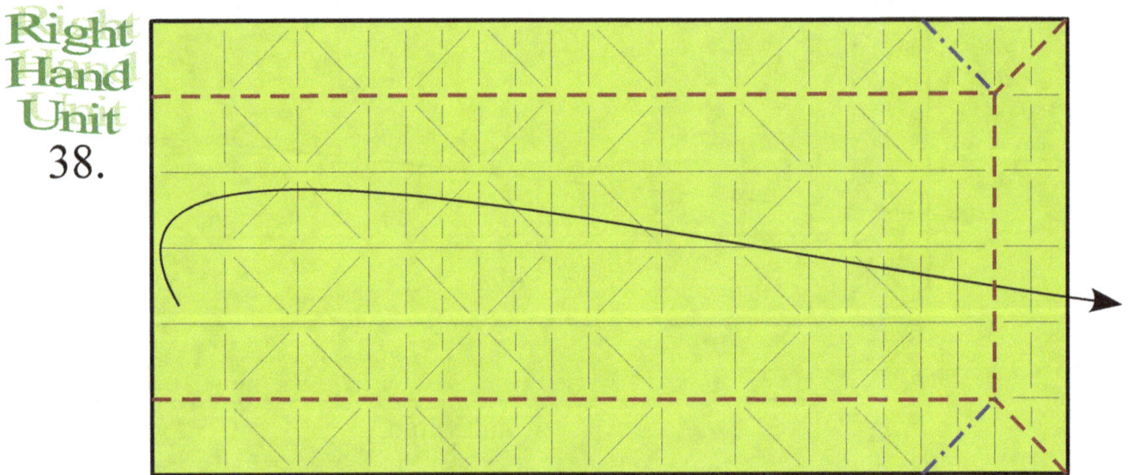

Inverse shovel fold. Essentially, this is a shovel fold performed in reverse.

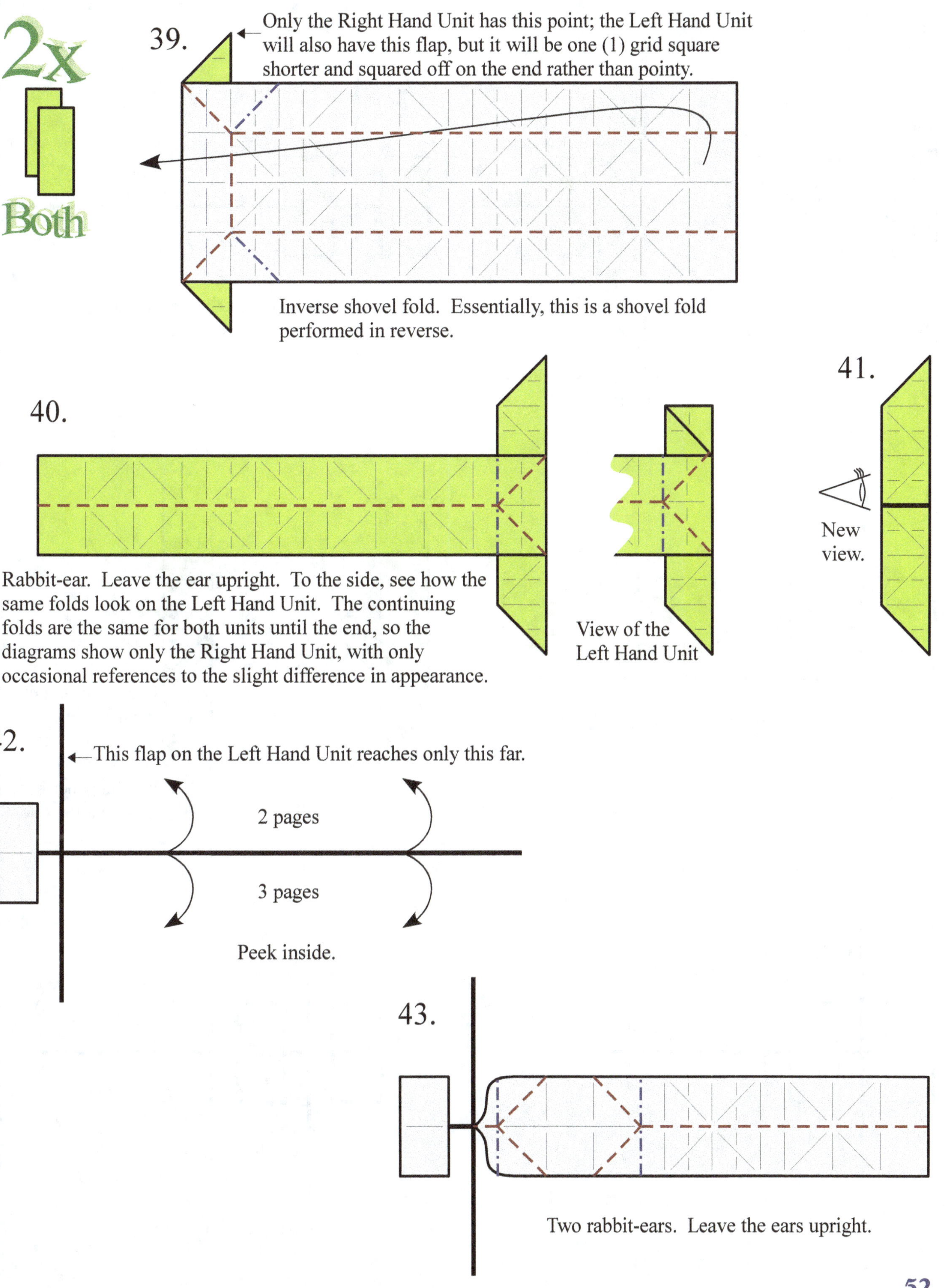

2x
Both
39.
Only the Right Hand Unit has this point; the Left Hand Unit will also have this flap, but it will be one (1) grid square shorter and squared off on the end rather than pointy.
Inverse shovel fold. Essentially, this is a shovel fold performed in reverse.
40.
41.
New view.
Rabbit-ear. Leave the ear upright. To the side, see how the same folds look on the Left Hand Unit. The continuing folds are the same for both units until the end, so the diagrams show only the Right Hand Unit, with only occasional references to the slight difference in appearance.
View of the Left Hand Unit
42.
This flap on the Left Hand Unit reaches only this far.
2 pages
3 pages
Peek inside.
43.
Two rabbit-ears. Leave the ears upright.

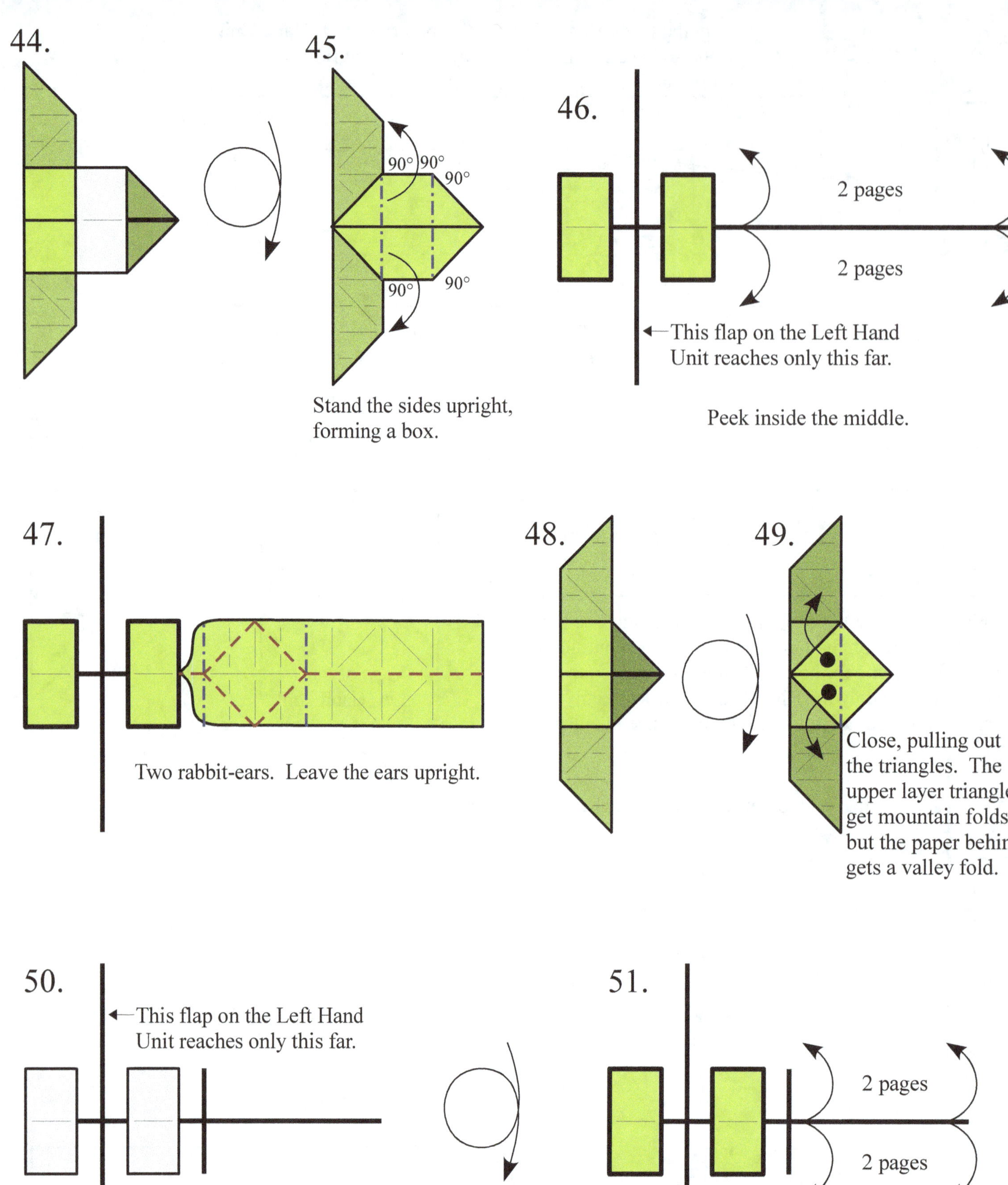

44.

45.

Stand the sides upright,
forming a box.

46.

Peek inside the middle.

47.

Two rabbit-ears. Leave the ears upright.

48.

49.

Close, pulling out
the triangles. The
upper layer triangles
get mountain folds,
but the paper behind
gets a valley fold.

50.

51.

Peek inside the middle.

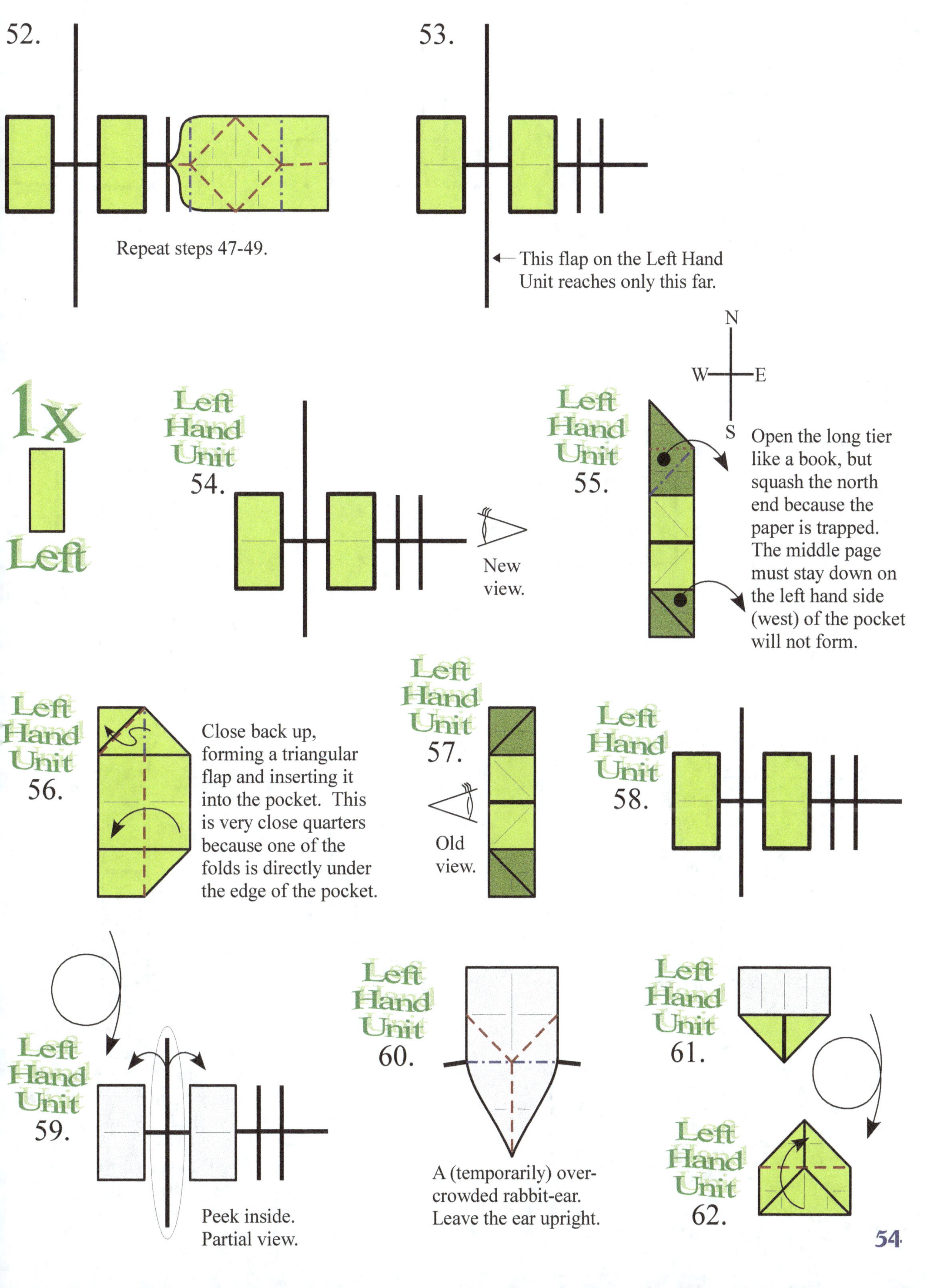

52.
Repeat steps 47-49.

53.
This flap on the Left Hand Unit reaches only this far.

N
W E
S

1x
Left

Left Hand Unit
54.
New view.

Left Hand Unit
55.
Open the long tier like a book, but squash the north end because the paper is trapped. The middle page must stay down on the left hand side (west) of the pocket will not form.

Left Hand Unit
56.
Close back up, forming a triangular flap and inserting it into the pocket. This is very close quarters because one of the folds is directly under the edge of the pocket.

Left Hand Unit
57.
Old view.

Left Hand Unit
58.

Left Hand Unit
59.
Peek inside. Partial view.

Left Hand Unit
60.
A (temporarily) over-crowded rabbit-ear. Leave the ear upright.

Left Hand Unit
61.

Left Hand Unit
62.

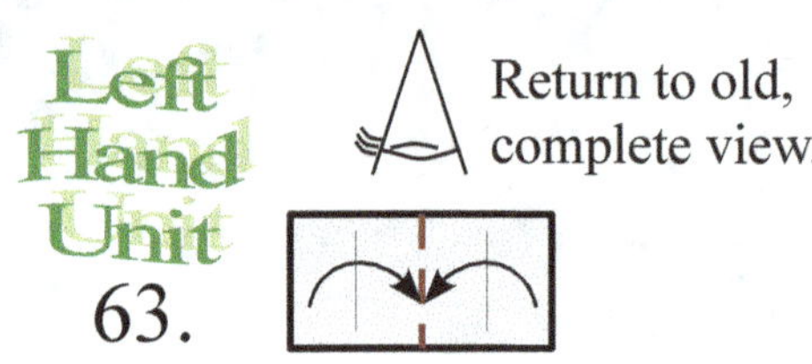

Left Hand Unit 63.

Fold in half from either side to relieve the overcrowding. Reshape the distorted boxes.

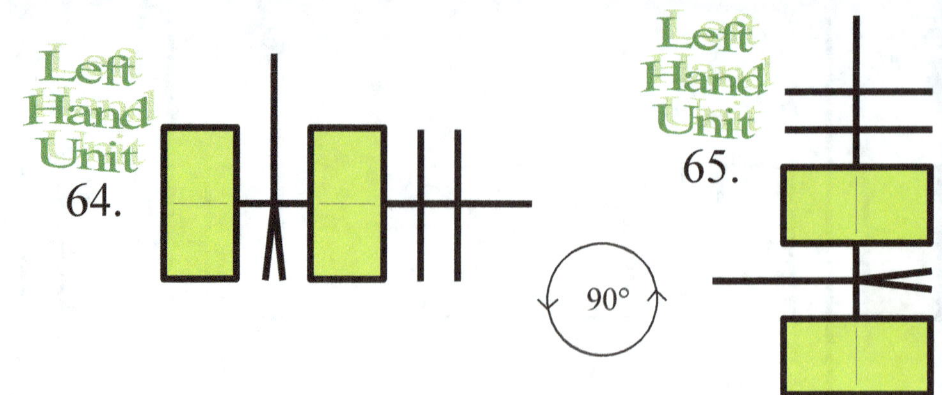

Left Hand Unit 64.

Left Hand Unit 65.

90°

1x

Right

Right Hand Unit 54.

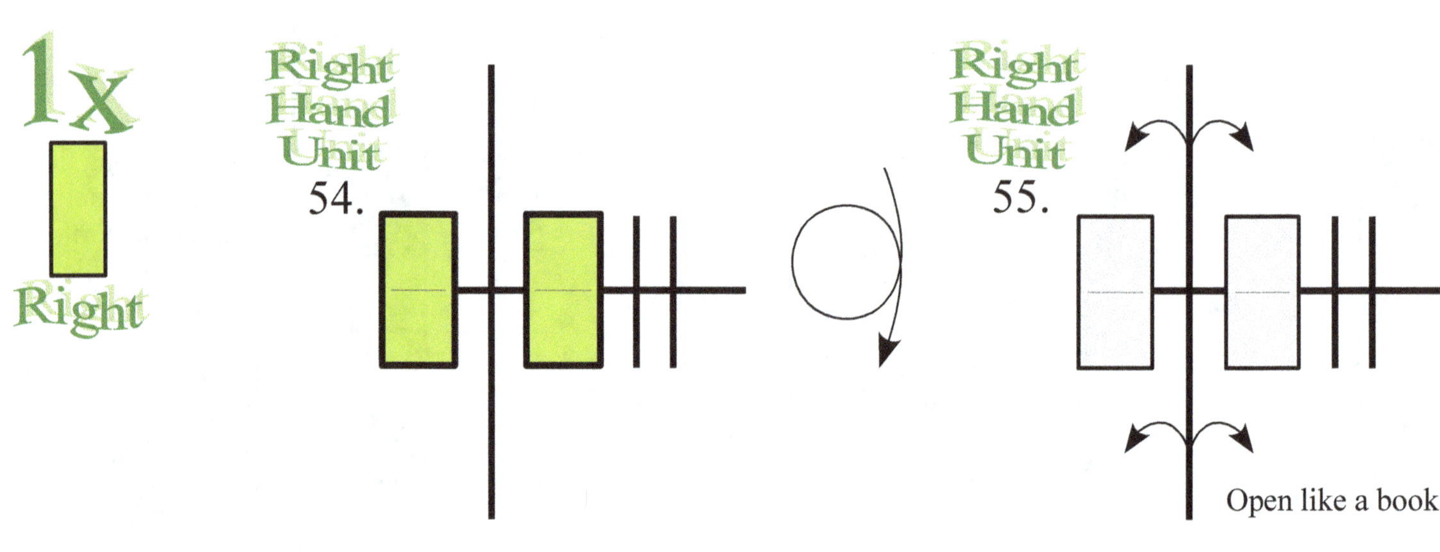

Right Hand Unit 55.

Open like a book.

Right Hand Unit 56.

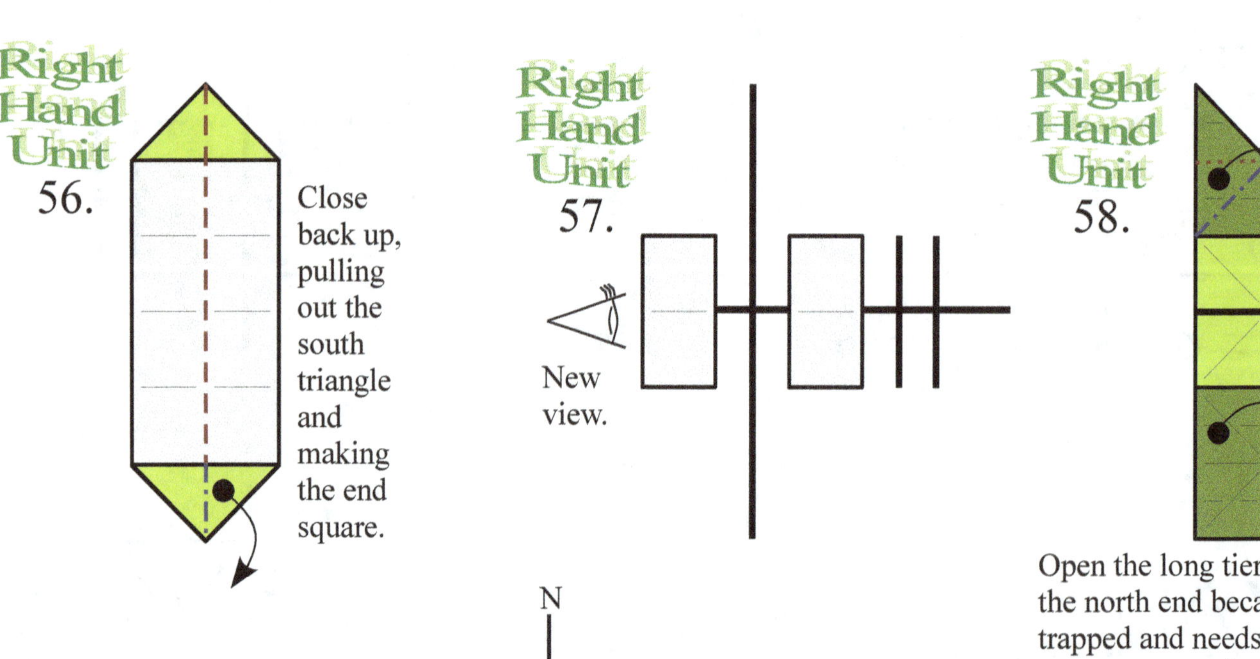

Close back up, pulling out the south triangle and making the end square.

Right Hand Unit 57.

New view.

N
W — E
S

Right Hand Unit 58.

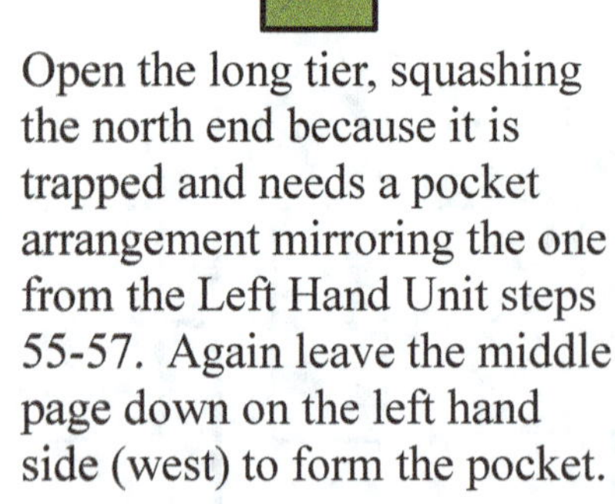

Open the long tier, squashing the north end because it is trapped and needs a pocket arrangement mirroring the one from the Left Hand Unit steps 55-57. Again leave the middle page down on the left hand side (west) to form the pocket.

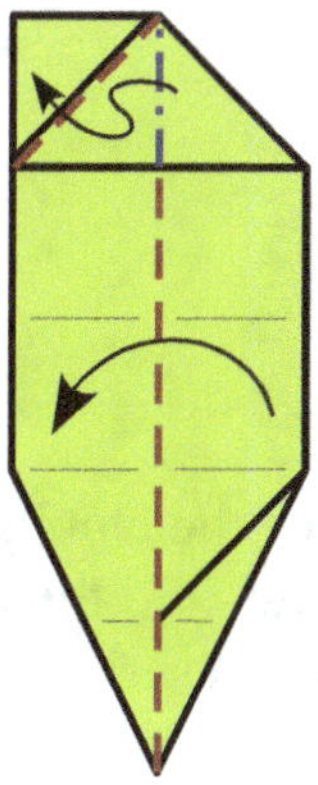

Close back up, forming a triangular flap and inserting it into the pocket. This is very close quarters because one of the folds is directly under the edge of the pocket.

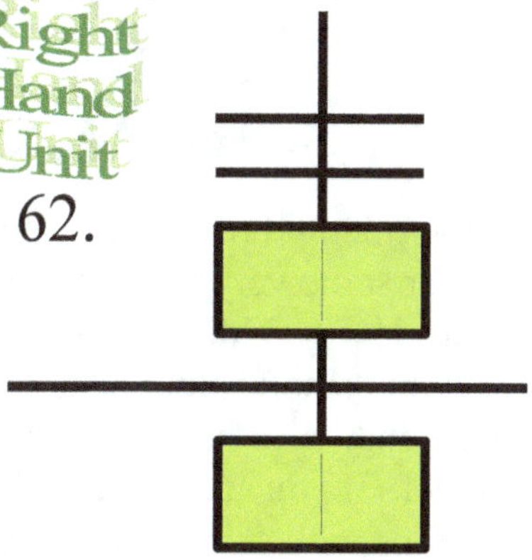

Assembly

A.

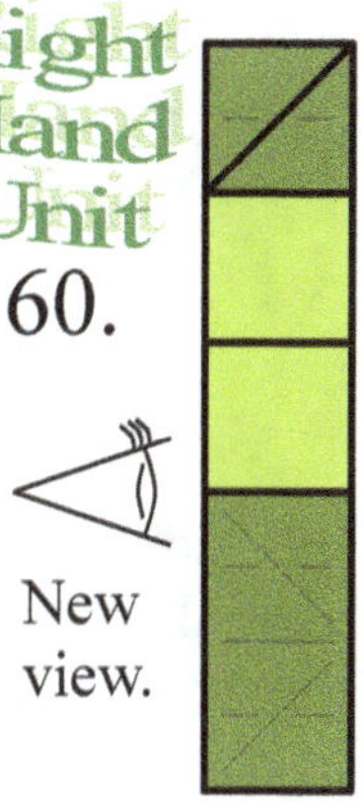

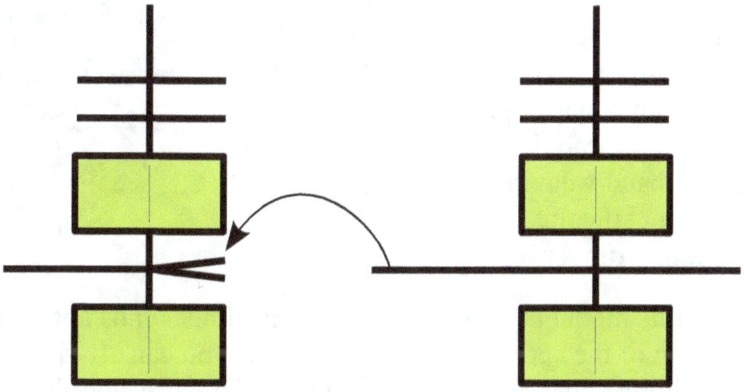

Hook the end of the long flap of the Right Hand Unit over the tongue sticking up in the middle of the double short flap of the Left Hand Unit. The Left Hand Unit should grip the right hand unit fairly tightly. Many of the folds happened close together, so the shape probably needs a little TLC at this point.

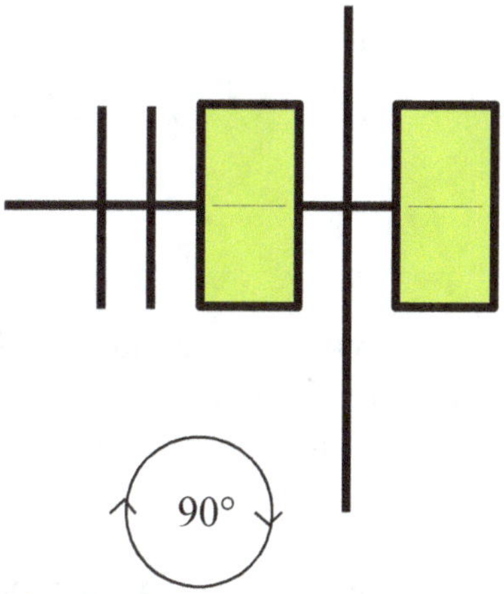

B.

Done!

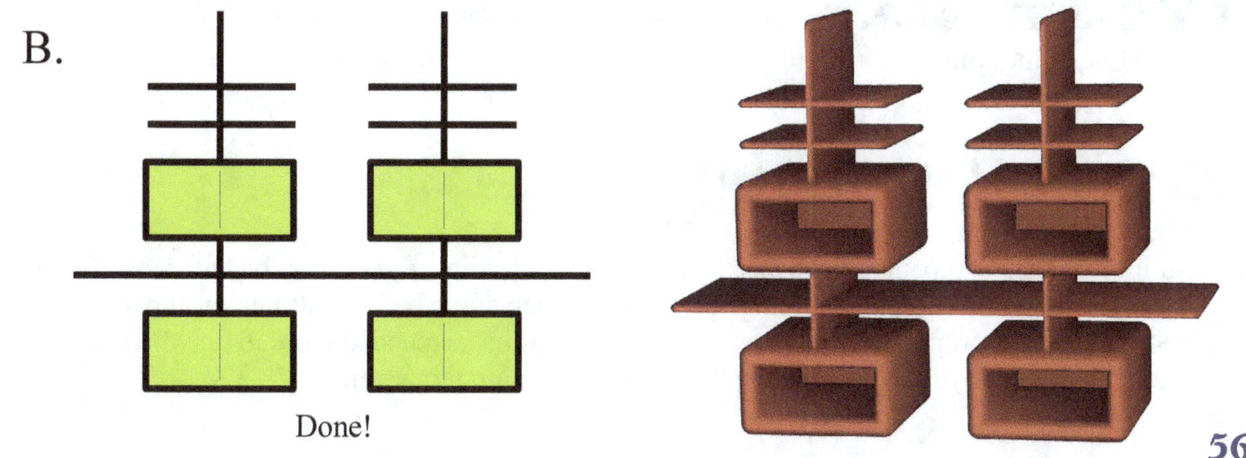

Wet-Folding and Clamps
so it doesn't puff out

To convince real dollar bills to hold the tight lines and intersections as shown in the photo of the Double Happine$$ model, it is necessary not only to crease sharply with a bone folder but also to wet-fold those banknotes. There is more than one way to go about this. Of the two recommended methods described here, the more difficult way gets better results, but the easier way gets pretty good results too and can be used to repair a previously folded model that has acquired a puffy configuration by tugging or exposure to humidity. Both methods need water and specialized clamps.

The Clamps

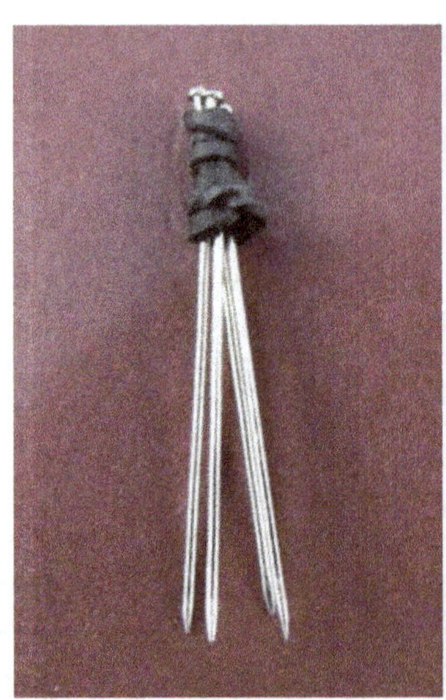

Pin-clamp.

Either method requires special, home-made clamps. To make these simple clamps, gather some very small rubber bands and the longest straight pins you can easily find. 1¼" (~32mm) should be fine; slightly shorter will work. Plain, flat heads are best, but small round heads will work, too. Rubber band the pins in groups at the head end. Another rubber band will hold the sharp ends once the clamp is on the model. If you are worried about poking yourself, you can cut off the utmost tips of the pins with side-cutters, nips or flush-cutters, but the pins will no longer be any good as pins. If you leave them sharp, it is also possible to poke the fully clamped model into styrofoam to hold it while it dries. Double Happine$$ needs six (6) groups of four (4) pins – which is to say twenty-four (24) pins and twelve (12) rubber bands. A few extra groups of three or four can also prove helpful. Craft, fabric, dollar, discount and other stores carry such straight pins. Craft stores now carry bags of just tiny rubber bands for rubber-band weaving. Small hair rubber bands also work if they are rubber bands and not silicone. Some collections of various-sized rubber bands also include such tiny rubber bands.

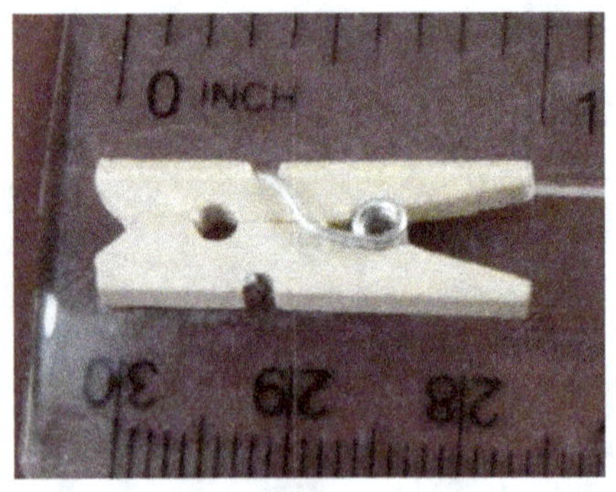

Mini clothes pin.

Clamping this model also requires some tiny clothes pins about an inch (2½cm) long of the spring-operated variety. If you can't find these or other small, toothless clips at your local craft or dollar store, additional four-pin clamps will work, but they get crowded, making it difficult to band the sharp ends without poking a finger. A stronger toothless clamp is handy to grip the thick connection. Have all your clamps on hand before you start to wet-fold.

Do not attempt to substitute paper clips for the clothes pins because they will add unwanted bends and can leave rust stains.

General Wet-folding

Wet-folding means dampening the paper at some stage of folding, which may be before the first crease, after some pre-creases or at the end just for shaping. It can even come before cutting non-monetary paper to the desired size, so that proportions are precise after the paper has expanded more in one direction than the other according to the grain of the paper. Usually the liquid is plain tap water.

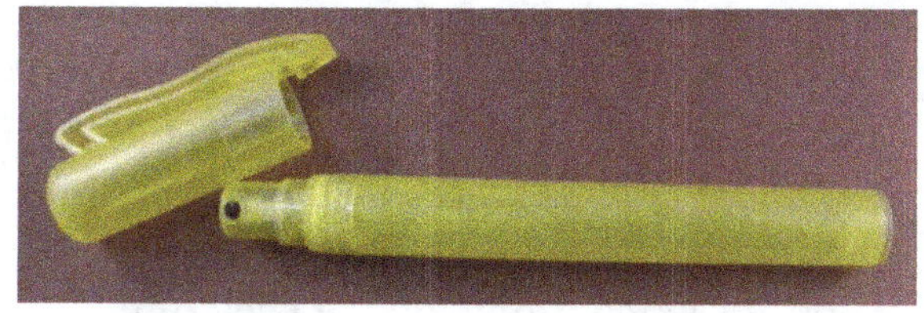

Hand-sanitizer spray bottle.

Usually sodden paper is wrong and Double Happine$$ is no exception. You will need some way to control how wet the dollar bill or other paper becomes. Do not just hold your dollar under the tap.

Misters or spray bottles are handy. The best for small models like this are the little spray bottles that come with hand sanitizer in them. Empty and thoroughly wash the bottle before using, including pumping one full bottle of water (typically 5mL) through the atomizer to rid it of sanitizer. Perfume atomizers are next best and can be purchased empty. They produce more water with each press but it is still a fine mist. They also often have a larger (but still modest) capacity. Craft spray bottles often produce a reasonably fine mist, too (and come empty) but produce even more water with each full press. Larger spray bottles leftover from cleaners or sold empty for household use often produce large droplets that do not evenly dampen the paper. They also put out larger quantities of water. The finer the mist, the more control. The hand sanitizer bottles produce the finest mist, in small, controllable amounts.

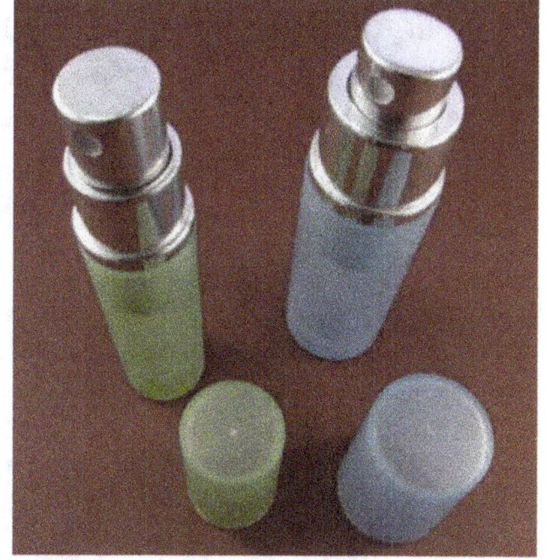

Perfume atomizers.

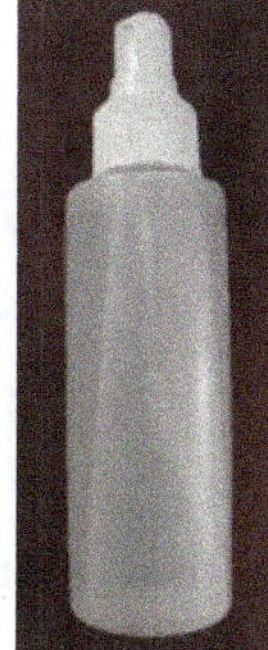

If no suitable spray bottle is available, wet a cloth or paper towel. Wring it out enough that it does not drip. This towel can now be lain or rubbed on the flat origami paper to transfer water in a controlled manner. This is less handy than the spray bottle, but more readily available in a pinch or for initial experimentation.

General craft
spray bottle.

Wet-folding Double Happine$$: Best Results

For the best results wet-folding Double Happine$$, rehearse the fold dry with practice paper or paper-backed foil until you are comfortable with folding it and can do so quickly and accurately before the damp bills dry out. It is best to fold each module completely and clamp it before the paper dries out. It is possible to add more water later, but shaping works best when the inner layers are still damp and the outer layers are dry to the touch but not thoroughly dry. Later addition of water dampens from the outside. To retard drying of the paper as you fold, intermittently dampen your hands; be sure to do this before the paper is already dry to the touch.

Use very crisp, preferably uncirculated dollar bills. Fold both dollar bills through step 22 (diagonal pre-creases) while the bills are still dry. Use a bone-folder to make very sharp creases. (Milk bone folders are good and you need not feel too badly when the free plastic gizmo absorbs green from many banknotes and fortuitously it doesn't like to pass the ink along to other papers.) Unfold one bill completely and dampen it evenly from both the front and the back until it feels leathery. Rub the water into the paper with your fingers to both speed absorption and check the level of dampness all over the bill. Restore the long pleats and fold the left hand unit. Clamp the uppermost intersections and add a clothes pin to the top. Temporarily clamp the connector; it is very thick and will dry more slowly clamped. Fold the right hand unit similarly, assemble and finish clamping. See the detailed description of clamping which holds true for both the best and pretty good methods of wet-folding this model.

If you try this method and the bills dry too quickly, rescue the model with the other, easier wet-folding method. The model will still benefit somewhat from the attempt.

Wet-folding Double Happine$$: Pretty Good Results & Repair

For pretty good results with fewer tools and less rehearsal, fold and assemble Double Happine$$ completely while the bills are still dry. Get a droplet of water on your fingertip. Pick the first intersection and apply the droplet from the front. Capillary action will pull the water inside. Apply a second droplet to the back of the same intersection. Repeat on the other intersections. Rub a little more water into the model with your finger where you want to do some shaping and on the tops and the connection. Clamp as described below. This technique also works to restore a model which has become puffy from tugging or exposure to humidity or dried too much while wet-folding as described for best results.

Clamping Double Happine$$

To clamp Double Happine$$, take a pin-clamp and put it around an intersection front-to-back with one pin in each gap. Press it on snugly. Rubber band the sharp ends together, being careful not to poke a finger. If a pin does jab a fingertip, set the model aside for a moment and pinch the fingertip to make sure it is not going to bleed. Red marks on the bill would not be good despite the lucky color. If it does bleed treat it before continuing; a band-aid will protect the model from blood and antibiotic ointment.

Next clamp the intersection beside the one already clamped; if you skip over one, trying to clamp the one betwixt them is unnecessarily difficult and likely to result in a jabbed finger. Repeat until all six (6) clamp-able intersections are clamped.

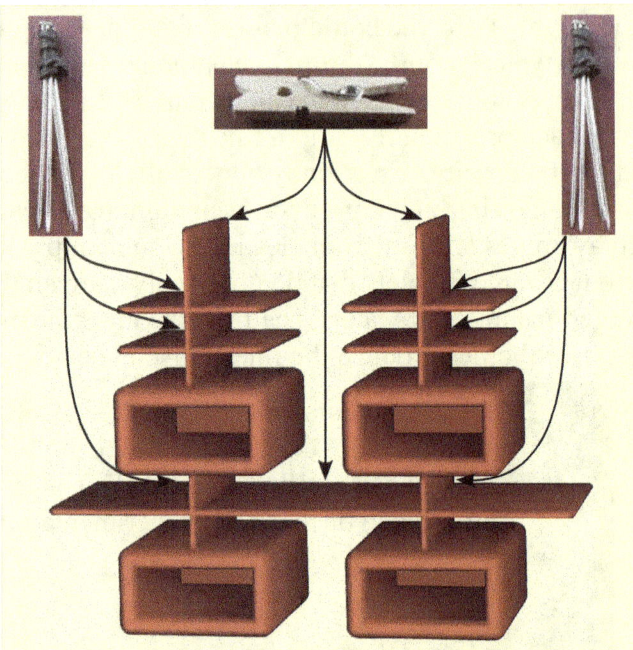

Pin-clamps go on these six (6) intersections. Mini clothes pins go on at least these three (3) locations.

Add the miniature clothes pins to the thick connection and the tops and anywhere else you think they would help and where they actually fit.

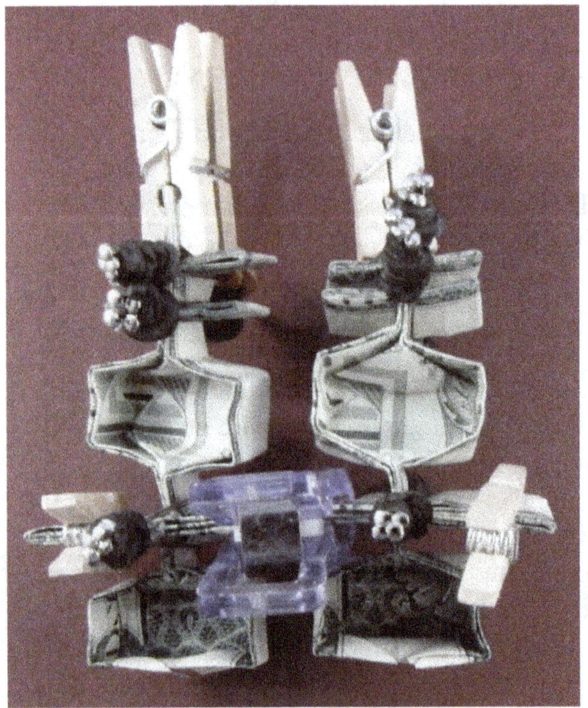

Double Happiness with clamps: front view.

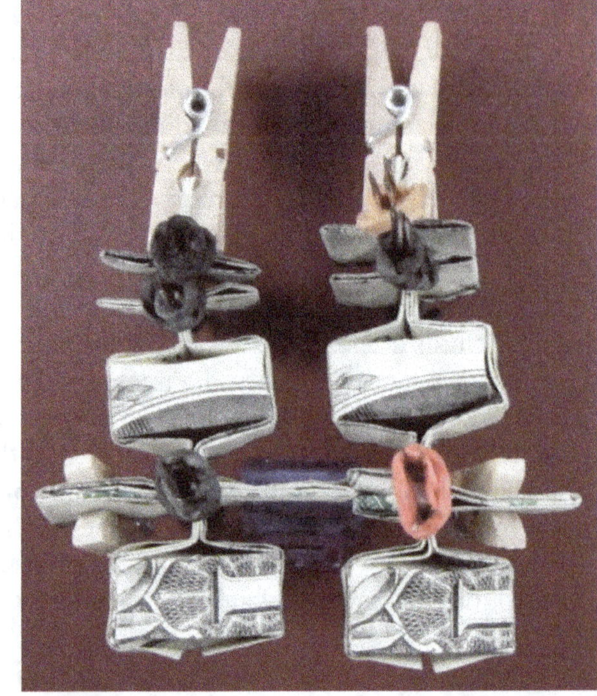

Double Happiness with clamps: rear view.

Fuss with the the shape.

To hold the shape even better, stake those pin-clamps into styrofoam and tweak the shape until it is just right. Brace the bottoms with either extra straight pins or pin-clamps. These pin-clamps require only three (3) pins each rather than four (4). The pin-clamps work better because they are more stable than single pins.

Let the model dry overnight. Remove the clothes pins then the pin-clamps. Be very gentle when you try to tweak the angles just a bit lest the intersections expand.

Preserving Double Happine$$

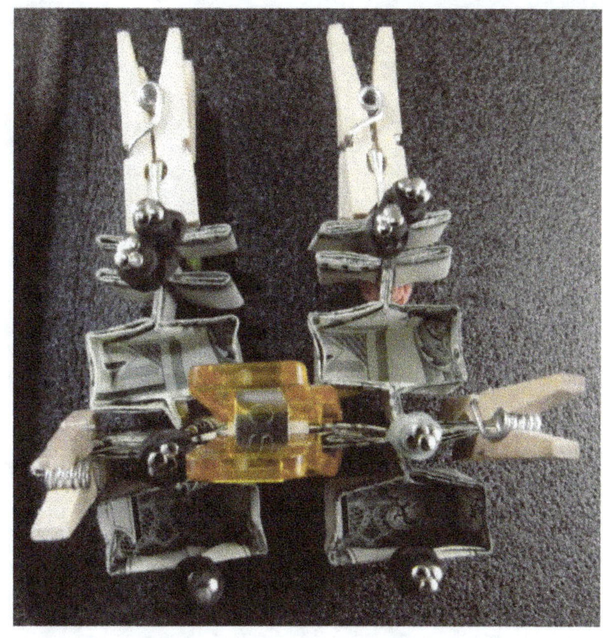

Double Happiness with clamps on Styrofoam.

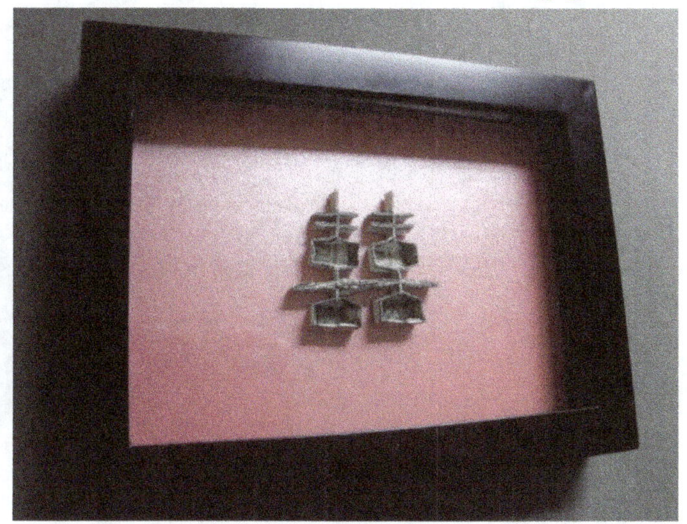

It would be a shame to let humidity undo all that fine work. An air tight container is all well and good, but a frame would show off the model better. Of course, the thick model needs a shadowbox not just a thin, flat frame which would hold a flat model tightly and keep most of the air away.

A shadowbox is not air tight. Gluing the model to the background would not only irreversibly damage the model, it would leave the model with little protection against humidity after exposing it to moisture in the glue. Invisible (nylon) thread, monofilament or lightweight fishing line solves both problems. Use a stiff background such as acid-free card stock (commonly sold for scrapbooking) which a sewing or embroidery needle can pierce neatly and stitch the model to the background without damaging it.

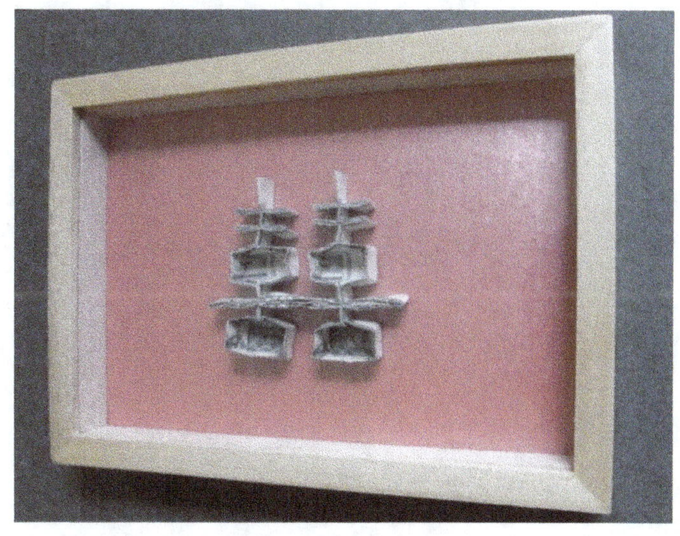

The stitches should go through the background and around each intersection twice in an X pattern. A single strand is sufficient and with the thicker options highly recommended. Stitching should always start and end on the back side, but poke the holes from the front to position them accurately and keep any exit-wound damage on the flip side where it will not show. Make the holes in the background very near the intersections so that they hide. Poke only the next hole that you will use next; do not pre-poke holes even for the same intersection. A second pristine layer of background behind the one with the stitches also helps hide the holes. Lighter colored backgrounds are more apt to benefit noticeably from a second layer. Size and proximity of the holes also affect whether a second layer will truly help. A thinner needle makes a noticeably smaller, less noticeable hole, but also has a smaller eye, making it more difficult to thread. Tying off after each intersection is reasonable; alternatively tie a square knot after the first intersection, continue without cutting and make three half-hitches around the lead-in line after each intersection to keep the completed work taut. Tape the ends down on the back.

www.ingramcontent.com/pod-product-compliance
Lightning Source LLC
Chambersburg PA
CBHW080503030726
47592CB00011B/3228